TANDEM COMPUTERS UNPLUGGED

A People's History

Gaye I. Clemson

Published by FastPencil

Published by FastPencil
3131 Bascom Ave.
Suite 150
Campbell CA 95008 USA
info@fastpencil.com
(408) 540-7571
(408) 540-7572 (Fax)
http://www.fastpencil.com

The challenge with oral history, especially when using social media is that the scope is limited by the nature of the kinds of stories that individuals are willing to post. As a result, though lots of people and events are included, lots of others that didn't quite fit the story line have been omitted, but not through any malicious intent. I have also found, that the human memory is a funny thing, so I don't pretend that every story is absolutely true. No doubt some embellishment has gone on. There may also be some stories that in today's vernacular might be considered not very politically correct. Apologies are extended in advance for any sensibilities, political, ethnic or otherwise, that get bruised. I also excluded my own and others' more 'juicy bits' to both protect the innocent but also because my sense is that these stories are much more suited to a fictional format. As I've often said, you just had to be there to get it all.

Cover photograph was provided courtesy of Yves Tournier, a formere employee from the Tandem France subsidiary. Cover postcard inserts were provided courtesy of Jan Seamons, Jim Katzman and Dennis McEvoy respectively. Cover by Troy Chasey of Capitola Design.

First Edition

To all fellow Tandemites who at one time or another proudly wore a Tandem Non-Stop badge.

⁊❧

Contents

Notes and Acknowledgements

IN 1974, WHEN JIMMY Treybig started Tandem at the age of 33, most pundits thought that building a new computer company was not a very good idea. But Jimmy persisted because he knew that the business problem he was trying to solve was one that was causing real pain at that time for businesses such as banks, tele-communications providers and airlines. But it wasn't just a new computer systems architecture that he cared about, it was also about creating a new way to manage people and lead a company. The values that he set out—for example that all people were good and the same whether they were workers or management, that every single person in the company needed to understand the essence of the business and that every employee needed to benefit from the company's success were ground-breaking. Management's job, Jimmy felt, was to create an environment where all of this could happen, which is what took place at Tandem Computers.

Like all things in life, some aspects of these ideas worked well and others didn't work quite so well. But as is so clear in listening to the voices of Tandem people that are found in this narrative, the impact on those who spent time at Tandem was and is significant. All of us are proud to have been a part of that legacy. We are proud of the fact that we helped lay the foundation for what has become Silicon Valley, proud of the individual contributions that we made, proud of the fun and success that we had as a group, proud of Beer Busts, TOPS, sabbaticals, TTN, email and stock options for everyone. We are proud of the trust that we all had in each other that led to an openness of thought, creativity, innovation and customer commitment that is rare today. We had a spirit and a feeling that lives on and I hope comes through in these pages.

This book is written in a way that reflects three different narratives. The first narrative is the history of the company that has been extracted from a mountain of press clippings and articles in various Tandem internal publications. A second narrative is my own voyage of discovery of Silicon Valley, a new management approach and more importantly of the world. Thirdly are the voices of my fellow employees, extracted from social media postings over the last decade and interwoven in different ways to tie it all together.

I started collecting these voices from social media postings by former employees of Tandem Computers in 2002 just after a reunion that was held at Bay Meadows race track in September of that year. Over the course of this journey not only did I have a chance to reconnect with all sorts of Tandem friends and former colleagues, I also had a chance to virtually meet many I had never known personally. Like my other oral history projects, it soon took on a life of its own and in the intervening years has taken me down many different and very interesting pathways.

But the challenge with this style of writing is that the scope is limited by the nature of the kinds of stories that individuals were willing to post. As a result, though lots of people and events are included, lots of others that didn't quite fit the story line have been omitted, but not through any malicious intent. I've also learned in writing many of these types of histories that the human memory is a funny thing, so I don't pretend that every story is absolutely true. No doubt some embellishment has gone on. There may also be some stories that in today's vernacular might be considered not very politically correct. I apologize in advance for any sensibilities, political, ethnic or otherwise, that get bruised. I also excluded my own and others' more "juicy bits" to both protect the innocent but also because, my sense is that those stories are much more suited to a fictional format. As I've often said you just had to be there to get it all.

Wherever I have been able, I've included employee numbers. Of course all Tandemites will know exactly why this is. But for those readers unfamiliar, the Tandem employee number (appearing on one's security badge) reflected the order in which one got hired. The smaller the number, the higher the person ranked in the Tandem family hierarchy. With that higher ranking came respect, honor and the deference of others—not quite a seniority system and certainly outside of the normal organizational power structure, but very important all the same. My number was #6410 as I joined the firm in 1984, 10 years after its founding. The company, at nearly $500 million in annual revenue, had just joined the ranks of the Fortune 500. When I left in mid-1992, revenue was close to $1.5 billion. This time period was perhaps not quite as exciting as the first few years after the company's founding but was a time of tremendous growth and change just the same. As a result, not much of the narrative covers the years from 1992 to 1996, at which point Compaq absorbed the firm. I will have to leave it to others to fill in this gap in some other way should what I have shared be insufficient.

There are so many to be acknowledged and thanked. First and foremost are Ed Martin, Dave and Fran Peatrowsky and Patty and Tony Turner without whose enthusiasm, support and occasional nudging over the years, this narrative would never have been completed. Second is to my fellow Tandemites who so kindly have allowed me to reflect their words in this way, provided photos and continue to express their keen support for this project. Mark Hammond, my editor friend who has helped with several other of my books to strengthen their readability in the most professional of ways and Troy Chasey, from Capitola Design, whose artistic help with cover design I deeply appreciate. Jan Seamons, whose memory, photos and help with final proofreading was immeasurably valuable, and Henry Norman, whose review caught lots of little technical corrections that I would have missed otherwise. Thanks also need to go to Dennis McEvoy and Jim Katzman, who shared photos, brochures and insight into many of the early players. Jim, who I had the pleasure of finally meeting for the first time just a few months ago, has been invaluable in reconstructing those early years, especially in putting names to faces. His fabulous contribution to the photo archive and willingness to let me take a look at his early engineering notes and the various versions of the original business plans was awesome. And last but not least is Jimmy Treybig whose enthusiastic support helped push the effort over the finish line. I deeply thank and honor you all.

Author in her canoe

The Journey Begins

THE CALL WAS ONE of those unexpected calls that come totally out of the blue. It took a bit of time to mentally connect voice and memory, but when the circuit was complete, hearing her voice was a very welcome addition to what had been a very stressful day balancing work and the raising of twin boys. On the phone was a former Tandem Computers colleague whom I'd worked with in Marketing in the mid-1980s, but I hadn't seen or spoken to in a very long time. She had access to some Tandem memorabilia and had heard from a common friend that I'd been working for some time on a book about Tandem. She wondered if I wanted to take a look at it before it went into storage. She thought that there might be some good historical reference material that I might not have seen. As she was explaining this to me, my mind's eye drifted to that scene in the closing minutes of the movie *Raiders of the Lost Ark*. All I could see was row upon row of boxes, piled floor to the ceiling, in this huge cavernous warehouse spreading into the distance as far as the eye could see. Those few boxes that captured some essence of Tandem forever lost. Needless to say, though this book had been on the back burner for some time, I jumped at the chance to take a look at this cache. We set up a time to visit a few days later.

Heading over the Santa Cruz Mountains from Capitola to San Jose that day, I reflected on my journey to California from Canada that had started out as somewhat of a lark back in the fall of 1983. My former husband, whom I'd met at high school in Toronto, had been consumed with wanderlust at the time and convinced me to abandon what seemed to be a very promising career with Bell Canada's Computer

Communications Group (CCG) in Ottawa, Ontario. I'd been working with a business development team whose objective was to bring to market what were known at the time as value-add services—email, voice recognition systems, database access and other services that were all new to the Canadian market. Unbeknownst to me, in Silicon Valley at the time, a midrange computer systems boom was under way. Personal computers didn't yet exist, so computers were based in data centers and connected to users via what we used to call "green screens" or "dumb terminals." Through colleagues at CCG, I had managed to obtain a job as a program manager at Tandem Computers, an upstart carving out a new market called online transaction processing. Though information technology had not been of interest to me in the business school at Queen's University where I'd done my undergraduate work, it wasn't long before I got caught up in the magic and excitement of the high-tech business.

Since Tandem had arranged a work visa for me, the transition to living in the United States and adapting to the culture of California was relatively painless. For the first few years I'd complain about missing certain consumer products such as Red Rose tea, McLean's toothpaste, decent maple syrup and Pop Secret popcorn, but my family in Toronto would ease those concerns by sending me care packages from time to time. Other than having to get used to not starting each conversation with a comment on the weather (as it was always sunny in California) cultural differences tended to be few. The funniest were bizarre conversations I'd get into about the differences between consumer packaging practices in Canada vs. the United States. For example: In the United States, milk comes in gallon jugs and butter comes in quarter-pound blocks, whereas in Ontario, Canada milk comes in plastic packages of three one-liter bags and butter in one-pound blocks. Or I'd talk about the lack of great "nippy" (as in old) cheddar and other imported specialty cheeses or farmers markets like Ottawa's Byward Market or the Lawrence Market in Toronto, where the weekly buying of fresh local farm produce had been integral to my life. Over the years, the differences became less acute (or perhaps I just became desensitized), though I am happy to note that farmers markets now abound everywhere and specialty cheeses can be bought in most supermarkets.

Meeting my former colleague was like taking a walk back in time. She had what seemed like a mountain of material and gave me free access. Over the next week, I spent long days going through her material, photocopying everything in sight. We shared a lot of laughs, a few tears and a lot of storytelling. In the end I came away with several legal-size boxes of "stuff." These I hauled home and shoved under my desk along with the other boxes of research notes, annual reports, magazines, Tandem internal publications and copies of various Tandem_Alumni Yahoo! Groups social media postings that I'd collected over the years. I then promptly forgot about it all.

My twin boys were 8 years old at the time, and I had little time for more extracurricular writing. I'd begun a research effort many years earlier, prodded by Ed Martin, a former Tandem Human Resources Manager whom I had met when he was working on the Focus Series of Tandem Philosophy training courses in the late 1980s. Our idea had been to survey former Tandem employees on the long-term impacts of the Tandem Philosophy. The line of inquiry was to ascertain, which of Tandem's people management values and practices had the most meaning to them over time and whether any were being adopted by their current employers. Though we collected some interesting data, the results weren't compelling enough to turn into a book or even a magazine article. I was never sure if this was due to lack of content, motivation or if I just didn't care any more. In addition, a year earlier I'd gotten engaged in writing what became my non-fiction Algonquin Series (now eight books). These were oral histories about various aspects of a community in Algonquin Park, Ontario, where I still had a cabin in the wilderness that I would retreat to every summer.

So there the boxes lay, under my desk until the spring of 2009, when Hewlett Packard (HP) decided to close the Fremont Manufacturing Supply Chain facility. For reasons I can't explain, the floodgates opened when I saw a note posted on the Tandem_Alumni Yahoo! Groups site advising of the facility's demise and a tongue-in-cheek précis of the supposed subsequent wake. As a sort of memorial, readers were encouraged to share their memories and a moment of silence. The response was overwhelming. Day after day for more than a week, person after person, some names that I recognized, lots that I didn't, weighed in with their thoughts and feelings across every possible spectrum, from sorrow to joy, from wonder to remorse. It was like nothing I'd ever seen—at least not in recent years. There had been a similar outpouring of storytelling in 2002 when a reunion was held at Bay Meadows Race Track in California and again in 2004—though I can't recall what triggered the 2004 postings. Though late to the party, I was motivated to add to the thread my 1986 story of working with Jimmy Treybig, Tandem's president, to create the company's first solutions marketing presentation called *"Tandem in the Marketplace"*, which I will share in a later chapter.

Now motivated, I dragged out the boxes, plus a few others full of documents I'd collected over the years, from under my desk and shipped them to Canada where, I was going on a summer sabbatical to my cabin in the woods of Algonquin Park. (For those unfamiliar, sabbatical refers to a common practice in academia and imported to Silicon Valley in those heady days of enabling an employee after some number of years of service to have paid leave). In Tandem's case, after four years of service one was entitled to six weeks paid leave. For some this meant traveling, for others it was an opportunity to rest at home and reconnect with the family. Still others used the time to give back in some way to their communities in a volunteer capacity. The goal was to do whatever one needed to do to refuel one's jets.

In the wilderness I spent days sorting through the various boxes, which included annual reports, old copies (from 1978-88) of Tandem's main internal communications mechanisms, the *NonStop News* periodical and the more philosophical journal *Center* magazine, and a host of technical publications, user manuals, sales guides, etc. The stack of press clippings alone was two feet high. There was even a copy of Jimmy's three-foot by two-foot philosophy cum business operating model masterpiece that he'd written in 1980. This document was the result of a bet as to whether or not it was possible for Jimmy to put the entire operating philosophy for Tandem on one piece of paper. (See Chapter 12 for pictures and a summary). Tucked in the bottom of one box was a copy of cartoon maps on how to get to Tandem from the San Francisco airport, as well as the original benefits brochure and customer support procedures manuals. The task was daunting, but there were enough rainy days during my sabbatical to slowly but surely make my way through the piles, taking copious notes and copying quotes verbatim into my laptop. A few weeks later I was done and once again the project stalled. Over the next two years, I would pick it up from time to time and work on different sections but again nothing jelled.

So here I am now in the summer of 2011. I've just taken an early retirement package from Cisco Systems, my employer of the last six years, and have migrated north once again to my cottage in the wilderness of Algonquin Park. I'm sitting on the porch, with a lovely view of Canoe Lake to the north. The sun is heading towards the horizon over my left shoulder, the low light casting lovely sparkles on the water. A few birds are chirping away, with the occasional squirrel having a fuss, likely over a dropped seed. Spread out all around me are my notes from the last 10 years of research and story collecting. With a glass of fine white wine at my elbow and some soft nature music playing in the background, I reach for my keyboard and the words start to flow. As my fingers fly, I wonder how on earth to capture one of the greatest love affairs of my life, my affair with Tandem Computers.

Young Jim Treybig Had a Dream

Song contributed by Carl Weber
(To the tune of Old MacDonald Had a Farm)

Young Jim Treybig had a dream   E I E I O
Non-Stop systems were his scheme   E I E I O
With a non-stop here and a non-stop there
Here a node, there a node, everywhere a node-node
Young Jim Treybig had a dream   E I E I O

And in his dream he formed a plan   E I E I O
Networks connected through EXPAND   E I E I O
With a link-link here and a link-link there
Here a node, there a node, everywhere a node-node
Young Jim Treybig had a dream   E I E I O

And in his dream the systems grew   E I E I O
Processors added to the basic two   E I E I O
With a CPU here and a CPU there
Here a node, there a node, everywhere a node-node
Young Jim Treybig had a dream   E I E I O

And in his dream the data was sound   E I E I O
For all discs crash as they go round   E I E I O
With a mirrored volume here and a mirrored volume there
Here a node, there a node, everywhere a node-node
Young Jim Treybig had a dream   E I E I O

Young Jim Treybig's dream came true   E I E I O
Tandem's systems do all this for you   E I E I O
With a non-stop here and a link-link there
Here a file, there a disc, everywhere a Tandem
Young Jim Treybig had a dream   E I E I O

Tandem - The Early Years

Tandem Core Four Founders L-R: Jack Loustaunou, Michael Green, Jim Katzman, Jimmy Treybig - Katzman Collection

ACCORDING TO THE OFFICIAL lore, Tandem Computers was formed in 1974 by a group of former Hewlett Packard (HP) employees who believed they could design and manufacture a computer system that would never crash. But the real truth is that though the initial founding"CORE FOUR" and later the "TANDEM TEN" played important and critical roles, the central vision for this new sort of computer company was due to the energy of one man. A man, James G. Treybig, who as *Industry Week* magazine said in 1984, had a *"gift for seeing the open window in already crowded markets."* Educated with a BA and an engineering degree from Rice University in Houston, Texas in 1963-64, and later (1968) an MBA at Stanford, "Jimmy," as he was known to all, started his career as a marketing manager at Hewlett Packard (HP). His first exposure to HP was while at Stanford when he got a summer job doing market research for Tom Perkins. At HP Tom, at the time, was in charge of marketing for the Computer Division, a group whose product had been developed by HP Labs at the behest of Dave Packard. Packard's original idea was to use it as an instrumentation controller to run arrays of HP instruments under the control of a computer. He didn't want to call it a computer as IBM was an important customer and he didn't want to compete with them.

Unfortunately to Dave's chagrin, after its first year not a single one had been sold. When Dave approached the team to try to find out why, all sorts of technical reasons were raised. Tom had remained silent during this entire exchange but when asked his opinion, raised the cryptic thought that maybe they should try selling the damn thing. Of course no one really knew what he was talking about as the standard process those days at HP was to publish a photo of the product in their catalogue alongside detailed feature/function specifications. Some time later, Packard approached Tom to better understand what he was talking about. Tom explained that most HP sales people didn't know how it worked and were afraid to stand up in front of a customer and make a fool of themselves. As a result, they tended to stick to what they knew. Dave then suggested that Tom take over marketing of the product. As Tom shared at a 2011 event:

"I then proceeded to change everything. I hired dedicated sales people (a first for HP), many from Digital Equipment Corporation (DEC) who arrived up and running. As it turned out, once the product got some specific attention, the offering was a great product. Customers would buy without asking too many questions. Sales took off and the division became a success."

After graduating Jimmy returned to HP to run sales support, training and service for HP's Computer Division. After a few years he transferred to the Mountain View Disc Systems Division to run marketing and later was responsible for the marketing of commercial computers that were focusing on banking, publishing and manufacturing. While working on a project for Holiday Inn, he saw a market opportunity that few others could see. The hotel chain wanted a computer that would process large numbers of transactions. When Jimmy looked at other industries such as banking, manufacturing and communications, it seemed that they also had a similar need. For applications such as credit checking, airline reservations, automatic teller machine networks and hospital systems, it just wasn't acceptable to have the computer go down. They all wanted the ability to capture, update, process and deliver voluminous amounts of information automatically without losing data when the computers did go down. Jimmy shared his thoughts many times, about the business problem that drove his early thinking about fail-safe, most recently in a 2011 movie celebrating Silicon Valley's roots called *"Something Ventured"*:

"In the early 1970s, the New York Stock Exchange would fail every day or every other day and something would go wrong. [The computer] would destroy data. People knew what the problem was but didn't have a solution. I knew that if I could figure out a different kind of computer architecture to solve this problem, I could create a big company."

So Treybig tinkered with the numbers and tallied up a market worth potentially as much as $800 million by 1978-79. His estimates were based on expected need for fail-safe applications across banking, retailing, communications, manufacturing, distribution, healthcare, hoteling and printing/publishing. As Tony Turner, one of Tandem's leading systems analyst and overall unique character said much later:

"HP suspects and prospects wanted to automate customer transaction-oriented business functions but would get mighty surly when you screwed up their transactions. With this market opportunity in mind, Treybig was able to arm twist some of HP's European systems engineers to build an approximation to a fault-tolerant transaction processing system out of HP assemblies for Europe's biggest cash and carry retailer. The result was not perfect, it would have to be built from the ground up to be that, but it worked well enough to be deployed in over 30 international sites. HP now had arguably the best online transaction system in the world."

But HP at that time was focused on the scientific, education and medical markets. They didn't envision a commercial market of any size for computers of this sort and had no interest in pursuing the market opportunity further. Jimmy was not ready to let his vision die so he tracked down his former boss, Tom Perkins. Perkins had left HP and in 1972 established with Eugene Kleiner, a venture capital investment firm called Kleiner Perkins (KP). KP was a pioneer in the venture capital industry that has since become Kleiner, Perkins, Caulfield and Byers and resides on Sand Hill Road in Menlo Park, California. Their partnership was unique because up until that point, most venture funding came from those with deep financial industry background. Kleiner and Perkins, however, were veterans of the high tech industry. Kleiner was a founder of Fairchild Semiconductor and Perkins was from Hewlett Packard. Their investment focus was then (and still is today) generally on early-stage category-defining companies—those that had high potential to become leaders in their respective fields. Today KPCB is a highly respected world leader with one of the best track records in building world-class companies, with investments in information technology, energy, greentech, utilities, life sciences and pharmaceuticals. According to the KPCB website, the firm has over the past 35 years been an early investor in more than 300 information technology and biotech firms.

It didn't take long for both Perkins and Kleiner to become intrigued by Treybig's ideas. As a result, they decided to provide him with space, time and a few resources to prepare a draft business plan for this new adventure. After a few months work, Jimmy had a business plan in hand and as he said later said:

"I got credit for putting together the foundation of the plan and Tom got credit for making it sophisticated. By that I mean he turned it into English."

Having a plan, even if it was very preliminary, enabled Jimmy to start the process of finding the right sorts of folks to help him achieve his vision. Two of his key early recruits were Jim Katzman and Michael Green. Katzman, a brilliant hardware engineer, had designed, while at HP, the HP3000 with Mike Green and many of the initial Tandem recruits. In 1971 he had moved on to Amdahl to manage the high speed I/O Channel Unit design for the Amdahl 470 V/6 computer system. Green was an equally brilliant computer scientist who according to Katzman:

"Almost single handedly designed the HP2000 time sharing system. He did it in a single summer while he was working on a PhD at Stanford in Computer Science. HP had never seen such a complex product designed in such a short time. He wrote the entire 16-user BASIC timesharing system in a summer and it ran on existing HP minicomputers. They made him an offer he couldn't refuse, so Mike never returned to Stanford. Mike was very low key and soft spoken (although he could display a temper). Revered by his peers, technical people loved working with and for him, mostly because they learned so much from the guy. HP folk lore had it at the time, that Stanford gave Mike a Master's in Computer Science even though they didn't really have a Master's Program in Computer Science. I think Mike Green is the only person to ever get that degree from Stanford."

Katzman's recollections of the day he and Jimmy met, as recounted in the *San Jose Mercury News* in 1989, provide some interesting color:

"In 1974, I got a call from Tom Perkins inviting me to lunch. I figured he was doing due diligence on Amdahl whom I knew was looking for investors. But when Perkins picked me up, he had another former HP colleague with him. This guy, Jim Treybig, started talking about an idea he had for a new computer company. With him was a thick notebook filled with newspaper and magazine horror stories about computers crashing, about the loss of business and occasionally life such technical failures caused. He told me that he was interested in developing a computer that wouldn't fail, that had backup systems in case of emergency. Did I think it was possible from a technical standpoint, to design hardware to do it? I said it would be a challenge, but it could be done, but the software was going to be very difficult. He asked me who was the best software guy I'd known. I said Mike Green, who had designed the minicomputer industry's first time-sharing system for the HP2000. 'I figured you'd say that!' Treybig said. 'I've got lunch with him tomorrow.'"

Needless to say, Katzman was intrigued and the next day called Green to ask how the lunch had gone. Green told him that he'd advised Treybig that developing the needed software would be straightforward, but that building the hardware would be tough. Of course, each thought that he had the easiest job, neither of which turned out to be true. All of it ended up being difficult—but not impossible. According to Katzman, some time later, Treybig divulged *"he had thought that both hardware and software would be terribly difficult, but that if he could get someone to build it he could sell it."*

With Katzman and Green on the team, albeit still doing their day jobs at Amdahl and HP respectively, it didn't take long for the basic hardware and software design specifications to be completed. Kleiner and Perkins were impressed enough in mid 1974 to invest $50,000 into the company, which enabled Green and Katzman to quit HP and Amdahl respectively and join the new venture. But to really move forward, venture funding needed to be secured. Unfortunately, in 1974, the country was in the midst of a deep recession. Venture capital sources were virtually non-existent and seed money was even harder to find. As noted in an *Inc. Magazine* article in June 1981 by Susan Benner, Treybig and the rest of the team had never started a company before. No one was sure that the technical problems of building a fail-safe, modularly expandable computer could be solved. Besides, *"who needs another mini-computer company"* was often the reaction of many potential investors that Kleiner and Perkins approached. Industry pundits were adamant that IBM had already won the mainframe war and there would never be another computer company. One funny story that Tom often shared was of their first experience going to Wall Street to seek investors:

"Jimmy was straight out of Texas, and I didn't think that he'd go over very well on Wall Street. So I took him to Brooks Brothers and bought him shoes, socks, suit, the works. Alas it didn't help as the first thing that came out of Jimmy's mouth when meeting the Wall Street bankers was, 'So how do I look? Tom dressed me!'"

Needless to say, the East Coast moneymen were likely a little taken aback by Jimmy. But Kleiner and Perkins never doubted the plan or the management and they decided the odds of success were good enough to invest $1 million of their own funds to carry the trio through 1975. This $1 million investment was sizable as Kleiner Perkins' total fund at the time amounted to only $8 million. As Tom Perkins shared many years later:

"If Tandem hadn't been a success, there never would have been a second Kleiner Perkins [venture] fund. "

At the last moment venture capitalist, Franklin "Pitch" Johnson from Asset Management Company decided to contribute $50,000 as well, which added much needed credibility. Johnson sat on the Tandem board for many years and made many contributions. He had a young associate, Brook Byers, who did the due diligence on Tandem and recommended that Pitch do the deal. Pitch suggested that he (Brook) also invest money in Tandem if he believed in the company. Byers eventually did and it was one of his first successful investments and he went on to become the Byers in Kleiner, Perkins, Caufield and Byers.

With this preliminary investment in hand, Green and Katzman were able to focus on recruiting the team that they would need to achieve the proposed development schedule. By the end of 1974, fourteen employees were now part of the endeavor. These first **"Founding Fathers"** (six of which were the top hardware and software people who had worked with Jim and Michael on the design of the HP3000), included: the **"CORE FOUR"** - Jimmy Treybig (#1 - President), Michael Green (#2 - Software Development), Jim Katzman (#3 - Hardware Development) and John Loustaunou (#4 - Finance and Administration) and the **"TANDEM TEN"** - Maria Cremerius (#5 - Administration - the only non-male "founding father"), Dennis McEvoy (#6 - Operating System I/O), Tom Blease (#7 - Tandem's Application Language - TAL), Steve Wierenga (#8 - CPU Hardware), Peter 'Rocky' Graziano (#9 - Microcode), Dick Bixler (#10 - Disk Controller), Joel Bartlett (#11 - Operating System Kernal), Dave Mackie (#12 - Product Management), John Despotakis (#13 - Manufacturing) and David Greig (#14 - Communications). One great synopsis of how the majority of this group was assembled came from Tony Turner (#624):

"Shortly after the pre-Tandem business plan was funded, HP shut down between Thanksgiving and New Year's, so that nobody would have to be let go. In a recession, that's the HP Way. However idle hands are the devil's playgrounds. By New Year's Eve, the 10 smartest sum bitches at HP worked for Tandem. That was the Treybig Way! In this manner 'The Tandem,' as in the product, was born."

In truth, as Jim Katzman (#3) and Dennis McEvoy (#6) explained:

"Our first few weeks we were in the plush offices of Kleiner Perkins and we called in all our HP friends for interviews in these offices and welcomed them to Tandem for an interview. Rather than lay anyone off, HP had implemented a forced furlough of two paid and three unpaid days off around Thanksgiving. On the first day back, the Monday after Thanksgiving, six people resigned from HP en masse - their best Research and Development guys who were instrumental in the design of the HP3000. Four were from software (Tom, Joel, Dennis and Peter) and two were from hardware (Steve and Dick). They all joined Tandem and became our first employees. Perkins

got a threatening call from HP executive offices about raiding HP and Tom responded that he was pretty sure that indentured servitude was outlawed in the United States and that these people were free to work wherever they wanted. However HP executives were not impressed and by Friday walked all six out the door. They even posted their respective pictures with security to ensure that none would be allowed back into the building. Later we bought an HP3000 that we used to design the initial Tandem System, which helped unruffle feathers at bit. We did not buy a maintenance contract for it however. We figured if we designed the HP3000, we could probably keep it running ok!

What was even funnier though was that the very first time Tandem appeared in print was in a trade magazine called "Electronic News". The reporter was one who covered HP. The headline of the story was "New Computer Company formed by HP Alumni", so Tandem's name wasn't even in the headline!" The first Christmas Party was held at Tom Perkins' house, where Green accidentally hit a pool ball through a glass window. Soon after we moved into an office located in the back half of the Spectra Physics building at 2909 Stender Way in Santa Clara, with Tom Perkins, through his Spectra Physics connections helping negotiate reasonable rent." (Author's Note: Tom Perkins had been a founder of University Labs, which invented the first commercial laser products and later merged to become Spectra Physics.)

One co-founder and key supporter was Jack Loustaunou (#4), who signed on as Vice President of Finance and Administration. Prior to joining Tandem, Loustaunou, had been an associate at Kleiner and Perkins but like Green and Katzman had also spent time at HP, where he'd worked for Tom Perkins in the Cupertino Computer Division. As Jimmy (#1) later said:

" One reason we were able to grow so fast and not have problems was that we thought through most potential problems before we started. With Jack's help, we worked out all aspects of running the business in advance—people, finance, manufacturing, everything. We could afford to do it because we weren't starving to death. We were camped out in the Kleiner Perkins offices."

One really important aspect was to come up with a good name for this new product and company. The first name that Treybig came up with in 1970 was "Numerex," but that idea went nowhere, when DEC and Data General (DG) announced plans for products with a similar name. To everyone's relief, those plans never materialized, but it was while putting the finishing touches on the first business plan using a code name Multidata, in the fall of 1975, that the team realized that they needed to get serious about finding a suitable name. They drew up a list and every day rotated a new name to the top to brainstorm amongst the team. As noted in an article called "The Name Game" from the winter 1986 edition of

Tandem's *Center* magazine, the contenders included Datadyne, Dandi Data (Perkins thought it would get attention), Redundant Computers (until Dave Mackie pointed out that redundant could mean unnecessary), and of course the name Tandem, suggested by Green. On the day that the call came from the California Securities Commission for a name to put on the incorporation papers, the name at the top of the list was Tandem, so Loustaunou gave them that name.

By December 1975 a formal and detailed business plan had been finalized including a much more detailed design of the system and a development schedule with specific milestones. With all of this in hand, the company was able to close the books on a second round of financing from Data Science Ventures (as well as Kleiner & Perkins, who added another $500,000). Data Science Ventures (DSV), an East Coast firm who specialized in early-stage financing, was founded in 1968 by Mort Collins. Collins went on to advise a number of U.S. Presidents on science and technology matters including Ronald Reagan and George H. W. Bush.

Over the years, other key board members included Tommy Davis and Bill Davidow. Tommy Davis, the founder of the Mayfield Fund, was another Silicon Valley legend. Before Mayfield he had founded Davis and Rock, one of the first venture capital companies in Silicon Valley, with Art Rock. Bill Davidow (from Mohr-Davidow Ventures) worked with all the founders of Tandem at HP including Tom Perkins. He had been, according to Katzman, *"a vice-president of Intel, responsible for Intel's Memory and Microprocessor Division whose microprocessors were not used in Tandem CPU's because they were too slow, much to Davidow's annoyance"*. Two others, Alvin Rice and Robert Stone were the first real outside directors who joined the Tandem Board after the company went public. In later years George Shultz (former Secretary of State), Walter Wriston (former Chairman and CEO of Citicorp), Jack Bennett (former Chief Financial Officer of Exxon) and Andrew Knight (former Editor of *"The Economist"*) joined this illustrious group of outside directors. All of these investors and board members were instrumental, not just in giving Tandem credibility with very large customers, like McDonnell Automation, but also were very supportive of Jimmy's new approach to people management, which will be discussed later on.

According to the company's first business plan, *"the intended market is the use of multi-processor computers in online transaction-oriented applications."* As Tony Turner (#624) later commented:

"Thirteen words describe architecture, application and market completely and unambiguously. Note the subtlety of 'the use of.' The seat of value is use, not product. As perfect a market statement has not appeared before or since."

The major components of the computer system itself were a bus structure, central processor, and an input/output (I/O) system. As was defined by Green and Katzman in the original plan product description:

"The bus structure provides a low cost and fail-soft method of configuring multiple processors in a single system and includes dual high-speed paths between any two processors. All processors are physically identical. Each processor occupies just one or two printed circuit cards and is oriented toward data handling and multiprogramming. The input/output (I/O) system features dual-port interfaces to all external devices to insure fail-soft access in case of failure of a processor. All the system components are designed for high-speed throughput in a data-handling environment. It is going to have a specially designed, high-level systems programming language as well as a standard, general-purpose operating system which can be configured for a broad variety of multiprocessing applications."

As Dennis McEvoy (#6) said many years later:

"Of course Joel, Tom, Pete and I had no idea how we were going to do that. But that was what made joining Mike Green at Tandem such a fun thing to do. We were enthralled about the idea of working on building a new computer from scratch - something that hadn't been done before. Inventing was a lot more fun than maintaining. We had all worked together (at HP), so there was already a level of trust and knowledge of each others strengths and even our foibles."

Joel Bartlett, for example, was a brilliant, eccentric, hippy-like, software engineer with long hair who would bike into Santa Clara and later Cupertino everyday from Palo Alto. He'd gotten a Masters degree at Stanford and during that process had been exposed to the work of Per Brink Hansen, the Danish-born chief who, according to Wikipedia, was the architect of the RC 4000 minicomputer and its multiprogramming operating system kernel in the late 1960s. Hansen then went on to write the first comprehensive Operating Systems Principles textbook in 1972. With Hansen's ideas in mind, Joel figured out a way to build a transparent, message based operating system kernel. Other characters in the initial crew included Peter Graziano (known to all as Rocky) who was a self-taught programmer and Tom Blease who was a clean-cut ex-marine corps member. Tom was a few years older and hence a little more mature than the rest of them, who were in their mid to late 20's.

Employee number 22 was Sam Wiegand, who was hired as the vice president of Sales and Marketing in September of 1975. Sam's corporate roots were in Honeywell Information Systems where he started as a systems analyst in 1954 and ended in 1967 as Director of the western region sales organization. He ran marketing for

Information Handling Services, a microfilm publishing company and Diablo Systems that produced peripherals for the minicomputer and small business system industries. Just prior to joining Tandem he was President of Ball Computer Products a subsidiary of Ball Corporation, which manufactured optical character readers and a variety of electronic interfaces for minicomputer peripherals.

Sam was unique because he was an expert at both sales and marketing and as a result contributed greatly to the early success of Tandem. He was responsible for the company's effective positioning in the marketplace including the first "launch" article in Business Week that generated the early sales and for the wildly successful early advertising campaigns. Most notable was the *"Seven Tough Problems in On-Line Data Base Systems"* and *"How Tandem's NonStop System Solves Them"* advertisements. He also knew sales and since Jimmy had an aggressive plan, for Tandem to build its own direct sales force, Sam had his work cut out for him. (Author's note: Interestingly enough, one of the first marketing brochures shows Cupertino and Frankfurt as the two office locations. This was because Tandem's first salesman was Horst Enzelmueller who predated Sam and was hired in Germany. Jimmy was very proud of this fact and would often use this hiring as a way to demonstrate Tandem's early commitment to the international marketplace.)

Within 18 months Wiegand had hired district sales managers in Chicago, San Francisco, St. Louis, Washington DC, New York, Houston, Denver, Seattle and Los Angeles. All were experienced sales managers and many came from Honeywell where they had known Sam. They included Dave Peatrowsky, George Eckert, Julie Rubenstein, Tom Bechler, Charlie Ryle and others. These were really the first Tandem salesmen. Sam negotiated most of all the early deals, established the standard contracts, the compensation structure and with Dave Mackie's help the first sales training program (really a product training program), as these people already knew how to sell.

To run manufacturing, Sam lured Bob Marshall (#32) from Diablo Systems where he'd held a similar position. Bob started his career as an engineer at Lawrence Livermore Laboratory after obtaining a BSEE degree from Heald's Engineering College in San Francisco. Later he went on to get an MBA from Pepperdine. Xerox had just bought Diablo and Bob was intrigued with the concept of a fault tolerant computer system. Like Sam, Bob had lots of experience and was really good with people. At Tandem he was popular and well liked and great at making things happen. Later when he became Chief Operating Officer, he and Jimmy developed a really strong symbiotic relationship built on mutual trust. Jimmy focused on the vision and the strategy and Bob focused on the execution side. Bob was especially great at soothing ruffled feathers and talking Jimmy out of things when he got a little carried away.

Jimmy was quite the character. Of average height, stocky in body type and always slightly rumpled, Treybig as described in *Fortune* magazine in May 1987 had this shock of fuzzy hair that would *"explode from the side of his head in a curly frizz. His eyeglasses refused to perch properly on the bridge of his nose, preferring to park themselves crazily on the other end."* He hated knotting his tie and only did so when he had to meet customers, or members of the financial community. His sleeves were always rolled up and his shirttails had great difficulty remaining tucked in. According to *Fortune* magazine in 1982, his *"hands-in-pocket slouch gave him this incongruous air of a teenager hanging out on Main Street."* With that look came a serious Texas accent and an "aw-shucks" manner. One employee shared a story about the challenges involved in getting Jimmy ready for a press briefing in the early days:

"The Houston Chronicle decided to run a story about Jimmy featuring the theme of local boy from Rice University makes good. Well, Jimmy and his public relations people from Cupertino came in and got dressed in the Houston office where they were going to meet the Houston Chronicle people. The admin noticed that Jimmy had no belt on. Jimmy looked down and sure enough he had no belt on. So grumbling to himself he went back in and came out with two belts on. Nobody said anything but later someone from public relations took one of the belts off just before they went in to do the interview."

This image disguised a man who was extremely bright and quick-witted. As *Fortune* magazine put it in 1982, *"freewheeling theorizing came naturally to Jimmy T., as Tandemites called him. He was no idle daydreamer."* Many would think on first introduction that Treybig was either just a shucking and jiving bullshitter or a country bumpkin totally out of his element. Behind the country-boy demeanor was a driven, aggressive and extremely competent businessman. But one of Jimmy's important gifts was an ability to see quickly and easily to the heart of a problem and an ability to apply a laser focus on solving it. Jimmy was a charismatic evangelist and a first-class salesman through and through. As Tony Turner (#624) shared:

"A few [technology leaders] have stood astride product, company and people. Gates and Jobs come to mind. At heart, these men are not extroverts, although they show off occasionally. But Treybig was and probably still is. He was like a young east Texan coonhound. He would try and tree anything and bay and bay and bay. You had to love him and get excited and run around, even though he had treed the ugliest damn coon you ever saw."

His main form of exercise was running, which he liked to do every day at lunch. One had to be careful when setting up a meeting with his administrative assistant to not book an important one in the early afternoon, as more often than not, Treybig would never make it back into normal work clothes after his midday run and would appear even more rumpled than usual. In his free time, Jimmy was a ham radio fanatic and loved to go to remote islands such as Tuvalu, a Polynesian island nation located in the Pacific Ocean midway between Hawaii and Australia, where there weren't any ham radio operators. Off he would go, hauling hundreds of pounds of equipment, including generators, where he would broadcast using various frequencies and research how radio waves propagated in the atmosphere. He was also a designer and builder of radios and antennas and had a 100-foot antenna atop his home in Los Altos Hills. One classic ham radio story came from Ghery Pettit (#5816), a fellow ham radio aficionado:

"I was sitting in the ham shack one late afternoon copying down addresses from the Call Book. You old hams will remember that phone book-sized publication. Rich Humphrey (N6NAE) was talking on the radio (to Jimmy, who was in Kiribati at the time, a small island nation of 100,000 or so people, straddling the Equator, in the central tropical Pacific Ocean when there was a knock at the door. Rich opened it and there stood Bob Marshall, the Chief Operating Officer and Dave Rynne, the Chief Financial Officer. I went back to what I was doing. They seemed a bit agitated and wanted to know if we had any idea how they might get a hold of Jimmy. Without looking up, Rich just held up the microphone and said, 'Here, talk! He's on the other end.'"

Jimmy's down-home way of being meant that he always had time for you and no one was beneath him. These qualities with his natural charisma made you want to follow him to the ends of the earth. As Jackie Kramers (#2766) shared:

"My parents visited one time, so I took them to Beer Bust in Building 2 in Cupertino. Jimmy was walking around as he normally did, with a beer bottle in hand greeting everyone. He came over to the table we were sitting at. He introduced himself, I introduced my parents, he sat down and we all started chatting. This went on for about 15 minutes or so. He asked my parents what they did for a living. They replied in kind. My dad then turned around and asked Jimmy what he did at Tandem. I nearly died or wanted to slide under the table. I had been with Tandem about six months. Jimmy just smiled and said: 'Well, some people think I run this company, but if you look around you, these folks run the company for real.' We all laughed and I felt relieved. He shook hands with my folks and told me he would see me on Monday. My father was impressed, he told me what an interesting character Jimmy was and how pleased he was that I worked for a man that was the 'salt of the earth.' This was a high compliment coming from my dad."

Or as Gail Ayres (#279) wrote:

"Jimmy was the most honest and finest man a young company could have as its President, its symbol. He was practically on a first-name basis with all his employees at corporate headquarters on Vallco Parkway and beyond and loved by all! Maybe it was the whole Texas thing he had about him, but employees really enjoyed being able to talk to their President one-on-one and not feel nervous about it."

Glenn Story's (#8968) related his experience at a new employee orientation, a standard part of the Tandem onboarding process:

"I first ran into Jimmy at the new employee orientation where he was scheduled to give a welcome talk. I entered the room to see this man fiddling with and cursing a slide projector. I figured he was some audiovisual guy. Lo and behold, it was Jimmy. His Texas accent and word usage didn't match my expectations of a company president."

Or as Charlene G. LaBelle (#2729) shared of her experience, also at a new employee orientation program:

"I remember it all quite vividly. At that time I smoked tobacco, so had a leather cigarette case sitting on the table in front of me as I sat in the front row. I remember 'some engineer type' in a white shirt (that wasn't even tucked in) asked if he could have a cigarette. I said sure. He took two, since he noticed I had a full pack. Boy was I surprised when this same guy got up and talked to all of us. In those days 'bumming a smoke' was no big deal."

Dave Sperry (#3913) remembers a time in 1982 when Jimmy invited all employees who participated in the *San Jose Mercury News* 10K Run to return to his home afterward for a buffet lunch. As Dave (#3913) recalled:

"The turnout was super. Approximately 100 runners converged on Jimmy's digs in Los Altos Hills for a fantastic meal. One minor detail—not a stick of furniture was in the house, but with rented tables, chairs and a cook we had a ball. The underwear found on the handball court next to the swimming pool, the glass dance floor and the huge ham radio operator antenna intrigued us all. As a new employee, I was amazed that a CEO would open his home to the masses."

Justin Simonds' (#4521) experience as a new customer engineer in August of 1982:

"I started and went almost immediately to Basic Analyst (BAT) training given by the incomparable Dennis Aiello. Long lives the Aiello gram. (A diagram showing the partitioning of memory code and data spaces, invented by Dennis.) It seemed like

everyday he'd fill up every board in the room and it all made sense while he was talking. The class ran for four weeks and I arrived back in Los Angeles exhausted with my head whirling, but was just in time for the Western Region sales kick-off in Santa Barbara. I almost didn't go but later was very glad I did. There were presents every day in the hotel room including towels, shirts, pewter beer steins, and pins. There were staggering parties including a beach party with a live band and all you could eat shrimp, crab and lobster. Did I join the right company or what?"

Jimmy cared deeply about his employees. As Dave Sperry (#3913) went on to say:

"The best example I can think of Jimmy's personal caring for his employees was this. At one point a Tandem employee was diagnosed with bone cancer. The only thing that would save him was a bone-marrow transplant, but finding a matching donor was very unlikely. Jimmy had Tandem pay for expensive screening blood tests for any employee who wanted to take it. I volunteered."

However, back to our main story. The office on Stender Way was basically one giant open bullpen of a room. There were no interior walls and no cubicles, just a pile of desks. Most of the time the team could deal with the general noise levels without getting too distracted, but as the pressure mounted and the deadlines became more real, distraction became a real problem. The solution was that one of the few offices that the team had became "The Barrel". Anytime a team member was on the critical path to meet a schedule deadline, they were relegated into "The Barrel"where they could concentrate and shut out distractions.

"Beer Bust" started in July 1975. As the hardware group had just completed the first wire-wrapped breadboard (cpu and memory), Joel decided that it was just as good a time as any to add the operating system. After several days of tweeking, he was able to get it up and running. The team was so excited that one of them ran out to get some beer to celebrate the success. From then on, the group started looking for reasons to celebrate at the end of the work day on Fridays. Eventually the "Beer Bust" became ritualized, not just for celebration, but as a way to reduce the stress and strengthen team cohesiveness. It also provided an opportunity to to talk about what each team member was working on, what was working, what wasn't, and sometimes even brainstorm solutions. Though Jimmy had to spend most of his time off-premise convincing investors, suppliers and landlords that Tandem was real, so as to obtain reasonable prices, contract terms and all that necessary stuff, he always made sure he was around on Friday's to host a compulsory game of Liar's Poker in his office. His objective he said was to teach the engineers all about the fine line between risk and opportunity – what he called a practical MBA.

In 1976, after 17 months of development and 15 years before the first Internet server appeared on the scene, the Tandem NonStop was launched. Progress had almost come to a grinding halt a few months earlier. Hardware and software were now integrated into the cabinets, but it soon became apparent that the small muffin fans weren't creating enough of an air flow to keep the systems cool enough. Steve Hayashi (#23) was determined to find a solution. After several weeks of experimentation he came up with a redesign with bigger fans and an air plenum chamber that forced the air higher in the cabinet to cool the processors. In order to make this all fit, Ken Barton (#20) had to redesign some of the packaging to accomodate Steve's changed components. As Jim Katzman (#3) shared:

"Ken Barton (#20) found a fan that met Hayashi's specs that had a very soft plastic blade, so that one could stick their hand in a working fan and stop the fan without any potential of harm or danger. It didn't even sting to do it. That was important because Ken felt that if we could leave off the finger guard (a wire mesh that went over the front of the fan to prevent one from sticking their finger into the fan) then the fan could push even more air through the cabinet. The wire mesh he felt actually impeded airflow by a significant percentage. Now the fans were only exposed when the keyed front cabinet door was opened, which would only be done by a field engineer. So the decision was made to leave the finger guards off since the only people exposed to the fans would be Tandem Field engineers who were trained that the fans had no potential for harm. Now Ken had lost the tip of his index finger years before we started Tandem, so he had only half of an index finger on one hand. When it came time to get UL (Underwriters Laboratories) approval for safety, the inspector came through to inspect our proposed final production product. When we opened the cabinet to expose the insides of the Tandem system, he noticed the fans had no finger guards and said that it was a problem. Ken declared with a big grin that it was no problem: "Watch", he said. He then stuck his index finger in one of the fans and stopped it. The UL guy then tried the same on another fan. Then Ken removed his fake half-finger from the fan and displayed it to the UL inspector (he hadn't noticed Ken's hand before this). Horrified, the inspector took his own finger out and saw that his finger was fine. Ken then burst out laughing. Our system was approved without finger guards on the fans."

With the company now settled on 20605 Valley Green Drive in Cupertino and as described so elegantly by Tony Turner (#624):

"What emerged from the hands and minds of the 'TANDEM TEN' was a way to tie 16 separate minicomputers together by means of a high speed bus. Called the Tandem T16 based on a unique operating system they called Guardian, it was built from the ground up as message-based, peer-coupled, shared-nothing piece of design excellence. Not only was it fault tolerant, it was also geographically independent and linearly scalable (almost) and contained primitives for data integrity and transaction

consistency. Where most computers were ugly through and through, 'The Tandem' was only plain on the outside. Inside it was elegant. You could look at the backplane and see how it worked and from there what it could be used for. How much of that was intentional would be a good discussion to have someday at a bar."

It was called "NonStop" because its multiprocessor arrangement provided non-stop computing such that if one of the processor's components were to break down, the other processors would observe the failure and absorb the workload of that processor. The first Tandem 16 system was delivered to Citibank in May 1976. Bob Marshall (#32) shared some perspectives on that first system:

"The first order to Citibank was for $116,000, a two-processor system in a single cabinet. Each processor had 64 kilobites of core memory with 32 bits on each of two 16" by 18" circuit boards, two 10 MB disc drives and a 60 line per minute printer (made by Control Data). The Disc drives were like mini- refrigerators."

Many thought this first system was to support online transaction processing in the innovative automatic banking machine network that Citibank had just intro-duced, but this wasn't the case. Citibank's first application was to automate its internal telephone directory—not quite so exotic an application, but online just the same. It wasn't until years later that the bank was willing to chance a mission-critical application to a new technology and company. However, as Jimmy (#1) said at the time, *"In those days, we were willing to sell to anybody for anything."*

In the beginning, the entire company was involved with the sale of the systems and often, Jimmy, Dave Mackie and Sam Weigand would be heavily involved with closing the initial orders. The early customers were really pioneers, taking a big job security risk in choosing Tandem over IBM and it was crucial that they knew that the entire company would support their success from Treybig on down. As Bob Marshall (#32) shared at a recent seminar:

"We had three parties for every order we got. First there was the party to celebrate when the sales person called to say that he or she had an order. Second was the party to celebrate when the system shipped and third was the party to celebrate when the customer paid."

Manufacturing took place in an open area thirty feet by thirty feet that included three shelves that were the stockroom, two long tables that were assembly, quality assurance, shipping and receiving. Since most of the subassembly work was con-tracted out to job shops, Tandem employees were responsible for system assembly, integration, testing and if needed rework. As Maureen Wallis (#63), production supervisor for the original 'Magnificent Seven' core assembly group, as they called themselves, said in a Center Magazine article in 1986:

"The place was so packed with energy, everyone wanted to give 300 percent. There was no holding back. Very rarely did you see someone not wanting to participate in whatever was going on at the time, from a potluck to staying late, or coming in early, to doing whatever it took to get the work done. It was fast. It was fun. We went at a pace that was unbelievable. Everyone made a total commitment to themselves for personal growth, enjoyment, and so on. As a group it wasn't viewed as an organization, it was a family. We felt each others hurts, we sympathized with each other, we celebrated each other. I think that people genuinely cared about one another. We were close from a professional standpoint and a personal one. The weakness of one person or group was offset dramatically by the strengths of another person or group. So you never had to worry about something slipping by and peers kept everyone from abusing the system. Now this is not to say that there weren't some challenging times. The group did have its share of toe-to-toe yelling and screaming with engineers or developers, trying to resolve product design issues. But more often than not, when the air cleared, the respect was still there."

Though the first year's business wasn't quite what had been expected, the systems performed so revenues and income soon caught up to the original projections found in that infamous first business plan. The original December 1975 press release announcing the first NonStop computer systems included ten pages of technical jargon, but Dave Mackie, the first product manager, captured the elegance of 'The Tandem' perfectly in an amazingly effective sales presentation that later took on a life of its own as the "Mackie Pitch." As Jim Katzman (#3) mused, *"Mackie was probably the best presenter the company had and was crucial to the company's early product marketing success.* As Tony Turner (#624) recalled:

"Employees could watch a video of the 'Mackie Pitch' presentation, look at the machine and relate it to their own experience and expertise and presto, instant synergy. There were some tradeoffs. 'The Tandem' couldn't run all things equally. More than a tad autistic, it was the 'Rainman' of processors as far as programmers and data were concerned. But once inside a transaction, it could whip around and be sure of getting out again."

One common and entertaining sales technique perfected at that time that freaked more than a few customers out was to take a customer to see a live system, preferably in some place like a manufacturing operation that was running real-time applications. The sales rep or systems analyst would open the back of the Tandem to let them see its inner workings and then would reach out and pull out one of the circuit boards. Customers would gasp, but be even more surprised when the system kept running as if nothing had happened. As was reported in *Electronic Business Magazine* in December 1978:

> *"Before Tandem came on the scene, a computer that did not go down was a rare sight indeed. Most commercial systems manufacturers had tried a different approach, offering triple-modular-redundancy (TMR) in which every board was replicated three times and every action by every piece of hardware were performed in triplicate. Three times the hardware and three times the price for the same performance. But by starting from scratch, Tandem was able to tailor its machine for commercial computing in a transaction-oriented environment by incorporating some unique features in the system such as intelligent input/output controllers and channels, two separate super high-speed processor channels at 13 megabytes/second each, and mirrored data-bases."*

Nonstop computing meant the system was never down, not even for routine maintenance. The key was to power down a module or failed part and leave the rest of the system running. To accomplish this, the capability had to be designed in at the architectural level. More importantly, the hardware and software had to be developed simultaneously. This was a unique way of building systems, with great attention paid to power distribution and cooling areas. In fact, more than 20 percent of the original Tandem patents were in power distribution and cooling. These were areas generally considered mundane by most technology companies.

Also critical in those days was upward compatibility. All technology executives (called in those days Vice Presidents of Information Technology or Electronic Data Processing) worried about running out of processing power, which would trigger the need to buy a bigger machine. But with a Tandem machine, if a user outgrew the basic two-processor system, all they had to do for more processing power was plug in another processor to get twice the performance. Up to 16 processors could be connected into a single system. Now after four systems were connected, the additional processing power available wasn't totally linear, but was about as close to it as anyone had been able to get up to that point. The customer didn't need to dispose of an old computer and none of the applications became obsolete. A marvel it was. A classic example of the impact of this technology on the market came from Henry Norman (#3827), who at the time was working as a programmer for a value-added reseller in Stockholm, Sweden, called Integrated Computer Systems (ICS).

> *"A group of us were visiting New York City to attend the National Computer Conference (NCC) Fair, when my boss came running up to us, very, very excited, saying that 'There's a small outfit in California that has implemented computer batteries. When you need more power, you just plug in more computers and go. You've got to check this out!' So we did and eventually hacked out a tentative agreement for ICS to*

distribute Tandem systems in Sweden. Vingresor (a subsidiary of Scandinavian Airlines) became the first Scandinavian Tandem customer.

"I was completely absorbed by the Tandem NonStop (TNS) architecture and later accepted an offer from SAS to work in their computing center in Stockholm in their 'new technology' group. One of my first tasks was to review a major market research project already conducted by SAS in search of a platform to base their ideas of 'distributed processing' (hot stuff at the time) for future applications. Looking at the system requirements (it came to me) that it was like reading the specs for a TNS system. But Tandem wasn't even on the 'short list.' So determined as I was to work on this great new concept in computing, I managed to get Tandem's name added to the list. Some time later Linjeflyg (the Swedish domestic airline, another SAS subsidiary) selected Tandem as their 'system of choice for everything.' There was only one catch—they required Tandem to open offices and support centers in Oslo, Copenhagen and Stockholm. This happened at a meeting that I was invited to as the one systems programmer who was to work exclusively with the new Tandem systems. It was a meeting between Thoralf Korsvold (the SAS Data Vice President), Knut Haernes (Director of SAS Data Stockholm) and from Tandem Samuel Wiegand, James Katzman, and the Vice President of Tandem Europe, Horst Enzelmueller. Thoralf Korsvold raised the issue of SAS requiring "Tandem support offices in Stockholm, Oslo, and Copenhagen." Jim Katzman looked at Horst Enzelmueller, and after an agreeing nod from him and from Sam, he said "Sure, we will do that, it's a deal"! High level and fast decision making. (and the three offices were promptly opened, manned and operational, very shortly thereafter)!

For my efforts in getting SAS to choose Tandem, I was later called in for a rather serious interrogation. SAS management wanted to find out if my adamancy in advocating Tandem could be connected with some sort of payola. Of course I was not "paid off," and my defense was the best. I told Knut Haernes (who did the questioning) that my job here at SAS was to try and ensure that SAS got the best possible system for distributed processing, and I was only trying to do my best for SAS to achieve this goal. Case closed. I spent four more years with SAS doing systems programming on their TNS systems. My favorite demo was to tell the visitors of the TNS development center, 'Watch this!' And then trip the computer room main power switch. No worries, watch again! And turn the power back on. And there it was, up and running. It impressed the heck out of everyone!"

Carl W., one of the core members of Tandem's customer support organization, shared his experience:

"In 1976 I had my first contact with Tandem in Frankfurt, Germany. Josef Broeker, one of the original systems engineers, did a demo for me on a Sunday, and I was more

than impressed. He simply turned on power—and the system continued working from where it had been when it was shut down on Friday night. The good old T16 with core memory had a wonderful and clean hardware design compared to what I was working with at that time."

As Phil Ly (#1067) said:

"The T16 architecture was so elegant that it was virtually impossible to come out with a better follow-up model. We were doing network computing (in a box) before anyone else. As an extension to that architecture, EXPAND (the networking system) too was ahead of its time. Requester/server was already a core Tandem concept way before the industry started the client/server craze. The list just went on and on of core features that were way ahead of the industry."

Or Al C.:

"I remember seeing the architecture of the Tandem for the first time. I had come over from Ford Aerospace by an invitation from an ex-technician there who was working for Tandem. I took one look at it and decided that I wanted to work for a company that made such equipment. Almost NO cables and the black monolith was awesome (I was working on Varian Systems at the time for Ford)! After going through nine interviews over three weeks, I was hired!

With this elegant technology also came a unique approach to people and management. Some was based on Hewlett and Packard's "HP Way," but to it Treybig added a unique Texan twist. Right from the beginning there were several basic principles that were fundamental to the founders' view of the kind of company that they were going to build. Firstly, people mattered. Secondly, vision and direction setting mattered. Thirdly, having the best technology mattered. Fourthly, having happy customers mattered and lastly creativity and innovation to drive growth mattered. Over the years these basic elements manifested themselves into the lots of different forms but the underlying philosophy was simple:

- All people are good
- People, the workers, the management and the company are all the same
- Every single person in the company must understand the essence of the business
- Every employee must benefit from the company's success
- Management must create an environment where all of the above can happen

Most technology companies today have similar statements that describe their culture, so it's hard for most people to understand just how unique and groundbreaking these statements were in the mid-1970s. The Tandem Philosophy, as it was known, came into being when the four founders (Jim Treybig, Jim Katzman, Mike Green and Jack Loustaunou) sat around on Friday evenings at the original "Beer Busts" discussing what kind of company Tandem should be. Jim Katzman (#3) kindly gave me a look at his original design notebooks and of course I was expecting a mad collection of engineering diagrams. I was shocked to see on the first page three bullet points about management philosophy not hardware design as follows:

- *Give a lot of direction at first and get them started on a good path then have occasional design reviews and do your own thing.*
- *Dole out project managerships freely and work for one, while managing the overall project.*
- *Get 'professional profile' data sheets out on each employee with past accomplishments and areas of interest and boredom and areas of aspiration.* [Author's note: This last one sounds a lot like modern day advice for a LinkedIn profile]

According to Richard Pascale, a Stanford professor and management expert, quoted in an article in *Newsweek* in June 1981:

"*The management style that was evolving at the time in Silicon Valley owed its existence to two vastly different companies. Fairchild Camera and Instrument Corp., the industry pioneer, flourished in its early years under a highly centralized management that pitted employee against employee in ferocious competition. But its managers did not foresee the boom that eventually created a shortage of skilled labor where turnover rates exceeded 100 percent in some companies. Fairchild didn't realize the need to hold onto people. It didn't understand that keeping experienced people was an immense competitive advantage. As a result it atomized and by the 1970s its best people were spinning off to Intel, National Semiconductor and Advanced Micro Devices. HP took the opposite approach. Founded in 1939, HP had a tradition of paternalism, hiring with meticulous care, generously sharing profits and imbuing its employees with Zen-like precepts of the company philosophy "The HP Way." The idea was that the company ought to 'make meaning' as well as money. HP managers decided early that they wouldn't run a hire-and-fire operation. When semiconductor orders slumped in 1970, everyone in the company took a 10 percent pay cut and no one was laid off. HP was a leader in instituting flexible work schedules tailored to its employees' individual needs. HP became the role model for the industry. Today Silicon Valley companies wage constant war on bureaucracy and hierarchical structures. The emphasis is on instant communications, the bias toward quick action. Perhaps more important, Silicon Valley managers believe in spreading the wealth. But Silicon Valley companies are hardly country clubs. Beneath all the camaraderie and teamwork are very tough, sophisticated management tools.*"

As *BusinessWeek* reported of the Tandem culture in July 1980:

"Employees have neither time clocks nor name badges, its workers have flexible hours, a swimming pool that is open between 6 a.m. and 8 p.m., a volleyball court complete with locker room and showers, an open-door policy that invites employees to drop in for a talk with their managers at any time and six week sabbatical with full pay that all employees are required to take every four years. Turnover runs less than 8 percent annually, far lower than the industry average of 23 percent. Job candidates are often called back three or more times for interviews lasting several hours, and salary offers are never made until a recruit accepted a job. As Jimmy said at the time, 'They've got to decide that they're not just coming for the money.'"

The company preferred to hire experienced people because they required less training. Jimmy himself participated personally in most new employee orientations with the goal to spread the management gospel, and used peer pressure to inculcate recruits in the Tandem way. Most decisions were made informally, with few formal meetings or reviews and executives would get together in spontaneous meetings as problems arose. As Romie Pickerill (#53) from manufacturing said in 1986 in NS News:

"There was such respect for peers and management. Managers were out on the floor with their people, not hidden in their offices. Jimmy and Bob always made it a point to meet and learn the names of new employees. Daily, they wandered around the manufacturing floor, casually talking to the employees. "Hi, I'm Jimmy, I work here. Where do you work?" was Jimmy's usual banter. And almost everyone in the group, upon joining Tandem had the embarrassing experience of asking him: "So, who are you? Where do you work?"

As previously indicated, hiring people was a big deal at Tandem and everyone got involved in the hiring process. Though formalized much later as part of the Understanding Tandem Philosophy Program, hiring was seen as an art that everyone needed to master. It included the following critical components:

- Individual should always visit us several times
- They should be interviewed at a higher and lower level
- Never make an offer until they have mentally decided they want to work with us
- Never hire someone who doesn't have "innates" such as honesty, integrity, a work ethic and desire for team winning, etc.
- Try to hire the very best we can attract and pay what they are worth

Joe Novak (#117) shared his experience:

"After interviews with Jim Campbell (a manager), Jerry Reaugh and Bob Marshall (both Vice Presidents), I was told I had to talk to Jimmy. For a shipping/receiving clerk's job?? Yes, I was told. Everyone who Tandem is considering for a position has to talk to Jimmy. I walked into Jimmy's office, after purchasing a necktie and getting a haircut. Jimmy had several cigarettes burning in different ashtrays in his office. His shirt was untucked, his glasses were crooked on his face and his hair looked like he had just walked out of a wind tunnel. He asked me why I wanted to work for Tandem. I don't remember exactly what I said. He responded by extending his hand and welcoming me to Tandem. His parting comments were—'Those women on the assembly line are all mine—keep you hands off them!!' Of course I told him I would." [Author's note: Sometimes it took awhile to get used to Jimmy's Texan sense of humor].

Another example of the lengths that the company would go to convince you to work there includes this anecdote from Polly Kam (#1177), who joined the company in 1979:

"I joined Tandem because of a VP's response to my question, Why should I work for Tandem? HP had a freeze on hiring at the time and I was worried that I would be hired and then be fired in three months. He answered me by saying, HP is a steady growth company, Tandem is a fast-growing company. Joining Tandem will provide you an opportunity to advance faster. It is not Tandem's policy to hire an employee and then fire her in three months, however if you are not satisfied with my answer, I can have you talk to our President and let him answer this question himself. I was totally impressed and awed by his response amazed that the President would take time out of their busy schedule to talk to a littler person in the hierarchy, a nobody, like me? With that, I sold my body and soul to Tandem."

The company had a relaxed and informal way about it, more pronounced on Fridays and a shock to some employees when they first started. As Bob Cron (#7061) shared:

"I started in 1984 in Hardware Engineering Computer Operations at Walsh Ave. Dianne Wylie hired me but first I had to interview with Nori Lemon. She saw me in my coat and tie and, very directly, asked me how I was going to pull cables, crawl under desks, etc. in those clothes! I guess I passed muster."

Or Pete Kronberg's (#6276) experience in November of 1983:

"I got a phone call from some guy named Joe Martinez at some company in San Jose called Tandem. I'd never heard of either. Joe told me that he understood that I was soon getting out of the Navy and wondered if I'd like a job! Well, I had planned to

be a ski bum for the winter after finishing my enlistment, but, well, something in my guts told me not to pass up a chance to check it out. We made arrangements for me to interview and, on that day, I got dressed in my sharpest winter dress blue uniform, and drove from Vallejo to the education center on Santa Ana Court (off of Arques) in Sunnyvale not knowing what to expect. So, I met Joe and several of his staff, including Dennis Rich and Kevin Calkins. We took a walk through the lab and some classrooms, and then back to his office to continue our very informal chat. Suddenly there's a knock at his door, and Joe says to me, 'Pete, I'd like you to meet Guido D'Ambrosio—he'll be your supervisor!' In walks this roly-poly guy dressed in faded jeans, riddled with old holes from a battery acid spill or something, green and yellow argyle socks, clogs and a bowling shirt! Guido says 'Hey Pete, good to meetcha! Whaddaya say we have a chat in The Swamp?' The Infamous Swamp. Guido's office (known as The Swamp) is more like a two-bit museum than an office. There was women's underwear and stuffed bras arranged on the wall, weird little statues all around and strange little signs with colorful sayings (some of questionable taste). Technical manuals were strewn about, empty beer cans, full ashtrays, half-dead plants, an old parking meter, a fish tank/terrarium that was completely green and countless other strange bits of junks including some provocative TANDEM posters on the wall (yep, the two bombshell blondes on the bike). I was SOLD. …. Besides The Swamp, I remember Bill Hanson's old-fashioned barber's chair, smack-dab in the middle of his office where he'd read the paper on breaks. To this very day I don't know exactly the chain of events and contacts that led Joe Martinez to me, but it was a life-changing event."

In the early years, customer information files were kept in shoeboxes. Shipment status was tracked by colors highlighted using a highlighter on a paper log. As Polly Kam (#1177) recalled:

"End of quarter crunch, you would see everyone at the ship dock helping. Sales commission splits were hand calculated. Donna Ducey had such a hard time maintaining commission because of its various rules. She sat at a cubicle next to me and we became good friends. So, to help her, I created a commission system using ENABLE. The cafeteria was in a little room manned by two young ladies and the lunch menu was limited to what a microwave oven and hand-crafted sandwiches could offer. Toast was made from a home appliance toaster and bacon was done in a microwave oven. Beer was stored in a regular refrigerator and for Beer Bust folks just grabbed a bottle, pulled up a chair and sat at any available table."

Jan Seamons (#442), another early employee, recalled one Friday that stood out in her memory:

"A tipsy colleague was standing on the counter. She had decided to change the menu (one of those black fabric cards with white stick-on letters) and added a new

item to the list—namely a 'Nooner' for about $2.00 with other menu items too risqué to repeat."

An example of the camaraderie and can-do work environment of the early Tandem can be seen in this recollection from Joe Novak (#117):

"Our first shipment to OCLC in 1977 was at the time by far the largest system (and $$$ order) Tandem had shipped in its history. After moving into the Vallco Parkway buildings in Cupertino earlier that year, we (the OPS Team) worked for many months to build and test the OCLC system. I believe it was our first system with only semi-memory boards (instead of the old core memory boards) and one of the first shipments with the new Apex 300 MB disk drives. On Christmas Eve, with Bob Marshall, Chief Operating Officer and a host of others, we packed and loaded two North American van trucks to the brim with the OCLC system. Before the doors on the trucks were closed, Bob Marshall asked me if I was sure there was a packing slip on Box #1 of the order. I told him I was sure there was. He wanted to be certain. I climbed into the truck trailer and inched my way to the very front of the trailer before locating Box #1 and confirming indeed there was a packing slip on the box. Just around midnight, the trucks were closed and pulled away. Bob arranged for champagne and beer for everyone. There were many tired folks—yet very satisfied that we had completed such an amazing accomplishment."

Al C.'s experience watching:

"Jimmy at end of quarter, pushing iron out the door at Cupertino's SIT (Systems Integration and Test) facility. An old 'founder technician' in an Army field jacket (never did get his name), walking around looking for something to do and fixing really weird intermittent problems on multi-layer boards at the Watsonville board testing facility. "

And another from Frank Sheeman (#100), who was hired into this startup that no one had ever heard of in January of 1977:

"Dave Mackie hired me as a flunky programmer on the Tandy Radio Shack warehouse automation project in Fort Worth, Texas and later around the corner from Disneyland. In retrospect I don't think I was qualified, but I learn quick. The first hurdle was 'the class'—three weeks in Cupertino taught by Bob Unanski. It was a great class. One got to learn everything there was to know about Tandem and read all the new and very well written manuals. I asked a lot of questions. Fortunately, Glenn Peterson (Agent #99) was hired the same day. I learned a lot from Glenn. Like programs should have no module bigger than one page and all modules should have exactly one entry and one exit. And thou shalt not use 'Go To.'

"TAL was the only language available. Status, Fup, Pup, Backup/Restore pretty much completed what we had to work with. Good rules. Off to Fort Worth. There were six of us. Things evolved. About April, the Tandy site manager called me into his office and showed me about half an inch of TAL printouts. 'Do you think you could take these over?' They looked pretty simple. 'Sure.' I had neglected to ask what they were supposed to do. They became 12 inches. 'Sure' had committed my waking hours from that date until mid-September. All of them. I also hadn't asked the authors. Much later, while disparaging the quality of my inheritance to Jimmy Treybig and Dave Mackie over beer, I learned that two of the programs had been written by Jimmy and Dave. Oops. In May we packed off to the pilot site in Anaheim. ENSCRIBE was very new. It didn't always work. By this time the programming team consisted of Glenn Peterson doing the two hard programs (Order Entry, Pull Tickets) and me doing about 30 easy programs (Invoice, Order Delete, Shipping Labels). The others had moved on. There was also Don Singleton from Tandy. And Mary Lou, who kept us from killing Don. Don had written the Spooler and 'TandyLib.' Print spooling, pretty much a copy of IBM stuff he knew. He was quite annoyed with us when Glenn rewrote it one night. Glenn's had only one real advantage—it actually worked. Said Spooler morphed into the Tandem Spooler and it stayed around for quite some time. Don was also annoyed with us when I finally decided I had enough of the naming standard that said that Order Entry was 'ACCT1201' and Invoicing was 'ACCT1428.' We only had eight characters for file names. Between 2 and 3 a.m. one night, Glenn and I changed all the names to things like 'OrdrENT' and 'Invoice.' And fixed all the software accordingly.

"By this time, Glenn and I were on a roll. We had our heads around this stuff. Changes were easy. Don Singleton wandered in around 8:30 a.m., pulled up the Status display and was visibly preparing to explode. Fortunately, the retired Marine Colonel running the warehouse looked over his shoulder, saw the display and said 'Hey, that's really neat. I can tell what's running now.' Tandylib? 2000 lines of utility library. It was a bit of a pig. Glenn got annoyed one night and rewrote it to run in 64 words of memory. Glenn and I got fabulous support. Joel Bartlett and Dennis McEvoy took most of our calls. (Sorry, no email until 1980. That's another story). We got major updates to ENSCRIBE in under 24 hours. Later in the process we were in the course of installing a major OS update, had completed the update, and were doing the restore when we noticed the tape reel doing endless retries. 11 p.m. Move a couple inches, backup, repeat. We were about to be screwed. We had to finish the restore and print pull tickets by 8 a.m. or we would shut down the warehouse. We called. Dennis drove to work, debugged the situation, and came up with a patch. 2 a.m. I carefully applied the patch—four commands in debug. No room for error. Bingo, tape took off—and stopped again. Dennis had found bad blocks that had to be patched to process success-fully. So I had to patch all the bad blocks, without making a mistake. There was no *time to do another five-hour restore. So I'm typing, Glenn and Mary Lou are watching carefully, ready to grab my hand away from Return should I make an error. Something over 150 patches later we got past the bad spot and it took off, finishing around 0700. Pull tickets were printed and delivered to the hopper just as the last prior ticket was removed. We didn't quite shut Tandy down. But that was September.*

"Back to June. We got the Anaheim warehouse application working to our satisfaction and to that of the Colonel who was running the warehouse. Then Charles Tandy decided to reorganize his company. The new model centralized all the 'Bottom 2000' items in one warehouse in Fort Worth. He didn't seem to think it was necessary to ask us if that was a good idea. Suddenly we were faced with the Fort Worth warehouse processing 1,000 orders per day at 2,000 lines per order. That was more than an order of magnitude bigger than what we had faced. Tandem's are modular expandable. Dave Mackie, faced with a strict budget from Tandy, configured a system that came within a few hundred dollars of said budget. That gave us five CPUs with about 256 KB memory (yes kilobytes) and nine hard drives. One was 10 MB in two units, the rest were four pairs of mirrored 50 MB (think washing machines) drives. We put the operating software (yes, the OS and the application) on the 10 MB with all the OS on one of the five CPUs. Then we did some back of the envelope calculations. The program that deleted old order details from completed orders was going to run 24 hours per day, dedicated system. This calculation inspired some 'concern' in Cupertino. Glenn and I were invited north. By the time we arrived we had a plan. Joel bought it. In the next two weeks, Glenn and I modified every program we had to use blocking of the order detail file and massive use of a new program we just had gotten from Cupertino —SORT—to speed up Glenn's two critical jobs. Massively. It was no longer truly online transaction processing with a normalized database. It worked. With some tuning. One night we were managing memory swaps—reorganize the code so the working set of pages would be smaller. We got the working set down to 10 pages. And moving files around on the disk to minimize seeks. I had my hand on the hard drive yelling to Glenn every time a seek happened. He'd move stuff around and retry. The ultimate in fine-tuning. System deployed successfully.

"The deal was pay when it worked. It worked in LATE September. On September 30 I (in Fort Worth) received a call from CFO Jack Loustaunou. Go pick up the $1 million+ check from Tandy. Take it to this specific building, this floor, this office—get there before 4 p.m. Our fiscal year ended that day. Revenue about $3 million. IPO was in November. We won. Tandy was lucky. They had bet on a startup. I can understand the bet. Once Jimmy Treybig, Dave Mackie and Sam Wiegand decide you are going to buy something you might as well just sign and save yourself the pain. The odds were maybe 10 percent of the bet paying off. Had we failed, they would have been unable to ship from that big new warehouse—their stores would have been screwed for Christmas 1977. But Tandem had a good team. Glenn and I were the visible point at *the customer, but without magic in Cupertino development we would have failed. One thing we learned in Anaheim—absent the sun, the normal workday is about 32 hours. Get up, eat big at Denny's (24 hour breakfast), work, order pizza, work, get tired, go have big dinner, sleep, repeat cycle. 32 hours per cycle."*

And Bob Strand's (#105) customer support experience in the early days:

"I was working in Technical Support in Cupertino and we got a call after normal working hours one evening. It was a very (self) important VP from McDonnell Auto-mation (McAuto). Theyhad been having a problem with their development system and wanted someone there immediately to fix it. I explained that we were aware of the problem and had a software or hardware fix that would be ready the next day. I also explained that I and others had reservations to fly to St. Louis the next afternoon and would install the fix tomorrow evening. That wasn't good enough for him and he demanded to talk to someone higher up. At that time, Jimmy and all the execs and sales staff were off in the Bavarian Alps at an annual sales meeting. Cell phones weren't around then so they were pretty much out of reach.

"After bullying me for about 20 minutes demanding that I fly out right away he finally realized that I was not about to budge. I wanted to fix his system and waiting until the next day for the fix was the fastest way to ensure it. Once he calmed down I said that our flight would land at about 6 p.m. the next night and we could be there by 7 p.m. Will the system be available to us at that time? His response was, 'Of course not. I will have 40 engineers and programmers using the system until midnight.' The system was not working 100 percent but was still able to be used by 40 people. We arrived there at 7 p.m. the next night, checked in with the customer and found lots of people getting lots of work done. We went to dinner. After dinner we went over to Frank Sheeman's house (who was living in St. Louis at the time) for a while and even-tually back to McAuto at midnight. We got the system at 1 a.m. and installed the fix and the problem went away. The point being, at companies before Tandem, when I arrived on a scene like this, I was given the whole machine as it would not be able to support one person let alone 40.

"The other story is more of the same. We got a call from Raytheon in Massachu-setts in the dead of winter. They were having a problem with their eight CPU system being used for developing software for the Washington Post. *This problem was not known to us and normally would have been handled by the eastern system spe-cialist. But Ken Piro was off on a company boondoggle cruise in the Caribbean. They were having intermittent processor halts so we gathered a team of people and all the diagnostic link boards we could find to head into winter's worst. They were using the machine 24 hours a day and continued to do so even after we arrived. They allowed us to test on two of the eight CPUs between 2 a.m. and 4 a.m. each day.*

"During the several days that we were there they had something like three or four processor halts—the other seven kept going and no one really noticed except us. Eventually we got a hit on one of our two CPUs and isolated the problem to a driver that Raytheon had paid a consultant $35,000 to write for their system. Again the point here was we had a single point of failure that took away one-eighth of the machine for a short time. On more than one occasion, we had reports from the field that they had gone to a customer's site and found a processor that had halted several days before. But because the system kept going and the customer did not do rigorous checks they did not even know it. Contrast that with a bright blue screen from Mr. Gates."

Photo of the first T16 Tandem NonStop from the original Brochure

First Tandem Logo

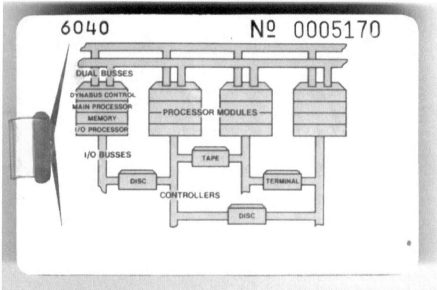

Top: Tom Perkins (l) and Jimmy (r) - The Tandem Story Video Bottom: The Mackie Diagram that was on the back of all Tandem identity badges

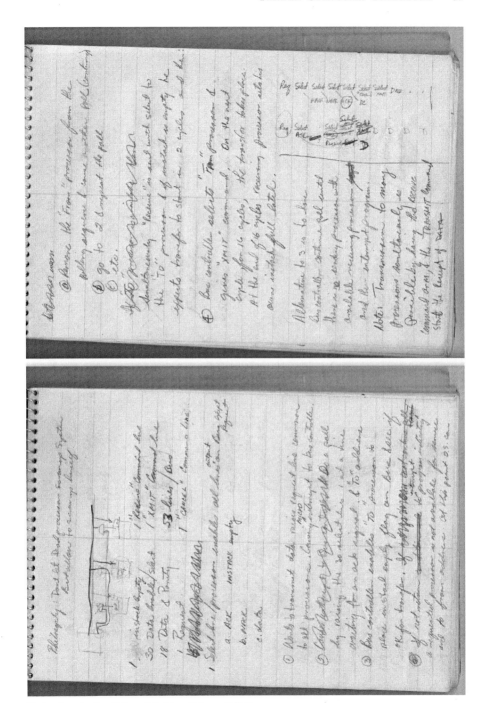

Engineering notes from Katzman's first day - Katzman Collection

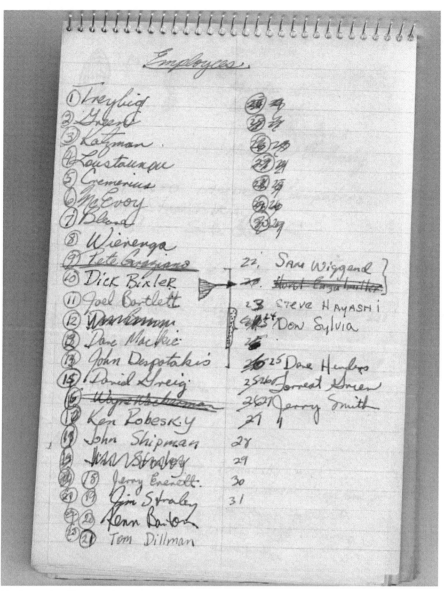

Handwritten list of first 25 employees - Katzman Collection

A summary schedule for product development is shown below in relationship to other key milestones:

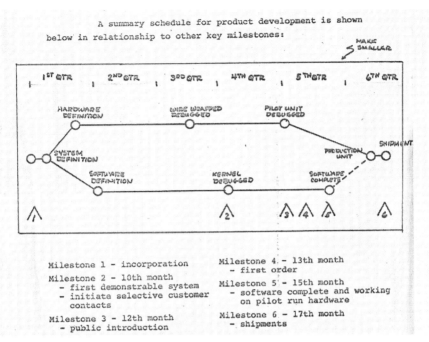

Milestone 1 - incorporation

Milestone 2 - 10th month
- first demonstrable system
- initiate selective customer contacts

Milestone 3 - 12th month
- public introduction

Milestone 4 - 13th month
- first order

Milestone 5 - 15th month
- software complete and working on pilot run hardware

Milestone 6 - 17th month
- shipments

Draft development milestones - October 1974 draft of the first Business Plan

Jimmy gives a casual speech - NS News November 1981

Jimmy's hand drawn development schedule - Draft Business Plan February 1975

Early brainstorming meetings in Stender Way offices L-R: Joel Bartlett, Dennis McEvoy, Pete Graziano, Michael Green - Katzman Collection

More Brainstorming L-R: Jerry Everett (First Field Engineer), Dennis McEvoy, Steve Wierenga, Jim Straley, Dick Bixler - Katzman Collection

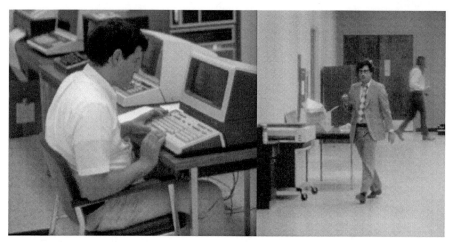

Peter 'Rocky' Graziano (l) working on microcode Jimmy (r) returning from the coffee room with Dennis McEvoy in the background - Katzman Collection

Stender Way was one giant room. Back: Dave Grieg Front: John Despotakis - Katzman Collection

TANDEM
COMPUTERS, INC.

2909 STENDER WAY • SANTA CLARA, CALIF. 95051 • (408) 984-1800

THE NONSTOP COMPUTER COMPANY

SEPTEMBER, 1975

COPY #__S-2__
ASSIGNED TO__JIM KATZMAN__

Cover of the original September 1975 Business Plan

-19-

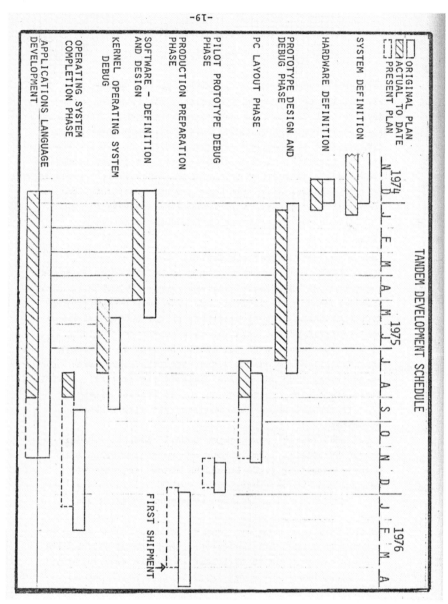

Final version of development schedule - 1975 Business Plan

Team offsite at Pajaro Dunes Front L-R: John Shipman (Software), Jack Loustaunou (Finance and Administration), Jim Katzman (Hardware), Dick Bixler (Hardware) Back L-R Steve Hayashi (Hardware), John Despotakis (Manufacturing), Steve Wierenga (Software)

Pajaro Dunes breakout session L-R: Jim Strayley, Peter Graziano, Mike Green, Dave Mackie, Steve Wierenga (back to camera) and Dave Hinders (on floor) - Katzman Collection

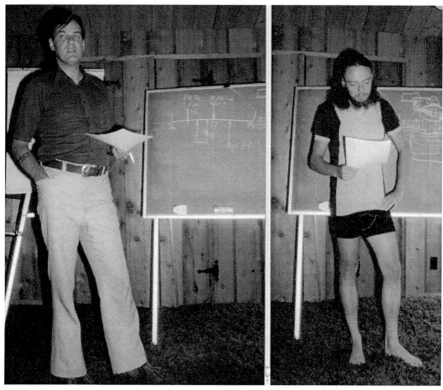

Pajaro Dunes Offsite - Top: Tom Blease (l) & Joel Bartlett (r) presenting Bottom: Steve Hayashi (l) & Joel Bartlett (r) taking a break- Katzman Collection

Pajaro Dunes Offsite with Dave Mackie (l) presenting and Sam Weigand (r) avidly listening - Katzman Collection

Another Pajaro Dunes Breakout L-R: Left Corner- Jimmy, Mike Green, Jim Katzman; Steve Hayashi (in profile on floor), Joel Bartlett (in chair), Maria Cremarias and Tom Blease (back) sitting on the floor - Katzman Collection

Test equipment and first breadboard in development phase - Katzman Collection

Top: First breadboard (prototype) in test mode. Circuit board layout was done by hand. Usually took 5-6 weeks with fabrication another 3-4 weeks - Katzman Collection Bottom: Jimmy gives the first NonStop demo - The Tandem Story Video

Sam Weigand (l) and Bob Marshall (r) inspect the first T16 - Katzman Collection

The move to Green Valley Drive meant lots more space - Katzman Collection

A computer that won't shut down

The proliferation of computer terminals at bank windows, airline counters, branch offices, and hotel reservation desks has brought a new problem for business: When an on-line computer stops, the business stops.

The surest and most obvious way to prevent such emergencies is to tie together two or more computers to create a "failsafe" system. Companies—mostly large ones—are already spending an estimated $200 million a year to avoid the consequences of computer breakdowns, and the expenditure is growing at about 35% annually.

But such failsafe systems are virtually custom built for the user, who must invest in specialized hardware and devise his own software to link the backup system to the primary computer. Such costs can easily double the price of the original computer installation. The so-called fourth-generation computers, which are expected to be widely available within the next five years, will solve some of these problems because they will rely more on networks of interconnected small computers, each assigned a specific task. For many applications, they will eventually replace current large central computers that do multiple jobs. In such multiprocessing systems, no one breakdown will shut down a company.

But until then, businesses that depend on continuous and reliable computer operation suffer from a technological gap. This week a fledgling computer company called Tandem Computers Inc. announced a product that will attempt to fill that gap at a cost lower than current solutions.

"Most computers are just not designed to run with each other," says James G. Treybig, Tandem's 35-year-old president. "We decided to start from scratch and design a different kind of computer—one that runs all the time." The Tandem 16, which Treybig says will be ready for shipment in April, builds on minicomputer technology. It is designed around a series of low-cost processor modules using stock components. Each module can jump into action if another fails or loses its power supply. Similarly, all the peripheral devices and their controllers are designed to keep going despite processor failures.

Tandem is intriguing computer in-

Treybig: "Tandem incorporates all the interface devices the others sell as extras."

dustry observers for other reasons as well. The Santa Clara (Calif.) company has managed to secure $3 million in financing at a time when most venture capital sources have all but run dry. And Tandem's concept of linking multiple processing units is widely expected to be the hallmark of the next generation of computers.

Raiding. With its Model 16 still in the engineering prototype stage, Tandem has little to show potential customers now except the résumés of its founders. But these are impressive because Treybig and his financial backers pulled off the unusual feat of recruiting top engineers from Hewlett-Packard Co., a company known for its ability to keep

Tandem Computer's new failsafe system will prevent costly breakdowns

people. Treybig, a Texan with an MBA from Stanford University, was marketing manager for H-P's minicomputer operation. He lured to Tandem Michael D. Green, vice-president for software development who designed H-P's first timesharing system; James A. Katzman, vice-president for engineering, who was a key architect of the 3000, H-P's biggest computer; and John C. Loustanou, financial vice-president, who was finance and cost accounting manager for H-P's Data Systems Group.

Tandem got its start early in 1973, when Treybig left H-P after a management shuffle and took his idea for a failsafe computer to Thomas J. Perkins, another former H-P executive who

is now a venture capitalist based in Menlo Park, Calif. Perkins was intrigued. "Jim had established that the idea was theoretically possible," he recalls, "but it needed development. So we hired him to work on Tandem and other ventures." Treybig worked about 18 months for Perkins and his partner, Eugene Kleiner, a founder of Fairchild Semiconductor, but he soon began spending all his time on Tandem. In mid-1974 Kleiner and Perkins put $50,000 into the company, allowing Treybig to recruit Green, who was still at H-P, and Katzman, who was then working for Amdahl Corp.

"The real start of the company was Mike [Green] and Jim [Katzman] sitting down and deciding which hardware and software combination would be the most efficient," Treybig says. Kleiner and Perkins were so impressed with the design that they anted up another $1 million to carry Tandem through 1975.

Last week Tandem closed the books on a second round of financing that brought in $2 million more from such sources as E. M. Warburg, Pincus, Princeton-based Data Science Ventures—and Kleiner and Perkins, who added another $500,000. Raising this amount of money at a time when few new ventures are finding financing is "a significant accomplishment," Tandem's Loustanou claims. "In fact," he adds, "we had to ask some potential investors to stop evaluating us."

Software support. What attracted the venture money was Tandem's unique approach to the backup market that today accounts for about 5% of mini-

Initial press after NonStop launch - Business Week Reprint December 1975

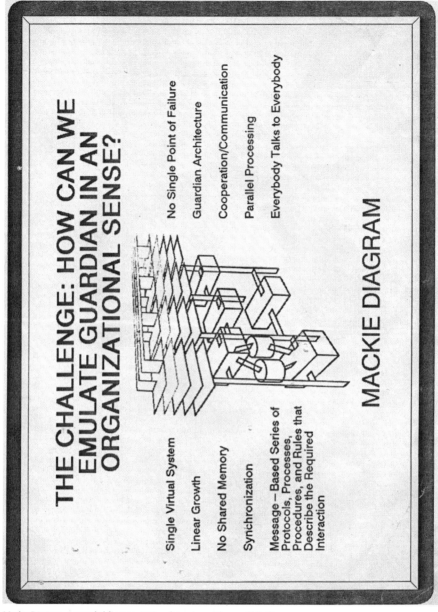

Mackie Diagram as a symbol for organizational structure - Clemson Collection

The First T16 System - Packaging designed by John Shipley - Katzman Collection

TANDEM 16

The NonStop™ multiprocessing data system for on-line, transaction-oriented applications.

- Unique system architecture designed for *NonStop* operation.
- *NonStop* means no individual component or subsystem failure can stop processing operations.
- *NonStop* means any system module can be removed and replaced without interfering with processing operations.
- *NonStop* means no hardware failure can cause undetected contamination of programs or data.
- *NonStop* because the unique *Tandem Dynabus*™ transfers data between processors at 20 megabytes per second.
- *NonStop* because even power supplies and cooling systems can fail and be repaired without affecting system operations.
- Modular expansion from 2 to 16 processors.
- The simplest Tandem 16 system will support more than 128 data communications lines.
- High-level programming language.
- An integrated, multiprocessing operating system.

The first T16 brochure

We placed early emphasis on presenting customers with facts about Tandem solutions for their business problems.

Sam Weigand's memorable advertising campaign - NS News 1983

Maria Cremarias demonstrates for the first brochure

Early production system with open cabinets - Katzman Collection

Shipping the first order for Citibank in 1976 - Katzman Collection

Six processor system ready to go - Katzman Collection

Production Models - Katzman Collection

Dave Mackie - Product Management and later Sales VP - NS News 1983

Dennis McEvoy - Software Development - NS News 1981

The OCLC system just before shipping - McEvoy Collection

Most of the Tandem Ten and the OCLC System L-R: Dick Bixler, Dave Greig, Jerry Held, unknown, Dennis McEvoy, Mike Green, Jim Straley, Ken Barton, John Despotakis, Rich Humphrey - McEvoy Collection

The drafting department before CAD - all done by hand - Katzman Collection

Ten processor system for OCLC - Katzman Collection

Manufacturing floor building the OCLC system - Katzman Collection

Manufacturing floor - testing disk drives for the OCLC system - Katzman Collection

Top: Katzman at a "Beer Bust" - Business Week 1981 Bottom: Jimmy at a Central Region Sales meeting - NS News 1983

Good Morning America, Ya'll — Jim Trybig, Traybig, Tigbray, Treybig.

F-4428-2-P

United States Patent [19]

Katzman et al.

[11] **4,356,550**

[45] **Oct. 26, 1982**

[54] MULTIPROCESSOR SYSTEM

[75] Inventors: James A. Katzman, San Jose; Joel F. Bartlett, Palo Alto; Richard M. Bixler, Sunnyvale; William H. Davidow, Atherton; John A. Despotakis, Pleasanton; Peter J. Graziano; Michael D. Green, both of Los Altos; David A. Greig; Steven J. Hayashi, both of Cupertino; David R. Mackie, Ben Lomond; Dennis L. McEvoy, Scotts Valley; James G. Treybig; Steven W. Wierenga, both of Sunnyvale, all of Calif.

[73] Assignee: Tandem Computers Incorporated, Cupertino, Calif.

[21] Appl. No.: 147,305

[22] Filed: May 6, 1980

Related U.S. Application Data

[62] Division of Ser. No. 721,043, Sep. 7, 1976, Pat. No. 4,228,496.

[51] Int. Cl.³ G06F 11/20
[52] U.S. Cl. 364/200
[58] Field of Search ... 364/200 MS File, 900 MS File; 371/66

[56] **References Cited**

U.S. PATENT DOCUMENTS

3,827,030	7/1974	Seipp	364/900
3,859,638	1/1975	Hume, Jr.	365/228
4,004,283	1/1977	Bennett et al.	364/200
4,015,243	3/1977	Kurpanek et al.	364/200
4,048,672	9/1977	Seiden et al.	364/200
4,050,096	9/1977	Bennett	364/200

Primary Examiner—James D. Thomas

Assistant Examiner—David Y. Eng
Attorney, Agent, or Firm—Donald C. Feix; James E. Eakin

[57] **ABSTRACT**

A multiprocessor system, the kind in which two or more separate processor modules are interconnected for two power supplies, provides the entire power for the device controller in the event the other power supply fails. The distributed power supply system permits any processor module or device controller to be powered down so that on-line maintenance can be performed in a power-off condition while the rest of the multiprocessor system is on-line and functional.

The multiprocessor system includes a memory system in which the memory of each processor module is divided into four logical address areas—user data, system data, user code and system code. The memory system includes a map which translates logical addresses to physical addresses and which coacts with the multiprocessor system to bring pages from secondary memory into primary main memory as required to implement a virtual memory system. The map also provides a protection function. It provides inherent protection among users in a multiprogramming environment, isolates programs from data and protects system programs from the actions of user program. The map also provides a reference history information for each logical page as an aid to efficient memory management by the operating system.

The multiprocessor system includes in the memory of each processor module an error detection and correction system which detects all single bit and double bit errors and which corrects all single bit errors in semiconductor memory storage.

7 Claims, 42 Drawing Figures

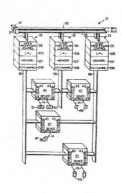

HIRING IS AN ART

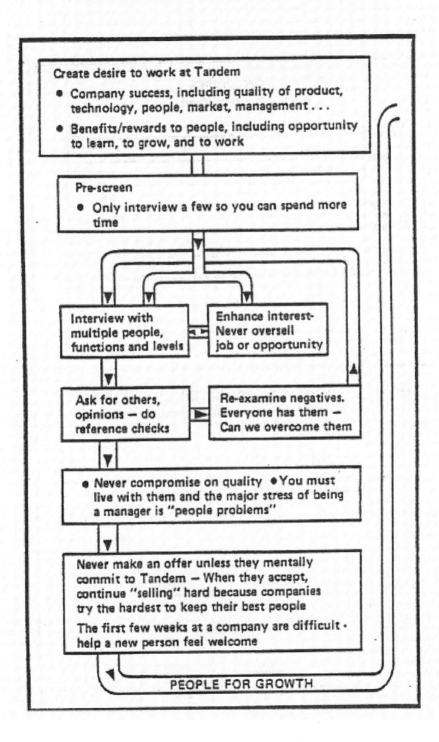

Create desire to work at Tandem
- Company success, including quality of product, technology, people, market, management . . .
- Benefits/rewards to people, including opportunity to learn, to grow, and to work

Pre-screen
- Only interview a few so you can spend more time

Interview with multiple people, functions and levels

Enhance interest- Never oversell job or opportunity

Ask for others, opinions — do reference checks

Re-examine negatives. Everyone has them — Can we overcome them

- Never compromise on quality • You must live with them and the major stress of being a manager is "people problems"

Never make an offer unless they mentally commit to Tandem — When they accept, continue "selling" hard because companies try the hardest to keep their best people

The first few weeks at a company are difficult · help a new person feel welcome

PEOPLE FOR GROWTH

The Public Company

Non Stop II Arrives - NS News Cover April/May 1981

WITH REVENUES OF $7.7 million and 170 employees, in 1977 Tandem became profitable, which was a first hurdle that needed to be cleared in those days to be ready for an initial public offering. Later that fall, with the help of Tommy Unterberg from L. F. Rothschild, Unterberg, Towbin, 770,000 shares of stock were issued, (equal to twenty-one percent of the company) at $11.50 per share, raising $9 million. The next year, in 1978, with revenues of $24.3 million and 540 employees, the company issued its first 100-share bonus option for all employees. This changed the dynamic of the company forever, putting company performance first and foremost in all employees' minds in a way that was deep and personal. As was reported in a June 1982 *Fortune* magazine profile:

"Generous stock options aimed at riveting employees' attention on the business's success are nothing new in high-tech companies, though perhaps none have gone so far as Tandem, where every employee gets gift options. So raptly attentive to corporate performance have employees become that Tandem now posts the stock price three times a day on its work station screens as formerly too many people were monopolizing the telex machines to find out."

Working hard and playing hard was also a hallmark of the Tandem employee experience. As Jimmy often said: *"People rarely succeed at anything unless they have fun doing it!"* The summer of 1979 brought the inaugural season of organized Tandem co-ed softball. A league that included 100 players on six teams, with a 10-game schedule, played at Cupertino High School three nights a week. The ultimate winner of the first trophy was the "Hardware Team." As Rich Giandana (#772) said:

"We also had fun after the games—P.J. Mulligans, the Night Owl in Santa Cruz. It was always worth the drive home to Ben Lomond just to play with those guys and the ladies, too. Julie Abreu, Mary Boettcher and others. The intramural league was also fun with Nick Yatsko, Rocky Ishida, Alan Bricker and many others I can't remember. I wonder how many pizza places we kept in business."

Or Henry Norman's (#3827) experience:

"I remember the Softball League. I was allowed to play on the "Swamprats" team (named after Guido's famous "swamp" office at Santa Ana Court), even though I (born and raised in Sweden) didn't have the faintest idea of what softball was! In my first game (against the "Master Batters"), I once took off from first base in the wrong direction, which everyone thought was really really funny."

Central to social efforts in those days was the Tandem Organized Activities Department, known as TOAD. It wasn't a department in a traditional sense, all participants volunteered, with meetings occurring whenever a problem or topic of interest arose. The group was, as they said themselves, a group of *"happy people hopping around the damp, dark recesses of Tandem making sure that the wonderful events you associate with Tandem actually happen."* Some of the key winner events in those days included the weekly Beer Busts, the Christmas Party, the Spring Hoe Down, the annual Company Picnic, the Halloween Party and of course Tandem T-shirts. Tandem T-shirts were a major institution in Tandem and after a few years, most employees had dozens in their closets celebrating all sorts of key events in the history of the company.

In 1979, in order to demonstrate to European customers that the company's continued commitment to the European marketplace, the company opened a manufacturing facility in Neufarhn, Germany. It wasn't cheaper to operate there and managing the business was certainly a lot more complex with respect to coordinating shipments and materials and maintaining quality. But the facility did become a support resource for marketing where spares could be repaired and customer engineers trained. [Author's note: in 1981 SIT facilities were opened in Reston, Virginia to support customers on the East Coast and Santa Clara, California. Later a terminal manufacturing facility in Austin, Texas and a subassembly manufacturing facility in Watsonville, California were started.

Another key to Tandem success in manufacturing was its use of a computerized tracking system to manage the entire process. Later the phrase the 'paperless factory' became fashionable, but Bob Marshall was committed to running manufacturing online right from the beginning. According to an article in Center magazine in 1986:

> "In the beginning the HP timesharing system was used for order processing, inventory control etc. But in 1980 Tandem decided to use its own systems for manufacturing and launched EMPACT, a homegrown inventory control and management system. EMPACT had eight modules including materials requirements planning (MRP), inventory control, order processing, bills of material, item master (descriptions and data about specific parts), master scheduling (what parts are needed by when, based on the market forecast), Work-in-process (WIP) and systems manufacturing."

But manufacturing wasn't without its challenges. The biggest being that the company made a conscious decision to have no backlog, (i.e. orders placed but not shipped) but had a sales process where most of the shipments happened during the last few weeks of the quarter. In addition, systems were infinitely configurable so there were no standard packages and the labour force was sized to support average not peak loads. The goal then was to "distribute the labour hours throughout the quarter and yet be able to ship a large amount of product at the end of the quarter." To make it all interesting, sales had issued a challenge to manufacturing early on to commit to shipping whatever sales could sell. This competition later became known as the Peterson Cup (named after Jerry Peterson, the VP of International and later Worldwide Sales). In order to consistently win the Peterson Cup, the manufacturing team had to constantly invent new approaches to manufacturing, such as pre-staging systems, so that when configurations got finalized they could quickly be assembled with the final elements, then tested and shipped. Though the competition was fun, it established right from the beginning an ethic and mindset that manufacturing could deliver.

By 1980, the company was on a roll. The Grumman-Cowen/Datamation poll had rated Tandem as No. 1 in customer satisfaction—a title it would keep for four successive years. With revenues exceeding $100 million, 1,632 employees and its 1,000th computer system shipped, Tandem was ranked by *Inc.* magazine as the fastest-growing public company in America. In December 1980, Tandem made a second public offering and raised $96 million.

Also in 1980, Tandem opened the Customer Conference Center (called the CCC), designed as a place to bring customers who wanted to make sure that

Tandem was a real company with real products and systems support behind the curtain. Over time, it evolved into an integral part of the sales cycle. Customers would come to the CCC for a variety of reasons. Some would come to find answers to outstanding issues and concerns prior to making a final purchase decision. Others would come to learn about Tandem's future product plans or meet company executives and discuss market and product strategy. For Tandem, most visits had two goals. The first was for the CCC program managers to strategize with the sales force about the best way to meet the objectives of the visit. The second was to provide the right resources to present and conduct sessions on market strategies and product plans that would meet the needs of the level and type of customer visiting. Some were executive-to-executive visits, others technical evaluations with each needing a different type of presentation style and content. In the early years visits were generally "come-as-you-are." But in later years a dress code had to be initiated (especially for the engineers). Though the presentability quality improved, some presenters could never totally get rid of the tie-dye socks and causal hippy look.

The company also started in 1980 the Intercontinental Division (ICON), mostly due to fact that Tandem's first real OLTP system in the banking industry was a foreign exchange application sold to the First National Bank of Chicago. With success in Chicago and New York, the bank wanted to expand worldwide and so of course Tandem had to follow. Skip Yazel, the founder of Tandem's forays into Asia, Japan and the Pacific, shared some of his early experiences:

"We started in 1980 with a bunch of castoffs and free spirits who wanted to travel —of course most of Tandem at that stage were mavericks of one kind or another. At first it was just Pete Peterson, then later I was able to steal old-timers like Forrest Grein, Gary Sabo and many others, to grow our fledging operation. Then after the small beginning, we started to attract the best from Tandem, and the rest is history. Most of it was a whirl of plane trips, eating strange food, meeting customers and prospective customers that I couldn't speak to without translators, discussions in bars all over the world. We had the best of everybody in the company—the best hardware and software guys who had to know a lot about everything because they would likely have been the only one in some remote spot under a lot of pressure, the best administrative people who had to put up with associates who were never there (of course, I'm open to the idea that they may have liked it that way). Working in an environment where everyone in the company was on the same page, and worked hard, and played hard— and at least from my perspective there was almost no corporate 'politics'—we were growing too fast for that."

Other highlights that made life very interesting for Skip included:

- *Having to referee golf games between the retired general from our South Korean Distributor and our General Manger in Japan, who were still at war with each other, and trying to stop Forrest from killing them both!*

- *Having meetings with existing and prospective distributors in various Latin American countries and becoming very embarrassed that they all knew more about our U.S. government officials and government policy than we ever knew.*

- *Arranging for the Mexico City Police Department's system to be placed on a private plane at the Brown Field airport (south of San Diego). Later we suspected that this was so they could avoid paying taxes to their own government.*

- *Being led into the Mexico City chief of police's office (through numerous soldiers with machine guns) and told that somehow all of the budget he had for the system was gone, and he didn't have any money to pay for the maintenance of the system. At first there were about 10 other data processing executives, my distributor and others in the room with everything going through the translator. Then he got mad and sent everyone (including the translator) out of the room leaving just me and a weird character in a trench coat and dark glasses sitting way over in the corner— who occasionally would nod yeah or nay to various comments I would make.*

- *Being a virtual prisoner of an armed Israeli colonel (who was negotiating with us for several systems to support the Israeli Air Force maintenance system) showing me around Israel (trying to get us to do some manufacturing there) and making sure I was safe.*

- *Trying to explain the sudden departure of one of our Philippine distributor's technicians from a Cupertino training class. His wife had just found out that he had two other wives!*

Employee communications was also becoming a hallmark of the culture of the business. *NonStop News*, which had started in 1978, was now an institution for keeping employees up to date on what was going on around the Tandem world and sharing the big picture. The focus as articulated in Fortune Magazine in June 1982, was to not just *"urge loyalty, hard work, self esteem and respect for co-workers, but by soaking employees in an endless stream of company boosting propaganda, vehement in its expression makes it clear how radical a departure the company's management style taken as a whole really is."* Not only did this boost company loyalty but also in Jimmy's mind lessened the need for management by pointing everyone in the right direction. As Jimmy said at the time: *"Most companies are over-managed. Most people need less management than you think."*

In addition was a commitment to promotion from within and to flexible working hours such that managers often had no idea just how long their employees were working except via the position of their car in the parking lot as all parking was first-come first-serve. There was no such thing as executive-only parking places. As Michael Green said at the time: *"We don't want to pay people for attendance, but for output."* And as Stanford computer science professor Edward Feigenbaum said in a June 1982 *Fortune* magazine article, *"The most creative computer people are semi-freakish—especially in the case of software designers who need freedom and solitude to perform their occult art."* John Boddie, a software consultant, said, *"When you have a good systems development shop, things always look to the outside observer as if they're out of control—and to some extent they are. Its semi-channeled chaos and Tandem's loose, flexible style reflects this industry reality."*

But it wasn't just that. It was also the youth of many of the employees. Most had gone to college in the late 1960s and early '70s and were aware of and often touched by the counterculture of the age. Sam Wiegand (#22) used to call Tandem development people "pseudo-hippies" and as was reported in *Fortune* magazine in June 1982:

"Not only are most terribly hard workers, but they also care about openness, spontaneity, non-judgmental acceptance, brotherhood, freedom and expressiveness on one hand, and technical proficiency coupled with personal ambition on the other. Tandem with its youthful style, beer bust rap sessions, high-flown egalitarianism, engineering excellence and hefty financial incentives resolves that conflict. It also enables employees to feel that they are moving toward the full development of all their human potentialities, filling their innermost goals of self realization at the same time as they are advancing the company's interests."

The depth and breadth of employee communications continued to expand. In the spring of 1981, Tandem established *Center* magazine, a quarterly journal that detailed Tandem philosophy, strategy and goals. Its intent, as articulated in the inaugural issue, was to *"provide Tandem employees with an informational and thought-provoking publication that would focus on and enhance their professional and personal development."* Topics ranged from company philosophy to management information, to health and people information, all to *"help people learn, grow and be happy."* The first volume included an article by Jimmy about understanding the philosophy of Tandem, one by Jerry Held, Vice President of Database Software Development, on hiring outstanding people, and another by Bob Marshall, Chief Operating Officer, on how to prepare yourself to be promoted from within. Al McBride, a Director of Hardware Development, wrote about the intellectual and emotional conflicts involved in taking the risk of leaving a big company and joining Tandem, while Heidi Roizen wrote success stories on personal growth and insight on what it takes to be a customer engineer. That first year *Center* magazine was honored in the International Technical Publications Competition with an "Award of Excellence," against 360 other publications.

Employee rewards and recognition also become more formalized in 1979. The "First Cabin Club," a rewards and recognition event for the top sales people, was launched and went on to be one of the company's most prestigious honors. It included an all-expenses-paid trip to some exotic locale for *"the employee and their spouse, spouse equivalent, significant other or loved one"* for three to four days. The first year's trip was to Europe, the second to Mexico and the third to Hawaii. Select company executives would attend and share the company strategy and direction along with first-class entertainment and meals. After a few successful programs, Jimmy felt that there also needed to be a program for all non-sales employees, as they were important as well. Jan Seamons (#442), head of employee incentives at the time, was given the task. As she shared in 2002:

"After the First Cabin Club was successfully launched, Jimmy and Bob called me in to say that they wanted to have another program for all non-sales employees. So one weekend up at the Tandem ski cabin in Lake Tahoe I was fixing dinner with Dale Lantz. While sharing a glass of wine, I mentioned that I needed a program name for Tandem outstanding performers. She replied, 'How about that, Tandem Outstanding Performers'... brilliant... see wine does do wonderful things. I buried it in the middle of a bunch of other suggestions and gave them to Jimmy, Bob Marshall and Li Garcia. You know the answer, of course TOPS was the easy winner! But there was one caveat. Jimmy wanted to be sure that we were never confused with some group called 'Take Off Pounds Sensibly.'" (Author's Note: One of the popular Cupertino-based Special Interest Groups (SIG's) was the Tandem Ski Club. The club members would collectively rent a large 8-10 bedroom ski cabin at Lake Tahoo each winter, which members could use on a first-come first-served reservation basis. This meant that for minimal cost there was a group to ski and socialize with all winter long. I participated in the club for many years and my competency in downhill skiing subsequently improved dramatically.

TOPS involved a nomination process whereby managers would suggest people on their team they felt were deserving of special recognition for some extraordinary work effort. Five percent of the employees were selected for each program, approximately equal to the % of sales people who attended the First Cabin Club, and it was designed to be a cross-section of the workforce. These people plus their spouses or a guest would go on an all-expenses-paid three-day trip to an interesting location. In addition, a few hand-selected guest managers would give presentations during the various business sessions. The objective was to both have fun but also share some of the company's goals and strategic direction and strengthen horizontal cross-functional communications. Jimmy's view was that by having the best people in the company form connections with each other, not just team building, but self-management would result. As Gary Bolen, Tandem's Creative Director shared:

"On my first TOPS trip I was teamed with an engineer who wrote software for disc drive systems. My first thought was how on earth am I going to talk to this guy, we have nothing in common. Well after a few days, we realized that both of us were really creative but just in completely different ways. We maintained a close relationship for years."

The first TOPS trip went to San Diego and was a smash hit. Over the years, groups went to lots of interesting spots including Naples, Florida, San Antonio, Texas, and Calgary, Alberta. For those who participated the memories are indelible, like the trip to Naples, Florida, for which Tandem hired a motion picture costume company that dressed everyone up as if they were extras for the plantation scenes in "Gone with the Wind." On another TOPS trip, the company rented a bowling alley, complete with 1950s costumes and make-up. According to one attendee, *"Some people went a little nuts running down the lanes and sliding headfirst into the pins."*

For Don Nelson (#4534), the Naples, Florida, TOPS trip was an experience. As he shared:

"It was over 100 degrees with 100 percent humidity. At around 2 a.m. a bunch of us were in the 'smoking' hospitality room having a fine time when the militia came in the door and asked us to quiet things down. They asked who was in charge and everybody pointed at me (everyone knows a sucker, I guess). I was assigned the impossible task and eventually did manage to get them to stop going outside and making noise. By the way, Jimmy much preferred the 'smoking' room to the 'non-smoking' room because that was where all the wild people hung out. Same for me—and I don't even smoke."

One vivid memory for Bob Horst, who was on the TOPS trip to the Calgary Stampede, was Jimmy leading everyone in a rousing chorus of "Oh Lord It's Hard to Be Humble, But I'm Doing the Best I Can." As Bob said, *"It may not have been great music, but there was plenty of enthusiasm."* Ray Glasstone (#5106) remembered his TOPS trip where:

"On the last day a bunch were drinking cocktails at the pool, a group that included an employee with a number less than 2 (meaning Jimmy Treybig). He asked who hadn't checked out yet. Foolishly I raised my hand. Guess who got a $300 bar bill. I had some 'splaining' to do when I submitted my expenses, but it got paid."

My own TOPS experience was a trip to San Antonio, Texas. At one point we were all on a wagon train of buses heading out to experience a typical Texan BBQ when the buses were halted and a gang of cattle rustlers with rifles appeared. They proceeded to kidnap all of the executives on the buses. It was a riot. They were all rustled into a row of jail cells at the event site and ransom had to be paid by all employees in order to get the "prisoners" released. My recollection was that this led to some very heated discussions as to whether the ransoms should be paid at all. Eventually we paid, with the contributions going to a local Texas charity.

TOPS, though an important part of the company's rewards and recognition effort, wasn't the only program. Lots of smaller-scale "thanks for your efforts" events happened all the time all across the company. As Kayo M. (#934) reported:

"One of my memories was being interviewed in the New Orleans airport by some girl from the Tandem magazine to be awarded 'Customer Engineer of the Quarter.' Then came the reward. Someone in Chicago arranged for our reward to be a Caribbean cruise for an entire week."

In Europe, boat trips were often a reward for extraordinary work efforts and special customer events. A few that Keith Payne (#1739) remembered involved cruising down the Thames River from Maidenhead with Old Time Music Hall entertainment, and a dinner cruise down the Seine in Paris in a glass-topped boat at an international banking seminar. But even better was a sailing trip along the English Channel on a nice summer day in the Barclays Bank sailboat. Other types of celebrations were team-specific. As Tony Duarté (#2209) recalled:

"My first year with the old Illustration Group saw us having tricycle races on the old basketball court, passing oranges with our necks as we held our own little party."

One famous reception was the "Data Bolt" party, held to celebrate the successful completion of a satellite system communications network code named "Data Bolt". It went on to live in infamy as the time Jimmy, wanting to commemorate the occasion, cut off the $150 Italian silk tie of Larry Laurich, the Vice President of Hardware Development, with Gene Cunningham's knife. According to Larry Laurich, Jimmy was chuckling as he finished the cutting with that goofy grin with which he could always make one laugh. However as another participant recalled, *"I'll never forget Larry's expression as the knife went by."* Later someone retrieved the two tie sections, framed them and gave them back to Larry as a gift.

Halloween was always a key event for Tandemites. One employee remembered going to a job interview to change departments on Halloween and asked her potential new boss if she could show up 30 minutes late as she had come to work as a potted plant and felt that she needed to change. He advised her that there was no need to change as he himself was costumed as a rabbit. What a way to meet your new boss! At another party, an engineer was asked if he was going to a job interview when he came to the party dressed in a costume that included a sports coat, slacks and a tie. At one big Halloween Party in San Mateo, Tony Duarté and his date came as punk rockers and won a prize for the "weirdest costume," beating out the infamous Glen Grimme, an early ICON marketing manager known for his off beat sense of humor, who came dressed as a baby.

Oftentimes some of the crazy things folks would do were an important release valve due to the stress that all were often under. Some of the highlight "pranks" included:

- Skinny-dipping in the pool behind Building 2
- Sailboat lessons in the pool… and sinking said boat with a certain VIP in the boat!
- Boat regattas held at Tantau's pond
- The mysterious pink flamingos that kept showing up in unlikely places
- Engineering figuring out how to tap a beer keg with a BIC pen and surgical tubing after Tandem's security took the keg taps away to signal Beer Bust "closing"
- Using the Tandem satellite network to watch adult movies after hours
- The "Get It Up" stickers we had about working to get our stock price up, when things dipped in the early 1980s
- A pregnant Candace DeCou (head administrative person for the VP of Sales Dave Mackie), on roller skates waltzing through the halls in Building 4
- AA (Attitude Adjustment) meetings in Watsonville
- Themed Hall parties at Forge Drive that resulted in lot of pictures of people in hula skirts, and Wizard of Oz, pimp and hooker outfits—and it wasn't even Halloween!
- The "Best Legs" contest at the Beer Bust before one of Tandem's 10K road races
- "No Talent" contests to humorously showcase participants' lack of show-biz talent (Author's Note: The "No Talent' contests took place for many years at Tandem Headquarters in Cupertino, usually on a Friday afternoon in conjunction with a 'Beer Bust' and provided a marvelous opportunity for team morale building and stress relief)

Henry Norman (#3827) shared one Tandem "party tradition" with which he was personally familiar:

"If anyone was given half a chance, the nearest Tandem executive had to be tossed into the nearest swimming pool. I had the privilege of witnessing this twice, once at the somewhat famous analyst symposium in Phoenix, Arizona, and once at the TOPS party in Newport Beach, California (that I got to attend because my wife was a nominee). Unfortunately, I missed a third first-hand experience at the Asia/Pacific Analyst Symposium in Singapore back in '89, as I was too busy drinking beer with Bill Newell, away from the Pan Pacific Hotel swimming pool."

Some of the pranks also provided an opportunity to make important political points. One such point was made in response to a life-size poster created by Tandem Germany that featured two beautiful blond Swedish women showing lots of leg on a Tandem bicycle. Though most of the male employee population thought it was lovely, most of the women thought it was pretty disparaging. To even the score, a woman in Marketing proposed "The Incredible Hunk Contest." It's impossible, of course, to even contemplate holding such a contest today, but at Tandem at that time it was considered a marvelous idea. Over 30 men decided to participate, at all levels of the company, parading around in gym shorts in a headquarters-wide beauty contest sponsored by all of the female employees. The blushing winners were Dennis McEvoy, Vice President of Software Development and engineer Steve Davoli, who were presented with enormous red satin sashes that bore the legend "Incredible Hunk." Dennis hung his on his office wall where it stayed for years, generating lots of conversation. The point of the unacceptability of sexism in the workplace had been subtly made.

At least for a while, Tandem was at the leading edge of equality for women, though that changed as the company grew larger. Later it seemed that new management and employees from more traditional companies didn't quite get it and they brought with them many biases and prejudices that had a negative impact. But at least in the early years, equality mattered: As Polly Kam (#1177) shared:

"John Hornby, a fellow IT analyst, and I went to the Chicago field sales office in Schaumburg, Illinois, to install the sales order processing system there. It was a cold snowy April around Secretary Week in 1980. We were in the elevator going down and one of the sales guys walked in and said to me, 'Oh, your boss is taking you out for Secretary Week, huh?' John said in a very firm voice, 'She is not a secretary. She is an analyst.' Now John didn't have to defend me, I was perfectly capable of saying something to the guy myself, but he did. This was the culture I came to know of Tandem."

The crème-de-la-crème social events were the Friday "Beer Busts." (The name in later years was changed to "Beer Parties" to allay the politically correct). As reported in the Tandem listing in the first *The 100 Best Companies to Work for in America* by Robert Levering, Milton Moskowitz and Michael Katz:

"All employees from president to assemblers go to the patio area outside the company cafeteria near the swimming pool and tennis courts to tip a few free cans of beer and talk informally. It's part of Tandem's conscious policy of promoting communication and egalitarianism within the ranks along with no reserved parking slot at company facilities, no time clocks and no organization charts. Every week 60 percent of the company drops in at the Beer Bust, held at all facilities worldwide, for an hour, joined sometimes by visiting customers or suppliers who take away indelible memories."

It's hard to explain how marvelous it was to know that on a Friday afternoon, anywhere in the world, if you went to the local Tandem office you'd find a welcoming group of people with whom you could share a glass of wine or a mug of beer. The reality was, though few would admit it publicly, the Beer Busts weren't really about the beer—they were about communication and collaboration and the opportunity to meet with executives and managers in an informal environment. Problems got solved, new ideas brainstormed, folks at all levels in the company and across all of the different departments had a chance to meet and greet and get to know each other better. It was also a great way to spread the word on any topic or issue of interest to the collective. Of course, sometimes things got a little carried away and most employees at one point or another heard of something funny that happened at or as a result of a Beer Bust, often but not always involving beer. Some of the classics included John Perera's (#1053) experience when he started in Facilities in 1979 at the tender age of 18:

"On Beer Bust days, Mark Castro would send myself and Paul Tracy to the Beer Bust to bring back a few cases for the shop. Well one day Bob Marshall followed us back to the shop and opened the fridge to find it filled from top to bottom with beer. That was the end of individual beers at the Beer Busts. Remember that transition? Yup, I was responsible for that." [Author's note: Prior to this event, beer for Beer Busts used to be provided in cans; after this event, beer was only provided in kegs, so it couldn't be taken back to offices and stashed.]

William Eberwein (#5366) recalled talking to Jimmy, who had a beer in each hand and his shirt tail hanging out: *"If you asked Jimmy a question or made a suggestion, his eyes would rack-focus and you got the sense of the man's love of accomplishment and sharing the process of making things work."* Don Nelson recalled one Beer Bust when:

"Some of us were standing around the beer kegs when the guard came to take away the taps. Rocky went up to his office and returned with his private tap. We proceeded to polish off at least that keg and maybe another. I wasn't OK to drive so I spent the

night sleeping on my office floor. My wife Lee was not pleased, though I was proud of myself for at least calling home! At another Beer Bust my wife and I were talking to Jimmy when he announced that he had to leave to go on a 'dayut' (two syllables). Lee asked him what that was. He spelled it out and she said: 'Oh—you mean date!' He said: 'That's what I said, dayut.'"

Or Mary Cashen (#3013) from the Indiana field office, who talked about the year that:

"We all gave up beer at our weekly Beer Bust so one of our own could get a handle on his drinking issues. No one complained and no one talked about entitlements. We walked the walk that we talked (teamwork in action)."

Sometimes Beer Busts were organized just for customers. One customer Beer Bust organized for a Midwest telephone company ended with all of the customers and Tandem folks having their ties cut off below the knot, in homage to the Data Bolt saga one presumes. Sometimes more than a tie was ruined. Mary Cashen (#3013) reported that after a Beer Bust in Michigan:

"Out-of-town guests were taken to a local bar, chaperoned by a local who owned a fancy Porsche sports car. When they came out later the car was missing. They walked around that building several times just to make sure that their memories were correct as to where the car had been parked (there were five who had squished into the four-seater). Eventually they called the police to report the theft and then a taxi to get them back to hotel. The next day the owner's dream car was found on blocks with nothing left but the shell."

Those based in the Houston office reported that often Jimmy's dad, a geologist with Texaco, would drop in during a Beer Bust, especially when Jimmy was in town. As Mike Smith (#1615) reported:

"One time he popped the tab on his beer and cut his finger really badly. Jimmy had us call the EMS emergency team who came and stitched his dad's finger up. Jimmy's dad just laughed about it and switched hands to drink his beer. Jimmy's mom just sat there shook her head and did not say a thing."

While Beer Busts were an important part of Tandem's Philosophy, trying to introduce the Beer Bust concept in foreign countries resulted in some very amusing situations. Skip Yazel, Vice President of the ICON division in the early 1980s, described a would-be Beer Bust at a newly established subsidiary in Tokyo, Japan: "Everyone sat around to the table quietly consuming sushi, and not getting it." Or in Germany, where as Henry Norman shared, *"for the first few years their*

Geschaeftsfuehrer, [Vice President] Horst Enzelmueller was known to ORDER his people to attend beer busts... it was MANDATORY! Not that anyone really minded."

Eventually Beer Busts crossed all cultural boundaries and became traditions all over the world—all employees knew where they could find fellow Tandemites on a Friday afternoon. Some of my fondest memories are of Beer Busts in London, Hong Kong, Amsterdam and Milan, usually followed by an invitation out to dinner or to see the sights of whatever city I happened to be in.

Though the Tandem Philosophy was initially spread through word of mouth to new employees, the company soon got so big that this became quite difficult and the decision was made to write it all down in black and white. Jimmy had always felt that Tandem could be explained on one sheet of paper, so early in 1980, he set out to do just that. The end result was a 2-foot-high by 3-foot-wide "philosophy map"—a chart showing Tandem's organization and Tandem's Second Five-Year Plan as one giant feedback loop. Each Vice President "owned" a particular area of the map and developed a presentation to support their specific area. This body of work became the official Tandem Philosophy. [Author's Note: See Appendix A for a transcript of the original presentation.] Its key tenets included the following, which were eventually incorporated into a New Employee Handbook:

- **Clear Direction:** Every employee should be aware of the business direction of the company, then he/she can make independent decisions for the good of the company.

- **Open Door/Open Manager:** Employees are encouraged to share their concerns, seek information, provide input and resolve problems/issues through their immediate management and as appropriate, consult with any member of management towards those ends. Managers are expected to listen to employee concerns, to encourage their input and to seek resolution to their problems/issues.

- **Err on the Human Side:** In making business decisions, consider the consequences to individuals as well as to Tandem's business. When possible, decide in favor of the employee.

- **Hire Outstanding People:** Managers must seek to hire people who are better than them. This is to guarantee an employee base that can contribute to an ever-increasing level of responsibility, productivity, innovation and creativity. This policy also creates a greater challenge for the manager as well as having individuals working for them who are capable of advancement. As the organization grows, people need to be ready to grow with it. When hiring, it's important for managers not to hire only in their own image. Diversity produces more good ideas than homogeneity and contributes to a better workplace.

- **Importance of Each Individual:** Tandem's success depends on the success of every employee. Therefore each employee should be concerned not only with his/her own success, but also with the success of others.

- **Open Communications, Both Structured and Unstructured:** Our employees and management share responsibility for maintaining a flexible structured environment—one that not only facilitates the free flow of information about Tandem's business, strategies and employee's concerns and suggestions, but also promotes creativity and teamwork through increased interaction between individuals and groups.

- **Promote From Within:** Providing advancement opportunities to those whose performance has helped Tandem grow is in Tandem's best interest because it rewards, challenges and helps to retain outstanding employees. Always hire the best candidate for the job, looking first for qualified individuals.

- **Delegate Authority and Responsibility:** It's important to minimize the manager's individual tasks by delegating responsibility to others in the group. This gives the manager time to hire outstanding people, to thing about strategies, and provide the kind of creative environment that supports individual and corporate success. And it gives employees increased responsibility for and involvement in the various functions in the department.

- **Sharing in the Rewards of Success:** All of the people who create our success should share in the rewards that come from achieving our goals. Unlike many corporations, which rely solely on salary increases as rewards and reserve stock options for a special few, we all are eligible for bonus stock options when they are offered as well as merit-based rewards, such as discretionary stock options and a recognition program for outstanding performers.

It's important to emphasize again that these weren't just idle statements, but were living and breathing values that were tested every day. Jimmy used to say, *"Employees are empowered to make mistakes, as long as they don't make too many of them."* Erring on the side of the employee meant deeply understanding that they were closest to the work and therefore their recollections of circumstances that later became issues were likely to be the most accurate and should be trusted first. There was also a hidden rule as one former employee shared on a recent blog:

"You can't say anything bad about a new idea for five minutes. If I bring up some hare-brained or unusual idea in a meeting, it isn't fair for others to shoot it down immediately—it needs to first be fleshed out and discussed for at least a short time, to see if there might indeed be a way that it can be implemented, or to see if it spawns other ideas that COULD be useful in providing insight, solving a problem, expanding a product definition, closing in on a solution, etc. The opposite reaction—to immedi-

ately say 'That can't be done because...'—will keep smart, dedicated people (the kind we hired at Tandem) from speaking up again, for fear of embarrassment."

This last point, the idea of sharing in the rewards of success was incredibly revolutionary and as Jimmy (#1) said at a recent gathering:

"One of my proudest moments was when a single parent, who wasn't a senior manager or anything, came up to me to tell me that she had just bought a house with her stock options. The ability to provide those kinds of benefits took leadership from the Board. Luckily I had Tom Perkins and a Board that were so supportive of these types of innovations."

The first formal presentation of the Tandem Philosophy was made to country and division managers in the summer of 1980. The two-day class soon became a monthly event for small groups of managers meeting in Cupertino and was presented by Tandem's executive staff. As Dennis McEvoy (#6) shared:

"Jimmy insisted that every executive staff member be able to present their own and another colleagues sections. It was hard enough to teach your own section, but to also be familiar enough with a team members area to teach theirs as well was a real challenge."

In May 1981, the Tandem Management Development Program was established under Jim Katzman and became the official home of the Philosophy. Unfortunately Tandem was growing so fast that running the classes monthly would never enable all employees to be reached. The class size was expanded to 150 employees and within 18 months more than 1,700 employees, nearly everyone, had attended the Philosophy class. In November 1982, Katzman left the company and the Philosophy program moved to Human Resources under Jan Jensen. He instituted an intensive redesign, rewrite and update of the materials with the name changed to the "Understanding Tandem Program" to better represent the content, which also included business strategies and organizational information in addition to details of the Tandem culture. One concern at the time was a growing divide between what employees were learning in the class and what they experienced in their day-to-day work environments. Some managers weren't practicing what Tandem preached. To fix this, managers were required to make "Understanding Tandem" presentations to their teams, so that every employee knew where they fit. The program included five main modules:

- **Introduction:** Tandem's origins and goals

- **Our People:** Expectations of managers and how individual contributors could be successful.
- **Our Product:** Strategies for each Tandem market, product development, marketing, support and manufacturing
- **Our Performance:** A review of Tandem's financials strengths
- **Our Future:** Changes and challenges the company expected to face

Through company communications vehicles such as *NonStop News* and *Center* magazine, the TOPS program and management practices, employee efforts were recognized in many ways. The challenge was to figure out how to retain that spirit as the company grew rapidly. As was so often stated, an open door policy was only as effective as the caring, interested management on the other side of the door. Especially in those early days, the vast majority of the time Tandem demonstrated its commitment to each employee by "erring on the human side" in difficult situations, as well as relatively minor matters. As was outlined in *NonStop News* in April 1982:

"Each individual is important to the whole company. Focus on integrity, a high standard of business practice, consistent fairness towards each employee, and an above-board open manner with customers is paramount. In a time when more people are choosing careers carefully in concert with their inner focus, one advantage of coming to Tandem is that one needn't compromise one's values one inch. The company's philosophy of fairness combined with creativity and productivity ensures that all employees carried with them a pride in contributing to something they could personally and collectively identify with."

And as Janet Bein shared in a recent blog posting:

"Tandem was the first company I knew where you could earn as much money and respect rising in the ranks as an individual contributor as you could by becoming a manager. They even gave individual contributors nicer offices with windows. We had large offices, not cubicles. Two individual contributors shared the room, but it was large enough that some people brought in additional furniture like sofas. Managers received smaller, private offices without windows. Jimmy Treybig, the CEO, was willing to talk to anyone. Not long after I had started working there, Treybig stopped me one day as I was walking in the corridor and asked, in his warm Texas drawl, 'How are things going?' He succeeded in giving me the impression that he actually cared what I thought."

No. 1 in Customer Satisfaction NS News 1986

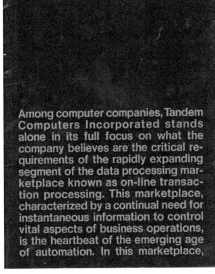

1978 Annual Report Cover - the first as a public company

CSAT Award from Hughes Radar - NS News Sept. 1983

Jimmy with customers - 1978 Annual Report

An early trade show booth. This was No. 3 - NS News 1982

Jerry Held (VP Database) and Dave Mackie (VP Sales) - NS News December 1981

Jean Wohlers (Treasurer) and Jimmy - NS News Feb. 1982

Executives at an early employee meeting sharing company results L-R: Jean Wohlers, Dave Mackie, Jim Treybig and Bob Marshall (standing) - NS News 1983

Watsonville SIT 86,000 sq. ft. with space to house up to 250 employees - NS News March 1983

Neufahrn, Germany SIT - NS News October 1983

Jimmy with a large system - The Tandem Story Video 2012

1981 Christmas share options bonus - NS News November 1981

Competitors in the 'Nobbly Knee' contest, which was judged by the children

Tandem UK's Nobbly Knee Contest - NS News May 1982

Sales Team Meetings - Mike Bateman (l) as King - NS News 1979: Jack Chapman (l) and Hosrt Enzelmueller (r) exchange native costumes - NS News May 1982

Cartoon from the Swedish Office 1981 - NS New December 1981

Lenora Harmon, Dave Needle, Maureen Wallis, Sandy Mendenhall, Candace DeCou, Lynn Cooley, and in the back Bill Schweitzer (Unavailable T.O.A.D.'s at the time photos taken: Rita Bloesch and Jerry Everett)

Toads Committee - NS News 1979

T.O.A.D.'S

These are the usually happy people hopping around the damp, dark recesses of Tandem making sure that the wonderful events you associate with Tandem actually happen. These people are members of the Tandem Organized Activities Department, commonly known as T.O.A.D. All of the T.O.A.D. members are volunteers who take time out from their busy daily activities to plan, organize, and make these events happen.

T.O.A.D. meetings occur whenever a problem or a topic of interest arises. While formal minutes are not taken, results and/or requests for help and opinions will be distributed throughout the facility. If you have a suggestion or a question you can contact your friendly neighborhood T.O.A.D. member or send it to the T.O.A.D. mailbox via interdepartmental mail. (All T-Shirt orders should now be sent to the T.O.A.D. mailbox).

Some of the events T.O.A.D. has planned and funded this year are:

Weekly beer party
Christmas Party
Spring Hoe-down
Weekly beer party
Company picnic
Interdepartmental softball league
Weekly beer party
The T-Shirts
New cafeteria evaluation
Weekly beer party
Halloween Party
The Tandem recreational area
And of course, The weekly beer party.

Each T.O.A.D. sponsored activity is designed with two goals in mind: to have lots of fun (cause we all like parties, Ya'll) and to encourage people to meet outside of their working groups and departments. The money for all of these goodies comes from the company provided fund of $10 per employee per month. This fund is supplemented by profits from T-Shirt sales.

T.O.A.D.'s are characterized by an interest in some of the Tandem events and willingness to work on the events that they are interested in. As usual with volunteer efforts, there is always room for more volunteers.

We, the T.O.A.D.'s, thank you for your support in our efforts to provide you with useful and enjoyable social and recreational activities.

SEE YOU AT THE HALLOWEEN PARTY, NOVEMBER 2nd.

Dave Needle and Bill Schweitzer, Cupertino

Toads article in NS News 1979

First Cabin Club in Cancun, Mexico - the next day nearly half the participants came down with Montezuma's Revenge and were all sick as dogs- Seamons Collection

Hawaii First Cabin Club Back Row L-R: Dave Peatrowsky, Keith Ulbrick, Mike Avery, others unknown - Seamons Collection

Jimmy (l) and Jim Katzman (r) learning to Hula dance First Cabin Hawaii 1981 - Seamons Collection

Top Left - Mardi Gras TOPS Trip - NS News April 1982 Bottom Left: Jan Seamons getting TOPS Award from Jimmy - Seamons Collection Right: Calgary Stampede TOPS Trip - NS News July 1983

Manufacturing would perform miracles. 23 systems shipped in 21 days to E-Systems who had a contract to build a nationwide private plane communications network for the Federal Aviation Administration Right: Softball League Champions announced in NS News

Building 1 on Vallco Parkway in Cupertino - Katzman Collection

Inpromptu gathering on the lawn - Original HR Benefits Brochure

Beer Bust in Germany - Tandem_Alumni Yahoo! Groups Posting

European Tandem Bike Ad which had a very short life span and spawned 'The Incredible Hulk' contest

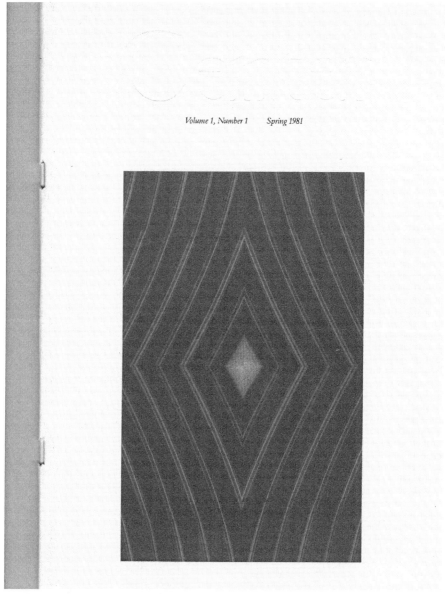

Volume 1, Number 1   Spring 1981

First edition of Center magazine

Incredible Hunk Contest Finalists - McEvoy Collection

Incredible Hunk Contest Winners L-R: unknown, Dennis McEvoy, Candace DeCou, Steve Davoli - McEvoy Collection

Executive Pool Toss Dennis McEvoy (V.P. Software) carried by Jimmy and Larry Laurich (V.P. Hardware) - McEvoy Collection

Dennis McEvoy (l) fully clothed and Jimmy (r) in his boxers in the Pool - McEvoy Collection

PROSPECTUS

Tandem Computers Incorporated

700,000 SHARES
COMMON STOCK

Prior to this offering, there has been no public market for the Common Stock of the Company. See "Underwriting — Pricing of the Offering" with respect to the method of determining the initial public offering price. The offering price has been determined by negotiation between the Company and the Underwriters and bears no direct relationship to the Company's assets, earnings or book value.

The Common Stock offered hereby involves a high degree of risk. See "Introductory Statement—Certain Factors to be Considered Before Purchasing Common Stock."

THESE SECURITIES HAVE NOT BEEN APPROVED OR DISAPPROVED BY THE SECURITIES AND EXCHANGE COMMISSION NOR HAS THE COMMISSION PASSED UPON THE ACCURACY OR ADEQUACY OF THIS PROSPECTUS. ANY REPRESENTATION TO THE CONTRARY IS A CRIMINAL OFFENSE.

	Price to Public	Underwriting Discounts and Commissions (1)	Proceeds to Company (2)
Per Share	$ 11.50	$.90	$10.60
Total (3)			
Minimum	$8,050,000	$630,000	$7,420,000
Maximum	$8,855,000	$693,000	$8,162,000

(1) See "Underwriting."

(2) Before deducting expenses payable by the Company estimated at $216,000 ($.31 per share, assuming the over-allotment option is not exercised).

(3) The Company has granted to the Underwriters an eight-day option to purchase up to 70,000 additional shares to cover over-allotments. See "Underwriting." In the foregoing table the minimum amounts assume that the option will not be exercised and the maximum amounts assume that the option will be exercised in full.

This offering involves immediate substantial dilution of the book value of the Common Stock from the public offering price. See "Introductory Statement — Dilution."

The shares of Common Stock are offered by the Underwriters subject to receipt and acceptance of such shares by them. The Underwriters reserve the right to reject any order in whole or in part. It is expected that delivery of certificates for the shares will be made against payment therefor on or about December 21, 1977.

L.F. ROTHSCHILD, UNTERBERG, TOWBIN

ROBERTSON, COLMAN, SIEBEL & WEISEL

The date of this Prospectus is December 14, 1977.

1977 Public Offering Prospectus - Katzman Collection

1980 1000th cpu party L-R: Jim Hunter, Jerry Reaugh, Mike Sanders, Steve Wierenga, Bob Marshall, Mike Green, Dennis McEvoy, Charlie Comstock, Jimmy Treybig, Jerry Held, Mackie DAve, Jim Katzman, David Greig, Dave Hinders, Joel Bartlett, Bob Huish

Testimonials, such as this 1983 ad, helped increase our credibility through our association with well-known customers.

This 1981 ad helped introduce the NonStop II system.

The 'Fenwick' ad series poked fun at the serious business of data loss.

The Down Side of Being Public

NonStop TXP - NS News December 1983

THIS SHINY GLOW THAT emanated from Vallco Parkway in Cupertino started to fade in the last quarter of fiscal year 1982, covering the period from July to September. Revenue growth, which had been over 100 percent every year since the company went public, slowed that summer to around 50 percent. Profitability sunk to 20 percent. On top of this, in December 1982, the company announced that it was going to have to restate earnings for the 1982 fiscal year, which had ended on September 30. Instead of recording $335 million in fiscal year revenues as announced in October, the company revised revenue to $312 million and profits were restated from $37.3 million to $29.9 million. Although $14 million in revenue was re-recorded for the first month of the new fiscal year (October 1982) and the balance a few months later, meaning that the reduction was not due to a loss of sales, just a deferral of revenue, the external market did not react positively. Investors fled the stock, with 6.8 million shares traded on the day of the announcement. By that day's closing bell, Tandem stock was down $5.88 to $23.63 a share and went on to sink as low as $22 a share in the weeks following the disclosure. As was reported in the *NonStop News* in 1983:

> *"Our old practices were designed at an early time in the company's history in a much stronger economy and have not kept pace with the tremendous growth of our business. The main issue is timing of the revenue recognition, not the quality of the business... nothing has changed our belief that we can achieve our long-term goals."*

Upon further investigation, it came to light that in the go-go atmosphere of Silicon Valley, Tandem customers were reporting special incentives, optional services or deferred payment plans were being offered in return for end-of-quarter orders. In addition, the company had occasionally recorded revenues in one quarter for equipment that wasn't shipped and installed until the following quarter. Company officials explained that these sales practices and accounting procedures were acceptable and typical throughout the computer industry. Unfortunately, Tandem's auditors felt otherwise, though most industry watchers at the time indicated that the rules governing these practices were very much a gray area. One of the contributing factors to the increased auditor sensitivity may have been a warning from the U.S. Securities and Exchange Commission (SEC) that it intended to more carefully scrutinize the reports of high-technology companies. In Tandem's case, when company auditors discovered the premature shipment credits in November 1982, they refused to approve the company's 1982 financial statements. As the *San Jose Mercury News* reported in December 1982:

"The announcement of the restatement surprised Wall Street investors Wednesday when Tandem revealed that its sales and profits for last year were substantially lower than reported earlier. It had improperly included sales of certain computers in results for the year ended September 30. It was intense pressure to meet sales goals that caused the firm to violate standard accounting practices and stricter methods for recording sales have been adopted as a result of the audit. In the past revenues were put on the books as of the date shipped only if the machine was installed within 60 days. Now that window has been reduced to 30 days. Security analysts consider the news a one-time occurrence that won't significantly affect Tandem's future."

The restatement resulted in an SEC investigation that was eventually resolved with no fines or warnings. Most press and analysts seemed to take it in stride as the fundamentals of the business were seen to be sound. This they felt was just a momentary blip, due mostly to naivety. The company was growing up and this event was *"one of those unfortunate things that happen to start-ups,"* said some. *"Not a surprise given Tandem's unorthodox way of doing business,"* said others. But for Jimmy it had a major impact and as he went on to say later that *"those times were the worst moments and most hurtful of my life."*

The net result of both the revenue recognition issues and the slowdown in revenue growth and profits was a series of cost-cutting moves. Salaries were frozen, the annual Christmas party was canceled and Beer Bust start times were pushed back to 5 p.m. on Fridays. In addition, the company introduced the "Pipeline Program," an email-based suggestion box in which employees could suggest ways to cut costs and increase efficiency. According to *NonStop News*, during that first year, hundreds of suggestions were received—everything from proposing travel restrictions to canceling all rented green potted plants in Tandem lobbies and offices. It was proposed that employees use Tandem's internal electronic mail system instead of phoning or sending items via interoffice or U.S. mail. WATS lines were proposed for all long distance calls. One employee proposed a "Bring in Your Own Coffee Mug" program. Employees were encouraged to return office supplies to supply stockrooms from offices and drawers and to turn off office lights if they weren't being used. Everyone pitched in to tighten his or her belt and get through what was a very difficult time. Rather than lay anyone off, management required all employees to take 2.5 days of unpaid vacation. This was announced in two ways. First, a long explanatory memo was waiting on everyone's computer terminal outlining the proposed cost reduction plan and detailing the reasons for the decisions made. Employees were then encouraged to express their reactions to the cutback by writing their own memos, which could be read by any Tandem employee. Even Treybig made himself available a few weeks later for dialogue through the company's internal teleconferencing network (TTN, or Tandem Television Network) that had just been established. Though perhaps not notable today, at the time the opportunity to provide specific and direct feedback, live on TV to employees from a management team was unique.

This is not to say that some were not upset. Len Fishler (#3103) was a freshly minted manager and a story he told illustrated the power of Beer Busts as a mechanism to both raise issues and encourage communications between different levels of employees in the organization. As Len shared:

"One of my key developers got into a LOUD 'discussion' with Jimmy about the handling of the (salary) freeze. In the midst of this argument, the developer in question told Jimmy that he (and his direct reports) should have taken a symbolic pay cut, as a gesture of solidarity with the employees. Jimmy and the developer both had been loosened up by beer drinking, and Jimmy really took exception to what was said. Angry words were exchanged, and at this point I kind of inserted myself between them and pulled the developer away. I sweated the whole weekend, expecting a phone call. Even worse, I was still worried when I came into work on Monday, expecting to find out that my key developer had been fired, and maybe me along with him. Not the case. Nothing happened. In fact, the next Beer Bust where the two of them attended, Jimmy made a point of coming over, and shaking hands with the guy and said no hard feelings, good fight. Tandem was the kind of place where you COULD have good fights, even with the CEO."

The Tandem Television Network was the first of its kind outside of the three broadcast networks (ABC, NBC and CBS). Mike Federico (#1492), one of the TTN executive producers, reminiscences of this difficult time that became the content for his first show on TTN:

"I got called into the large conference room in Building 2, where every Vice President, Jimmy and Tom Perkins (the Chairman of the Board) had all gathered together. They were in the middle of a heated and loud discussion about what to do about the fact that it was looking like the company was not going to make the quarterly financial numbers. Dave Rynne had just joined as the new Chief Financial Officer. He'd been brought in to provide some discipline and process the organization. All of a sudden Dave jumped up and shouted 'VACATION TIME!' The conversation in the room came to a sudden stop. 'What are you talking about?' said a lone voice in the corner, 'It's on the books,' Dave said. 'Let's get everyone to take their vacations. We've already accrued all of the cost, which we can write off to make the numbers.'"

More than 1,500 people viewed the first TTN teleconference, which featured those year-end results and was hosted by Bob Marshall. The third one, called Tandem Talk, was beamed to 1,700 people at 16 sites and focused on the cost-cutting measures. Tandem Talk was designed to be a forum for company-wide issues that would enable efficient and effective communications of important information to everyone simultaneously, with immediate feedback and interaction. Tandem Talk became a regular monthly program that Treybig hosted. Its focus remained as a two-hour opportunity for the officers of the company to share information on and discuss openly key issues of the day that were important to the company. Employees were encouraged to call in and ask questions on the air.

From these beginnings, TTN studio facilities soon were available to any group wanting to communicate its message. It was honored that year at a TV industry-sponsored awards dinner for "Outstanding Achievements in Ad Hoc Video Teleconferencing." The number of users soon multiplied, and a variety of regular teleconferences were established. TTN was usually on the air three to five times a week with training programs, divisional meetings and marketing presentations. It took awhile, though, for executives and others who participated to get used to the medium. As one member of the TTN team said:

"We had to learn how to use the medium. How to get it to be human and how to make people feel relaxed. We found that if you just sit people down in front of a TV camera they felt naked. So we put a table in front of them and that set them at ease. We also began using videotape, invited guests to appear, tried to make the language less technical. Secrecy was also a concern as at that time, anyone who knew the right frequency could tune into Tandem's broadcasts—including competitors. Later special encoding devices were installed so as to keep the broadcast private."

Over time, the various uses of TTN sometimes overlapped in content and audiences, and often were seen as too technical. The team at TTN solved the problem by creating an entertaining way to package various messages clearly and efficiently called "First Friday." It was a two-hour program that appeared on the first Friday of every month that became one of the major information channels for Tandem. The first hour and a half was aimed a specific audience (marketing, sales, engineering etc.), with the last 30 minutes set aside for a segment called "On-Line Exec," targeted at all employees. Members of executive staff served as hosts for this segment. It was used to present general company news from each of their perspectives. The show that took place on the first month of the quarter covered marketing topics. The program that took place in second month was aimed at field sales organization and the program in the third month was oriented for customer engineers and other technical folks. Every First Friday began with a short humorous sketch playing on current events, personalities or TV shows. The level of creativity driven by Baron Sarto, who led the TTN organization, was amazing. Some of the best episode titles included *"The Bob Father,"* with Bob Marshall as a Mafia gang leader, and *"Fantasy Friday,"* a takeoff on the TV show Fantasy Island, as well as *"Star Trek - Next Generation"* and the *"Battle of the Mainframes,"* to name a few. [Author's Note: Many can be found on YouTube by entering Tandem First Friday in the search box.] As William Eberwein (#5366) commented:

"What other company would make such high-quality, sometimes hysterically funny, opening segments using the company's own officers? Ed Sterbenc will always be Buck Profit. If Carolyn Krawczyk called to say there was a segment I could work on, I was happy for weeks. Bill Kochuk was our own Tim Conway of TTN. He was always cool and collected on camera, but would tell you some story or joke just before you were to go on that would crack you up to dangerous laughter levels. For example: I worked on the 'Star Trek Next Generation' opening segment with Bob Marshall. He was famous for showing up two minutes before he was asked to appear, learn his lines COLD in those two minutes, and do his part in one take, or maybe two if Carolyn or Baron wanted a different reaction or angle. One scene required the 'Jordy' character to say: 'Captain, I detect an alien life form,' but Bob kept saying 'alient.' Ten, 15 takes. 'Captain, an alient life form.' Bob started to boil, but then it struck him as funny and it took another 10 takes for us all to stop laughing. I was wearing blue makeup all over my face, and it had to be reapplied because I was crying with laughter."

In addition to these tactical responses to the restatement issue, the executive team also took a serious look at the company's organization. In March 1983, co-founder Michael Green retired, following Jim Katzman and Jack Loustaunou who had left the previous year. As reported in *NonStop News*, the company realized that to be successful, more attention needed to be paid to:

- Understanding the sales and support needs of major global customers that spanned continents

- Improving the company's responsiveness and decision-making
- Providing clear product direction
- Establishing more consistent policy

As Bob Marshall shared with Forbes Magazine in 1986, *"We had to reposition ourselves from being a maker of NonStop minicomputers to being a big computer company with a broad range of products."* At the same time, decentralization remained a guiding theme for sales management, the idea being that responsibility for customer sales and support needed to be positioned as close to customer installations as possible. These needs resulted in a restructuring of sales and marketing. Names that became key influencers of sales and marketing policy over the next few years were at the core of the new organization. Larry McGraw was brought in from IBM to be the Vice President of U.S. Sales and Marketing, Jerry Peterson was chosen to run International Sales and Marketing and Steve Schmidt was brought in to run Manufacturing. Jerry was supported by Skip Yazel, Jack Chapman and John Louth. Skip ran the ICON Division that included, Australia, New Zealand, Japan, Asia Pacific and Latin America, Jack Chapman (who had started the United Kingdom office), became the Division General Manager for Germany, France, Italy and Switzerland, and John Louth took over responsibility for the United Kingdom, Scandinavia, Holland and Belgium. This theme of being close to customers applied not just to sales, but also to Tandem manufacturing. As Jimmy (#1) said at the 4th Annual ITUG (International Tandem Users Group) meeting in 1981 where 600 participants (twice as many as at the 1980 conference) from 15 countries met in San Francisco:

"We build our factories near our customers as a matter of basic philosophy to support their needs anywhere in the world. We don't put our factories where there are low taxes or low labor costs, but where they will be most efficient to our customers."

For most of its existence, Tandem had impressively high customer loyalty and took very seriously the annual Datamation Survey for Customer Satisfaction. In 1980, customer satisfaction (CSAT) amongst Tandem users was reported by Datamation to be the highest of all computer users. No Tandem customers were planning to switch their systems, which was the best record of any computer manufacturer. This level of loyalty continued with Tandem for more than four years, but in 1984 the company lost its #1 position and efforts were begun to better understand customer perceptions of Tandem customers. This desire took programmatic form in 1983 with the creation of the Key Customer Symposium and the Customer Satisfaction Survey. Today these types of customer feedback programs are common among high-tech companies, but at the time it was rare in the industry, especially on the scale undertaken by Tandem. Kirk Cunningham and Yvonne Mathieu of Tandem Marketing conduced the first "Profile on the Customer" survey. Questions were formulated and submitted to Tandem's top 40 customers. The next year, in October 1984, a second survey was conducted with questionnaires sent to senior people at all customer accounts. Over 500 responded (62 percent), which was at the time an impressive response rate. The feedback generated was well received and led to a number of important changes in Tandem's sales and marketing approach.

Another approach to get closer to customers and for Tandem executives to share the company's future product, technology and marketing directions was the Key Customer Symposium, a hallmark program launched in 1983. For the first one, senior executives from Tandem's top customers (with their spouses or a significant other) were invited to three days in the sun at Caneel Bay in the Virgin Islands. The idea was to combine business and social activities. Tandem executives shared details of future marketing and product development strategies. In addition to formal presentations, lots of time was set aside for informal breakout sessions to better understand customers' top technology and support concerns. Interspersed were all sorts of social activities, including a special 'spouses program'. Though not an appropriate setting for the resolution of individual issues, it did provide an opportunity to brainstorm strategy and obtain direct input from the highest levels of the company's most important customers.

One suggestion from customers familiar with IBM's sales approach was that Tandem engage in joint planning activities with customers. At the same time, Tandem was starting to see that its strategy of supporting large customers with different team members at different sales offices in different countries around the world (who never or rarely talked to each other) wasn't working very well. This assessment led to the adoption of a Major Account Sales Planning System. The objective of what later became known as the Major Account Program was to encourage collaboration between team members from all locations and disciplines including sales, systems, engineering and support functions. Central to this was a two and a half day offsite meeting to review status of the account, discuss problems and develop a plan of action to be used at all of the offices. The review also included establishing the present and potential value of the account to Tandem so that team members could take a more strategic view of the customer relationship. Each account was appointed a Tandem "Executive Sponsor," the primary interface with the customer in resolving customer support issues. Supporting the Executive Sponsor were Early Warning Reports (EWR) used by the field and the customer support organization to advise the sponsor of any chronic customer support issues.

Planning sessions started with a visit from a high-level customer representative who would provide perceptions as to how well the account was being managed. This process often would provide invaluable insight into the quality of Tandem's relationship with the customer. Then the planning team would collectively establish sales, team investment, and quality and performance goals. Then brainstorming would take place that focused on the identifying any obstacles or issues that were holding the team back from meeting those goals—be they related to product, sales team, the customer or management. The team would develop specific action plans flexible enough to allow for change with deadlines, assigned resources and follow-up measures identified. With the Executive Sponsor, the plan would then be presented to the customer so that everyone involved was aware of the new plan. Periodic status reports were generated to keep track of the progress. Executive Sponsors were expected to meet with customer senior executives from time to time, host CCC visits and be on top of any customer support issues that arose.

It didn't take long to see that there were some major benefits from such a structured sales planning approach. As reported in *NonStop News* in December 1985:

"By giving systems analysts a voice in the sales planning decisions, sales reps were able to see not just obstacles that they might not otherwise consider, but also areas where other non-sales team members could play a valuable role in helping break down roadblocks. By developing sales plans using the full resources of Tandem, to make the sale in the most effective way, everyone started to feel that they were an important part of the sales and the marketing process. Each team member could learn each other's perspective, focus on common goals and solidify the power of the team concept."

Though expensive to initially launch, the long-term payoff was significant. Tandem was able to penetrate more deeply into these accounts and build much better relationships with key customer decision-makers and influencers. The biggest immediate byproduct was better sales forecasting, communication and cooperation amongst account team members who all felt that their input was valued. By being able to see common goals, team members could more effectively work together. It never totally eliminated the "hockey stick" effect at the end of the quarter, but did help.

It's hard, so many years later, to sort out if the culture attracted unique people—or if the uniqueness of the people created the culture. Either way, Tandem was a completely different environment with a completely different approach to people management than was common in Silicon Valley at the time. Some cynical folks have proposed that most of it was because we were all young and most were just starting out on their careers. We had little experience and hence didn't know any better about what to expect. Others have said that it was only because Tandem was fast-growing and profitable that these kinds of programs and practices could be undertaken.

Nevertheless, attracted by its culture, Tandem had more than its share of really interesting characters, who were all accepted, which was one of the things that made the company so unusual. Everyone fit in, no matter what his or her peculiarities. Take, for example, Brian Robinson, a University of California at Berkeley grad in electronics and computer science engineering. In his spare time he was a competitive Rubik's Cube competitor. Who would have suspected that there even was such a competition? As reported in *NonStop News* in September 1983, many people could solve the cube in two to five minutes, but Brian's best unofficial time was 16.44 seconds—topping the international record by 4.4 seconds. Brian's top official record was 28.73 seconds, which won him second spot in a Los Angeles regional contest at which over 2,000 players competed. As Brian said in the NS News at the time:

"I don't think about solving it while actually spinning the cube. Each move is so natural now that I don't consciously plan them ahead. It helps my spatial perception —I can think in three dimensions now, when most people think in two. To solve the cube you have to solve several problems simultaneously."

Another character was Dave Mackie, one of the original 'TANDEM TEN" and as previously mentioned, the creator of not just the "Mackie Pitch," but also what became known as the "Mackie Diagram." This visual representation of the Tandem systems architecture showed all of the Tandem benefits such as no single point of failure, no shared memory, a single virtual system and near-linear scalability. The image lived in perpetuity on the back of everyone's security badge, though few knew where it came from after Mackie left the company in 1986. Dave's favorite local watering hole was the Duke of Edinburgh, a British pub near the Cupertino campus. One could find him there pontificating as only the British could do on the weaknesses of Americans. One story, repeated so many times that it took on a life of its own, came from Chuck Stobing (#2356) and went something like this. Dave would invite a group of the unsuspecting out for a beer, and as Chuck related:

"Dave would make some comment like, 'So you know, you Americans do not drink correctly. Drinking done right puts you in fine physical condition.' The audience, hanging off of every word he uttered, would look at one another puzzled, but hey he was the boss, so everyone listened carefully. 'Sure the problem is you Americans also do not drink enough. You have to drink, drink and drink until you get sick. Then you heave up your guts, really heave up your guts. It is great for the abs.'"

Needless to say, the audience was shocked and would leave the pub never knowing whether or not to take him seriously. Dave was also the inventor (rumor has it) of the Tandem "cork trick," a mainstay of any Tandem gathering as the years went on. The idea was to hold two corks between thumb and index finger on each hand and separate them without having them get stuck interlocking. Dave would demonstrate in a bar somewhere and then hand the two corks (preferably those that had just been opened from bottles of wine) over to an unsuspecting participant, then sit back and watch the action. Most engineers who saw it for the first time would go crazy and of course, not wanting to be told the solution, would spend hours trying to figure out the trick. The answer of course was all in how you placed your thumbs and index fingers on the corks. By twisting ones hands before you grabbed the corks, it was easy to extract without the two corks interlocking.

An interesting character in field sales in the early years was Julie Rubenstein of Chicago. Julie was one of the original Tandem salesmen and certainly did more than his share to ensure Tandem's early success. Stories about Julie are many and varied. Bob Strand, whose wife Joyce was working for Carol Hubler in marketing at the time, relayed a good one. The group had gotten a new administrative assistant and on her first or second day on the job, she appeared at Joyce's desk obviously flustered and at a loss for what to do. She told Joyce this story:

"Carol's phone rang and I answered, 'Good morning, Carol Hubler's office.' 'Is Carol in?' 'No, I'm sorry sir, she's not here at the moment. Could I take a message?' 'Yes. Tell her the fat Jew from Chicago called.' Click. This was long before caller ID or whatever. Joyce just smiled at the admin and said, 'Tell Carol that Julie called.'"

But the classic Julie story came from John Haverland (#4512).

"It was 1978 and I was a partner at ACI doing technical pre/post sales support (this being before I joined Tandem). Anyway, Mike May (ACI VP Sales at the time) and I met Julie in Chicago to make a sales call at First National Bank of Chicago. The sales call sticks in my mind for two reasons—the first being that First Chicago was talking about buying 10 systems (no, not a 10-processor system, 10 systems) and Julie's attempt to accelerate the close. We were meeting with a senior IT decision-maker but Julie took the gambit of telling the customer that he was not going to sell any Tandem equipment to them because Tandem was a small company and we couldn't afford to have a failure at a major account like First Chicago. Furthermore, based upon what Julie knew of First Chicago, he was convinced that the bank was not competent enough to successfully implement a Tandem/ACI solution. Needless to say, Mike and I were more than a bit taken aback by this closing technique. The call ended with the First Chicago executive begging Julie to sell him a proof-of-concept system and to let him prove that First Chicago was competent and worthy enough to being a Tandem customer. [Of course as we all know], First Chicago went on to become one of Tandem and ACI's major customers—as I recall they eventually had 50+ Tandem systems installed [in countries all around the world]. Yup, Julie was definitely a 'big' personality."

Another of Tandem's many and sundry eccentrics was Tony Turner, one of the technical gurus. Tony was brilliant and his command of the English language superb. He had a way of translating highly technical subjects into easy-to-understand concepts with amazing analogies. A favored speaker at the Customer Conference Center, one of Tony's classics was his explanation of the Tandem architecture using a photo of Stonehenge. As Mike Greenfield (#4168) shares:

"Think about it... the pillars across the top of the stones as the Dynabus! Tony exemplified the brilliant, individualistic, sometimes eccentric people at Tandem who thrived in an environment where they were team players while maintaining their individuality."

But Tony always looked like he'd just returned from some exotic adventure in the wilderness. In all the years he worked at Tandem I don't think he was ever seen in a suit. The best one could do was to get him to wear a tie, which he would only do under duress. He loved Hawaiian shirts, suspenders and purple socks with sandals and you never quite knew what might come out of his mouth. My favorite was a video he created to explain the messaging system, which if my memory serves me correctly, was based on an English maypole with all of these messengers dancing around it. Another Tony story from Mike Greenfield (#4168) says it all:

"I joined Tandem in May 1982 as the sales rep in a remote office (Greensboro, North Carolina) reporting to Vic Para who was based out of Atlanta. My instructor at sales school was Barry Ariko. I recall Bob Marshall describing my location as an outpost rather than an office. My first visit to the Customer Conference Center took place a few months after joining Tandem. I was accompanying a number of senior MIS executives from R.J. Reynolds, the tobacco company. RJR was a very formal company, the kind that still served visitors (even sales reps) coffee on china with silver teaspoons. The afternoon of the visit, a reception was held and various executives dropped by to greet my guests. Our Executive Sponsor who was scheduled join us for dinner had been called away, but arranged a substitute. At the restaurant, the folks from RJR were still in their three-piece suits, when someone resembling Grizzly Adams entered (big beard, suspenders, jeans, sandals) and wandered over to join us. A Tandem colleague poked me in the ribs and told me that that was Tony Turner, our substitute host. Tony looked like he was ready for a day in the woods. The RJR guys sat there speechless. I decided to break the ice by starting the conversation, saying to Tony: 'So we met our Executive Sponsor earlier today. For someone with all his responsibilities he sure seems calm. How does he do it?' Without missing a beat, Tony responded: 'That's easy to answer, he's an f*&%ing idiot!' I would have liked to see the look on my face! Anyway, Tony gained instant credibility and after that, I always found a way for Tony to participate in my CCC visits."

Another mad man first in the field organization (and later when he moved to corporate) was Chris Christedes, a sales manager also from Chicago. I'm not sure what was in the water in Chicago that generated these characters, but there must have been something. Though a common look now, Chris shaved his head so that he was completely bald. He had a sense of humor that would have everyone in stitches and impersonations were his shtick. Lee Calamaio (#7243), a Chicago sales rep who once worked for him, shared this story, which would be completely unacceptable in public company today:

"We were at a sales rally in Phoenix in the late 1980s. Christedes was holding court at a Mexican restaurant with his team including Pete Hackensen, Rick Gardner, myself and Harlan Lee to name just a few. Chris loved to do his 'Ming from Cling' or 'Ming the Merciless' impersonations. This time, while waiting for our orders, Chris took the taco shells and cut one up to form a point that he licked and glued to his forehead and then wrapped two more around his wrists. He looked just like Ming from an old Flash Gordon movie. He goes on to impersonate Ming for five minutes. We laughed until we cried. When he was finished and removed the tacos from his head, I told him that they had left a giant grease stain forming an almost permanent impression on his bald head. He got suddenly serious until I told him I was kidding."

Another unique character in the late 1980s was Ed Sterbenc whose day job was to run Sales Operations for Mike Moore, the Vice President of the ICON Division who had replaced the departing Skip Yazel. A professional stand-up comic in his youth, Ed was constantly making jokes out of any situation that occurred. His main claim to fame was as the recurring star "Buck Profit" on First Friday. This was a segment where Buck would stand in front of a map of the world and review major sales wins in various countries and slapping 'happy face' stickers all over. It was stand-up improv comedy at its best. You never knew what he was going to say, only that he'd have you rolling in your seat as he recited his common refrain at the end of each segment: *"And I've a yearning to tell you, that whether it's a yen or a pound or a peso or a lira, a Buck is always a Buck!"*

It's hard to describe how self-motivating it was that all of these characters were well accepted and that humor had a place in business. Here was a company that cared so much about the health of its employees that it not only built a swimming pool and a basketball court, but started a department called Total Health Services, whose objective was to help ensure that employees maintained a good work-life balance (though that term wasn't in common use at that time). They made sure, for example, that financial planning was available to rookies who knew nothing about stock options and had classes to discuss the importance of 401retirement planning. Families felt supported and were even allowed to use (at their own risk) the facilities.

As Bob Horst shared, *"When our kids were little, if it got too hot at home, we would go into the conference room in Building 3, above the pool and have a picnic."*

For Steve Rhodes, Special Interest Groups (known as SIGs) were of major impact. They could be started by anyone and usually had a theme. There was one for ham radio operators, a book club and many others. As Steve shared:

"I started a parents group and ran lunchtime meetings for most of my career at Tandem. I divided them into groups called Small (ages 0-5), Medium (ages 6-12) and Large (ages 13-18), based on the ages of the worker's kids. Once a month each group would meet in a conference room at lunch, and we'd discuss a pre-selected topic. I hosted all the meetings and learned a lot about parenting in the process, as my only child grew from Small to Medium in the process."

This commitment to people generated a work ethic and group commitment to company success that I don't think will ever be duplicated in Silicon Valley. As Brian Green, the New York Regional Sales Director, said in 1982, *"Whatever discipline Tandem people are working in, they never stand back and watch. They pitch in. Our people do what needs to be done and they don't worry about the role that they have."* Some examples of this attitude are shared below:

- *"I had Boeing up in Building 2 for a discussion of a very complex satellite tracking application they were trying to write. They had some detailed database questions. Jim Gray, one of the database gurus, was walking down the hall in jeans and sandals. I flagged him down. He joined the meeting and did a 30-minute impromptu talk on the white board. It was stunning. He asks what their budget is. They claim no limit, so he says 'A 16 processor ought to handle it.' Nice Jim!"* [Justin Simonds #4521] (Author's Note: Jim Gray was lost at sea on Sunday January 28, 2007 during a solo sailing trip to the Farallon Islands near San Francisco on his 40-foot yacht "Tenacious" to scatter his mother's ashes. Searches were carried out for several weeks but no sign was ever found of the vessel or Jim—may he be resting in peace.)

- *"I met a lot of great people and everyone tried to help you get sales and always asked, 'What can I do?' I always remember my first chance to come to Cupertino and my boss sent me out on a Friday in 1980 (I came from Honeywell) and I remember walking to the pool area, looking out and seeing people skinny-dipping in the pool. I always met people who really carried about helping and getting you everything you needed. I honestly felt that the people at Tandem were the smartest people I have ever worked with."* [Michael Smith #1615]

- *"The tandem bicycle in the front lobby. The God-awful pizza that came at end of quarter that increased my waist by five inches!! Ping-Pong at lunchtime. Beer Busts with imported beer (at least at first). Performance benchmark testing for Scandinavian Airlines and OCLC (an Ohio-based organization whose systems help libraries acquire, catalog and lend materials). The swimming pool behind Building 2. The really neat parties, where nobody really got too carried away. Clowns and face painting for the kids. The great HEART that the people of Tandem showed. Starting my first two weeks at Tandem playing GAMES on the system (and learning it very well). The excitement in the air when people felt THEY owned the company and were making something worthwhile. People sleeping in chairs, on the floor, in sleeping bags at the SIT at end of quarter. If you needed something to do your job, you got it! Managers that took criticism at meetings from employees and then really TRIED to do it better. If you were sick, you took as much time off as needed, regardless of how many 'sick days' you were authorized. A place where being a human being was honored. Third class mail, where I sent out 'Franklin's Corner' messages to the company to inspire them and boost morale—discuss issues and sell old cars. Where else would you see these things, but the Tandem was a Giant among pygmies." [Al C.]*

• *"But what I remember most is the times we weren't carousing, the times we were talking, the times I met people I would have never met in the rest of my life. I talked to people (in person, email, phone) around the world. I'd never been outside the U.S. before I came to work for Tandem. I learned that the world was both bigger and smaller than I thought, and I could be a part of the world, in ways I never imagined. The machines, the architecture, the fault tolerant thing. I thought the architecture was, for want of a better word, 'thrilling.' To this day I don't know if this is because I don't have a hardware/system internals background or if it really was thrilling. I tell you—massively parallel fault tolerant—still has a nice ring to it, don't you think? People really cared about the machines. I know—just because you care about something, that doesn't necessarily mean it's good. But I still think that we were making something wonderful." [Mary Szvetecz #8914]*

• *"I was only 22 years old when I started at Tandem. It was the first real company that I worked at. The culture and the wonderful people shaped me as a person and as a professional. It taught me so much about valuing people and really being a part of a team. I remember being a temp and getting a performance award in the quarterly review. What kind of place was this? I remember seeing my Vice President Mike Moore having lunch regularly with Don the security guard. As low on the totem pole as I was, I never felt it from the people and the company. I actually have never felt more valued, which has made it difficult to work in other places that do not share these values. Tandem was the only place where its actions and words lined up. So many times you hear the company line, and think they are like Tandem. They NEVER are! I take you all with me wherever I work, and pull from the memories and those wonderful Core Values. Tandem is often referenced as the benchmark for culture. If I hadn't worked there I would have thought it was all an urban myth." [Valerie Bunnell]*

One tool and technology that tied the company together was the internal telecommunications network. Today it's hard to imagine that there was ever a time when employees didn't have access to email. Tandem was one of, if not the first, company to make email available to ALL employees in 1983. As reported in *NonStop News* in July of that year, the Tandem network included 140 Tandem systems (or nodes) totaling more than 600 CPUs, networked together via more than 200 telephone lines. It served 125 locations and reached 98 percent of employees. Built on fault tolerance, data integrity and modularity it had a backbone ring with seven nodes that provided the best balance of cost and availability, resilience and manageability. Central to its operation was the Network Control Center (NCC) in Cupertino that was operated by five staff (three in the U.S. and two in Germany). Each site took turns being on call. There was even a mechanism for the operators to monitor the network from home during off-hours so that they could take care of any emergencies that cropped up.

Called Network MAIL, it was, at the time, one of the world's largest distributed database applications with more than 3,000 messages sent every day. As shared in an article in *NonStop News* in December of 1983: *"NCC is where our worldwide network is monitored minute by minute. The control room lights are dimmed, giving operators clear visibility of the five large screens that cover one entire wall. Images from the monitoring terminals are projected on these screens, allowing a single operator to view data from all of the systems in Tandem's Network without moving from his or her terminal. From here we can see that if a processor fails in Singapore, we can move an entire process to another in London. The Operations Room is also used for customer demonstrations. The network is monitored in three shifts between Cupertino, and Frankfurt Germany (expanding to include Melbourne Australia, a few years later). It enables us to monitor the system 24 hours a day without anyone staying up all night to do so. Operators at each site can access and control the network at any time."*

Its origins were in a piece of software called TEMAIL. As Frank Sheeman (#100) shared:

TEMAIL was based on some code done by the documentation guru in development. In 1981, a group working for me in Building 3 and later Building 4 wrote the code, all TAL of course, upgraded it a bit and made it a company-wide tool. Candace DeCou did the magic that made it all come together—she got TELE [the company internal online telephone and email directory] properly populated with contact information, including email address for everyone, including the executives. That took a lot of individual negotiation and pressure. She had to ensure that Jimmy's assistant printed his email for him—he was still into paper. The fact that we got the backbone network working running EXPAND (using a basic architecture that Jim Gray tossed off to me in a hallway conversation) was also critical. Once Jimmy started expecting people to have read his emails we were done! Did anyone besides me use the encryption feature? i.e., specify an eight-character code and we'd run it through DES before sending it. You had to have the code to read it—even our guys couldn't read it. Of course, it was illegal to send those messages outside the U.S., but we were either too dumb or too arrogant to know that. Sadly, the guys who migrated us to the Transfer/Pathway did know that. Another lost and valued feature—like the front panel lights."

Email, now ubiquitous, was a remarkable application, which, as we all know, changed the world. It's hard to imagine in 2012 that there was a time when email didn't exist or if it did it was restricted to a small group of users. As was declared by William Eberwein (#5366) in 2009:

"We had email before the world knew what email was and you can always tell a former Tandem employee because they tend to refer to 'email messages' rather than 'an email.'"

And echoed by Phil Ly (#1067):

"Looking back, it is amazing how 'connected' we all were: between the field and corporate, as well as among field people. Software like MAIL, PRS, and TELE allowed us to communicate and share information effectively. Who would have guessed that COURIER and TRANSFER were actually [precursors to] the very first Worldwide Web and would serve the whole company so well?

In April 1983, another advance was made in the area of email. An upgrade occurred that year that made available three classes of mail:

- Post1 was for "First Class" mail, i.e., messages to individuals or small groups
- Post2 was for "Second Class" mail, i.e., business-related messages broadcast via distribution lists
- Post3 was for Third Class mail, i.e., non-business related messages, broadcast to wide groups

What was even more remarkable was the ability while traveling to access mail on your home Tandem system node, where your inbox was stored, from a system node in a remote office. This was an unheard of innovation at the time. As ubiquitous as the Internet and email have become in 2012, Tandem was the first to use email and the network as a company hierarchy flattener. As Jerry Reaugh, the Vice President of MIS, at the time said:

"I'm not aware of any other company that offers all employees access to the company network or that has a network that spans the entire corporation. Often more effective than telephone, Tandem's Network Mail has helped many feel more a part of the company as a whole. Being the trend setters that we are, we often find ourselves in situations where there is little or no prior experience to help us understand what is happening."

This was especially true when it came to dealing with MAIL and trying to set policies for its use. As an article in *U.S. News and World Report* said in December 1983, quoting observations from several professional behaviorists about people's use of email and computer systems:

"Mail is a great equalizer because it affords everyone who uses it the ability to compose and review their message before transmittal and lets the message stand on its content without being biased by the ability of the presenter. It also appears that people tend to be much freer and more open when dealing with an inanimate object, the terminal than they are in dealing with people directly."

But it didn't stop there. Professor Sara Kiesler of the Carnegie-Mellon University Social Sciences and Social Psychology Department, got a lot of press with her research into the *"Social Aspects of Computers and the Impact of New Technology on Organizations."* Her basic premise was that email dramatically altered the way people related to each other. Little did she know that online dating sites, Facebook, LinkedIn and Twitter were just around the corner in a decade or two. In an article that Kiesler wrote at the time:

"On a telephone you hear the other person's tone of voice, face to face you see a person's smile, see who takes the head seat at a meeting that provides cues as to status. No such feedback takes place in computer exchanges. There are no nonverbal cues and no social norms built up around email the way there is when you meet someone in person or talk on the phone, so computer exchanges are less predictable. People are likely to be less inhibited when communicating by computer, willing to reveal more about themselves as few cues inhibit self-disclosure and are less likely to hold back strong feelings and communicate in an abrupt manner. Computer users tend to get totally absorbed in what they are doing on the machines and often become much less self-aware. Workaholics will get worse as a result of using computers because they forget that they ought to stop."

On the other hand, Kiesler's research suggested that some people might be helped by the use of technology as a communications medium and *"in some cases they may promote the development of deeper relationships and even might help people cope with embarrassment because no one is looking at them. They may communicate more with superiors and with people to whom they don't usually talk, which might lead to more face-to-face meetings because people will raise issues they would not have raised otherwise."* They could meet on the computer and then get together face-to-face thereby *"stimulating rather than reducing human contact."* These were all key benefits that Jimmy certainly saw of email.

In addition to improving the level and types of communications up and down and across the organization, MAIL profoundly improved productivity but also gave immediate feedback. Jimmy used to love to tell of the experience of a Vice President who had just joined the company. The new VP sent out message sharing information concerning a new company policy via electronic mail. That very same day he received over 400 messages from employees, all of whom were against it. He said he believed in Tandem's people philosophy but it would take awhile to adjust to this democracy. My own initial experiences with Tandem email affected me profoundly. The idea of being able to send a message to any one at any level in the organization was shocking. But what was even more shocking was the fact that more often than not people would reply and do so with kindness and respect. One of my first exchanges was with Dennis McEvoy, the Vice President of Software Development. The message that I had sent had arrived garbled because I didn't understand some of the technical features of composing a message. Instead of ignoring my message, he not only replied, but gently gave me some guidance as to what I was doing incorrectly. He didn't need to do that and the fact that he did so personally was very impressive. Here are a few other employees' experiences that have been shared over the years:

- *"Once someone asked me why our processors didn't restart after failure. I had no idea. Next day I asked someone and they suggested sending an email to All Tandem because someone out there knew. Well, at 8:30 a.m. I sent out the message and my first response was a half-hour later from someone from Zurich. THAT WAS 1984!! Fantastic. We were way ahead of our times!"* [Steve Cole #5776]

- *"I had friends and advisors from all around the world and I was constantly amazed at how much people would help others be successful. [One colleague] would send pages of explanations that helped me get going when I first joined. We all wanted everyone to succeed. You spotted kindred spirits from their remarks and made friends long before you met face to face. I was there 13 years and I think MAIL was down twice!"* [William Eberwein #5366]

- *"But by far my most memorable moment was when I installed the Sales Order Processing System in Frankfurt, Germany but I was physically in Cupertino. You have to understand that was way before the Internet was introduced to the world. I had to check twice to make sure if it was real. Yes. I was running the system on the Frankfurt node indeed." [Polly Kam #1177]*

- *"I worked at Tandem from 1980-1998 in NYC, Cupertino and Atlanta, mostly in MIS. I loved the technology and having access to all those brilliant minds was unbelievable. In 1981, I was part of a team developing an accounting application on \Corp and our software compiles were taking a very long time due to the fact that \Corp was a general purpose computer used by many departments for development and production. The compiles were slowing production. So, we decided to ask our teammates in Germany if we could use their node \Germany during our day and their nights to compile and test our software. They said sure as no one was using the system at night. So all we had to do was set up security, go to \Germany via the file system, Fup dup and we were in business. Those were the days. The Tandem architecture was so great and fun to work on." [Steve Engel #1702]*

- *"I remember when Tandem decided to use Transfer/Mail internally around 1985. All Tandem nodes around the world had to upgrade their hardware and software. System Managers had to learn Transfer and TMF. A bridge was built between TEMAIL and Transfer/Mail. Then at some point there was only Transfer/Mail. PSMail, M6530 and then GUMBY were the clients. We had guaranteed delivery. We had automatic email distribution lists built every night from the TELE database. Having TEMAIL, Transfer/Mail and TELE as tools to enable quick worldwide communication was the best." [Steve Engel #1702]*

- *"There was a large mail node in Cupertino supporting email for Senior Management, Marketing, Accounting and several other organizations. Transfer/Mail had a new release that required a database conversion and it was complicated and took time. The business window for the change was a weekend—Friday evening through Monday morning. It was determined it could not be done with the current hardware and size of the database within a weekend. We asked the Benchmark Center if we could use one of their high-end configurations—faster processors, 16 of them, more memory and disk drives. We shut down Transfer, disconnect \Mailman from the network, backed up the data to tape, reinstalled everything on the isolated benchmark node, it became \Mailman for the weekend, did the conversion and upgrade, backed up the data to tape, reinstalled Transfer and restored the data on \Mailman in Loc. 3. We finished Sunday evening. This type of sharing and support was the norm at Tandem." [Steve Engel #1702]*

- *"Tandem had the best 'favorite books to read list' file (that was built by entries from the Tandem employee population). I remember looking for a hard to find sci-fi book called* Genus Homo *by L. Sprague de Camp and posted something in 2nd or 3rd class mail about it. A kind Tandem employee in the Austin office located a copy for me at a book show (signed by the author, no less), bought it and sent it to me. Amazing people at Tandem." [Paul R. P.]*

With email being so new, Tandemites had to learn the rules on the fly—or make them up as we went along. One phenomenon that emerged was "distribution list inflation," or what we at Tandem called CYA (cover your ass)—copying others to whom a sender would not normally send messages. Another as we all become more proficient in the use of email, were the "email wars" that would occasionally erupt. Someone would post something that rubbed feathers the wrong way and an electronic firestorm would erupt. Some of the mail wars were legendary, but the classic was our collective response to the firing of two employees who had engaged in likely the world's first cyber-sex exchange. One was in the in the U.K. and the other on the McCandless campus in the U.S. It was scandalous at one level and hilariously funny at another. It sure made for good water cooler and across the network conversations for a very long time. It also heralded the introduction of the "Mail Police," whose key "Sergeant at Arms" was Ron Lapedis. This team monitored what was going on across the network, spotting and halting misuse of email, especially third-class mail. One trick was the sending of "Emily Latella" messages, a pseudonym for mail police member William Eberwein (#5366), who used the Emily Latella messages to coerce participants into "good" email behavior. As he shared:

"My main motivation on 'Emily' was to take a mail-war that had gone on too long, and launch an impassioned opinion that would render the entire thing ridiculous before too many feelings got hurt. Man, that was fun! We were using email to 'brain the company' and connect with one another before the Internet burst upon the scene."

TXP launched in 1983 - NS News Cover October 1983

Tandem's trade show booth with a 4-cpu system at the 1983 Hannover Fair, the world's largest industrial trade show at the time with 650,000 attendees and 6,000 firms from 47 countries - NS News 1983

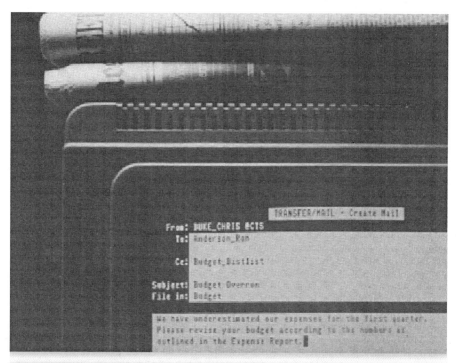

Mike Moore, VP of ICON (l) and Jimmy (r) learn about email from RIck Clayton (l) and Jim Bisordi (r) - NS News
February 1984

Suzanne and Tom Dix sometimes ride to work on a tandem to save gas—she pumping, he reading.

Frank Sheeman and Stephanie Schwartz save electricity by using window and lantern light during meeting.

Cost savings measures at work - NS News March 1983

Clockwise, top photo: Teleconference panelists who introduced INFOSAT include Ann Doerr, Tom Gabriszeski, Vice President of American Satellite Co., and Jerry Peterson. Satellite dish in Cupertino transmits teleconference signals to the field. INFOSAT developers include Gene Cunningham, John Atwood, Steve Hayashi, and Mike Kearny, shown examining a transmitter spectrum.

Tandem American Satellite unveil the first integrated computer satellite communications network (code named Data Bolt) - NS News June 1982

Watsonville at Work: L Nancy Jakobsen, Yvetta Rusler, Mark Ellison, Natalie Clark and Pat Larrecou. Bottom Right: Rick Medina Recording Completion Rates- NS News March 1983

Top: Mike Bateman, Skip Yazel and Larry McGraw
Bottom: Steve Schmidt, Tom Bechler and Mike Moore
on the Executive Question-and-Answer Panel

Barry Ariko (l) and various executives (r) on a Q & A Panel - NS News

John Louth, GM United Kingdom, Scandinavia and Benelux (l) and Ernst Lotz, GM Germany (r) - NS News

Randy Baker, VP Customer Support (l) and Jerry Reagh, VP Information Systems (r) - NS News

Jan Jensen, VP Human Resources (l) and Jimmy's official portrait (r) - NS News

Dave Rynne, Chief Financial Officer (l) and Jerry Peterson, VP International (r) - NS News

Larry Laurich, VP Hardware (l) and Jack Chapman, GM Europe and later VP Global Sales Operations (r) - NS News

Executives preparing for 2nd Teleconference broadcasting from Ann Arbor, Michigan 1982 L-R Dennis McEvoy, Chris Duke, Jerry Peterson and Larry Laurich- NS News May 1982

Nine of the original 13 patent holders L-R Sitting: Michael Green, David Greig, John Despotakis, Steven Hayashi, Joel Bartlett L-R Standing: Dennis McEvoy, Jim Katzman, Dick Bixler, Steve Wierenga Fortune Magazine June 1982

Matt Cullen, Jim Bourgeois, Bruce Dougherty, and Forrest Grein.

TTN Presents:

Ed Sterbenc as Buck Profit in Action on First Friday Telecasts

First Friday intro collage (ttp://www.youtube.com/watch?v=UzTPugKx8Xw&feature=related)

Mike Federico and Gregg Hansen at the controls for the inaugural 'First Friday' broadcast - NS News December 1985

L - Julie Rubenstein (Striped Shirt) R- Carol Hubler

Tony Turner, the Sage of Tandem - all dressed up!! Next Page: Jimmy on the cover of INC Magazine and TXP Ad!

My Introduction to "The Tandem"

CHANGES AND

THE THIRD
FIVE YEARS

CHALLENGES

Cover of the Third Five-Year Plan

MY LOVE AFFAIR WITH Tandem didn't start until early 1984, nearly a decade after the company had been founded. I didn't know that much about the company when I joined, being a transplant from Canada and totally unfamiliar with Silicon Valley. Though raised in Don Mills, a suburb of Toronto, Ontario, I had been living prior to moving to the United States in Ottawa, the nation's capital and a slow-moving government town. Nothing in my experience prepared me for the high-octane experience that was the computer industry in the mid-1980s. Tandem was just a computer that my technical colleagues at Bell Canada's Computer Communications Group liked better than Northern Telecom's voice switch for online data transfer, but it's technology was central to the Intelligent Network (INET) public database access application solution that Bell Canada was building. The idea was to enable remote users to access a "cloud" via a user-friendly graphical user interface and be routed through the "cloud" to third-party database information providers for stock quotes, bibliographic information and more. INET, though never really successful commercially, was a precursor technology to the Internet. Much of the language used at the time to describe the service is the same vocabulary used today to describe both the Internet and cloud computing.

As INET project manager, I was responsible, in 1983, for the running a marketing trial to test pricing, usability and customer demand for this new service. Alas, to everyone's horror, when completed, we found that we'd built a service that left users unhappy and unwilling to pay any price for the service. This was because the databases available through database information providers didn't contain information that users were interested in and the users weren't the kind of user that the database information providers wanted. The only winner in the whole thing was a funky little outfit called America Online (AOL), which seemed to be the only information provider that users loved. How I wish I'd bought its stock at that time, though it was a decade later before AOL became a household name.

My first experience of California in coming off the plane in San Francisco from the frozen north over the Christmas season in 1983 was overwhelming. Accustomed to huge office buildings in both Ottawa and Toronto, I was blown away by the short stubby, architecturally uninteresting buildings that were Silicon Valley. Later I understood that concerns about earthquakes had set the tone for building standards, though it wasn't until five years later in the Loma Prieta earthquake that the significance of earthquake-resistant buildings truly hit home. As so articulated so well by *Newsweek* in June 1981:

"Silicon Valley stretches along the western shore of San Francisco Bay, from the tree-lined suburban streets of Palo Alto through the urban sprawl of San Jose. Its starkly modern, crisply manicured campuses house the highest concentration of Ph.D's in the world. But California's Silicon Valley is to the burgeoning semiconductor industry what Pittsburgh was to steel, a birthplace and manufacturing Mecca of a technology that will drive America's productivity engines for years to come. Silicon Valley is not simply a geographical location, but a kind of heightened industrial consciousness."

In September 1983, my husband accepted a job at a startup in Felton, California, about 30 miles south of Silicon Valley. I wasn't willing to leave Ottawa and join him without a job and work visa. After a potential transfer to Bell Northern Research's Mountain View facility fell through, I reached out to the technical lead of the INET project to ask if he could introduce me to someone at Tandem, the computer platform that the INET service was running on. This he did and kindly introduced me to Keith Ulbrick, who was the Ottawa sales rep for Tandem at the time. Keith in turn put me in touch with Adra Ross, the Tandem Manager of Industry Marketing, with whom I did an informational interview. I had no idea until much later how much hype had been generated in the press about Tandem and how hard it was to get hired there. I hadn't read a single press release about the company, though had some information from Keith. In hindsight it's a wonder that I got hired at all. One contributing factor might have been that I was working for Tandem's largest Canadian customer. Either way, a few days later, Adra called me and told me about an opportunity in Marketing Support. The Tandem Executive Institute was looking for a program manager. They figured that my telecommunications and finance experience would be helpful in the next phase of TEI's development, which was to expand to different market segments and countries. So with not much hope, I ventured to Cupertino and spent a day of interviews with all sorts of people including the TEI director, Ann Perlman, her manager, Kathy Weiner, her manager's manager, Barry Ariko, and all of the other members of the TEI team—Susie Farber, Ellen Anderson Herbst and Rose Tokugawa. It was an amazing day, with an interviewing process that was standard in the Tandem culture, but the likes of which I had never experienced before. Lo and behold, not only did they offer me a job, but they also agreed to obtain the necessary visas so that I could immediately start work, which I did three weeks later, in early February 1984.

The year 1984 was a watershed for the company. Not only did Tandem get listed on the Fortune 500, but more than 150 systems were now installed worldwide, which was a pretty impressive track record. A High Performance Research Center opened in Frankfurt under the tutelage of the legendary systems performance expert Joseph Broeker. Two key members were Harold Sammer, a programmer extraordinaire, and his wife Geate "TMF" Sammer. These two were the main drivers behind what became incorporated into the Guardian operating system core as the "expedited message protocol," which significantly sped up performance of the message system. Also that year Tandem systems were used at the 1984 summer Los Angeles Olympics to keep track of the scores and medal counts. Not only that, an employee, Chris Cavanaugh, won a gold medal in the 4x100M freestyle swimming race, which just put the icing on the cake of a wonderful Tandem systems performance and opportunity for market visibility. Tandem now had a place in the "big leagues" and was able to poke a few competitive holes in strategies of IBM and DEC. Revenues that year came close to $450 million and over 5,100 employees now wore Mackie Badges. The early part of 1984 also brought a hiring binge of which I was a part. That spring the company held its first-ever open house, attended by more than 900 people hoping to find the right position at Tandem. It was the biggest recruitment event ever held in Silicon Valley involving software, hardware, marketing and MIS departments all at one time, resulting in 120 follow-up interviews.

I think another reason for interest in me was my familiarity with the computer and communications needs of various industries including financial services, energy and manufacturing. I had gained this knowledge as part of CCG's foray into industry market management, a new field at the time. In the mid-1980s, Tandem was just beginning to understand that technology features and functions weren't the only important selling attributes and was starting to move to more customer-centric marketing. As mentioned previously, some of this change in thinking may have been due to the slide in revenues in 1982.

As the sales force started to better understand customers, so came the realization that Tandem customers were often at the leading edge of their own industries. This meant that when they bought Tandem systems, it was often for an application that was the "next cool thing" in that particular industry. These included applications that automated shop floor control in manufacturing, enabled automatic teller machine networks (ATMs) and foreign exchange systems in banking, supported point-of-sale devices in retail and interactive communications systems in the tele-communications industry. One company at the leading edge was Knight Ridder newspapers. Its Viewtron service, like AOL, was an early iteration of an Internet-like platform (based on videotex technology) in which a multitude of services including banking, shopping, news and advertising was fed directly into homes and work-places via a high quality, color, user-friendly communications system. With intuitive graphics and text, consumers could make flight arrangements, follow stock quotes, buy from key retailers, obtain recreational information such as menus and concert guides, and purchase from classified ads.

TEI as a marketing program was leading edge for its time. It was based on a sales model just as true and viable today as it was over 25 years ago. It positioned Tandem as a business partner, not simply a vendor, by emphasizing the importance of merging business strategy and technology. It provided opportunities for participants to brainstorm future trends in an industry's use of technology with leading-edge consultants and showed why non-IT senior management needed to stay involved in technology decisions. The ultimate in peer selling, Tandem customers were invited to a three-day seminar to talk about their systems, how they benefited, why they made the decision to buy Tandem and how they implemented the system. Of course there was some technology training, but it was done by Tandem senior executives and typically was on topics such as the future of online transaction processing, and database and data communications technologies. By the end of the seminar, partici-pants not only understood the compelling reasons for using a relational database or geographically distributing a network, but had a chance to share ideas with peer executives in their industry as well as interact with the best and the brightest from leading academic institutions and consulting firms.

The initial idea for TEI came from the field sales organization based on a desire for an integrated set of presentations designed specifically for upper management. The first few institute programs were customer-specific. One program was requested by the president of a major West Coast bank, who wanted his management team to learn together about technology trends and Tandem products. The second was a customized session for a major airline in Sweden to help increase their confidence that Tandem, a tiny company in Silicon Valley, had systems solid enough to run a major part of the airline's business. In 1982, industry-oriented sessions were held for banking, the non-bank finance industry, manufacturing and transportation. Thirteen banking executives attended the first Data Processing for the Banking Industry Institute, held in Monterey, California. As Susan Rohrer, TEI's first Director, said in an article in *NonStop News in* April 1982.

"TEI is an educational and marketing resource for major account selling and support designed to influence key senior non-technical decision-makers to choose Tandem for their major business systems. It does this by giving them an in-depth understanding of Tandem's management system, corporate strategy and products over multiple days in a soft sell sort of way via presentations, discussions, outside speakers, case studies, demonstrations and labs."

Since the programs were expensive to run and designed for non-technical senior executives, the screening process for invitations was handled by the field and very strict. Each geographic region was given several seats with the objective to find the right balance between customers and prospects with an eye to inviting those with the highest potential to contribute to Tandem's revenue growth. It was interesting to see over the years that often those companies most interested in coming were those facing serious technology or competitive-driven change. Sometimes these companies had a new management team on board, or new and stiffer competition, or a changing regulatory environment that resulted in lost revenue or slipping profits. In these situations, taking advantage of new technology effectively could totally reshape a customer's worldview.

As industry and solution-oriented marketing started to take hold, the "Alliance Program" that had been started the year before started to aggressively recruit Tandem-based software applications. In this way, Tandem started to be able to sell hardware and software application solutions as well as build capability in understanding the businesses that its customers were in. The company had previously never given much thought if any, to the applications that ran on its hardware. However, by mid-1984, this mindset had changed. An executive Q&A in *NonStop News* stressed that it was *"very important to have agreements with software houses as 25 percent of Tandem systems were being sold to be used with software packages now,"* rather than with applications customers would build themselves from scratch.

For a quiet Canadian, to walk into the maelstrom that was the high tech industry in general and Tandem in particular in early 1984 was like walking into the middle of a tornado. By that point I'd been in the workforce about eight years, I'd had my first ups and downs with corporate life in the late 1970s and early 1980s. I'd had my initial tangles with sexism in the workplace, like the time my boss introduced me at a large team meeting as his "lovely assistant," or the time his boss's boss "stole" my view-graph presentation to teach me a lesson about leaving it on the table in the conference room (something he never would have dared do to any of the other men on the team), as well as the day-to-day challenges of gaining credibility in a technical organization where women were seen as not smart enough to even be on the team. We marketing types had to operate in a world that couldn't understand why marketing and sales were even needed. As was often implied, if the technology was cool enough, customers would come. Who needed to spend time thinking about how to sell it or better understand the needs and business problems confronting a prospective customer, or how to clarify the business value.

My first experience with the management practice of "promoting from within" came pretty fast and furious. Though originally hired as a Program Manager, I completed just one program before my manager, Anne Perlman, was promoted to a bigger and better position. Without any hesitation, even though I'd only been with the company a few months, they promoted me to be her replacement and run Tandem Executive Institute. I had a $1 million budget, six staff and a mandate to go conquer the world and I was just 28 years old. This was for me the perfect job—I was able to stay on top of trends in various industries by the program's relationships with key industry consultants and hob-knob with academic gurus in various areas, including Ram Charan, a very popular strategy management consultant whose approach I adored. He later went on to collaborate with Honeywell CEO Larry Bossidy to write a 2002 book, *Execution: The Discipline of Getting Things Done*, which spent over 150 weeks on *The Wall Street Journal's* bestseller list.

What an experience! Yet it wasn't unusual for Tandem to assign projects and programs to employees who at other companies might have been considered unqualified for the tasks. As Polly Kam (#1177) shared:

"I was the Western Division Representative at ITUG [the International Tandem User Group] and was assigned to film a short video for an advertisement to be broadcast in teleconferences prior to the discussion of Tandem's new local area network

(LAN). Having no film experience I reached out to the creative geniuses in Tandem TV (TTN) who were happy to help me script and film what become known as 'The Promised LAN.' The film began with a nomad (who was) wandering in the desert tired and thirsty looking for an oasis. He tripped and fell onto the sand. Suddenly, he found two coaxial cables coming out of the sand and he started to dig feverishly. At the end of the coax cables was a bunch of gold block letters that spelled out 'The Promised LAN.'

"To film this, we found a summer intern from the Marketing department who was willing to play the part of the nomad. So on a summer day with a camera crew of two, the director, summer intern and myself took off to Monterey, California. We stopped at a state park along the sand dunes off of Highway 1 and were ready to get to work. I was so excited because I never had the opportunity to experience something like this before. But there were a few problems. First of all, there shouldn't be any seagulls in the desert. The director said, no problem. We would dupe the sound out. Then, the weekend prior it had rained so the clouds were still lingering. The desert should be sunny. So, we ate sandwiches on the beach and waited for the clouds to clear. We had problems filming the last scene because the block letters were foam blocks sprayed with gold paint so they were lightweight. The letters were off position whenever the nomad tried removing the sand to reveal the letters. So, finally we had to film the last scene first so the letters were in perfect position. All that hard work to produce only a 60-second spot. The Tandem LAN teleconference was a success and I still have a copy of video somewhere listed me as the Executive Producer. That was really fun."

Mike Frederico (#1492) talked about getting a chance to travel the planet to shoot and edit videos in exotic locales for about 20 TOPS trips and sales rallies, Cupertino's annual Tandem-sponsored 10K Running Races and of course the Los Angeles Marathon. Wally Robertson, who previously had spent three years in Washington, D.C., working at the World Bank and the International Monetary Fund came across Tandem, signed up and was immediately sent to London where he spent three years doing customer support, performance consulting, design consulting, customer seminars, market research and strategic planning. As he said, *"Where else was it possible to learn so many roles in such a short period of time?"* Or Mala Chandra's experience of finding *"so many opportunities to either lead or participate in for the first time, from setting up the Support Program Management group with Larry Cockerell to leading the OMA task force, working on the first GUI programs, NonStop availability program, SNAX get well program, the TPC benchmarks, DP2 conversion program, TMF3 rewrite..."*—all without being rejected for not having enough experience. Also as Henry Norman (#3827) shared:

"By 1982, my desire to become part of this extraordinary Tandem organization at long last became too strong and I left SAS and joined Tandem Sweden as a field sup-

port analyst. In late 1983, I was asked to relocate to California to join the SSG Guardian Support Group. What a group of people. The famous Guido's office, The Swamp, with his incredible collection of Tandem memorabilia scattered all over the place. I specifically remember a homemade 'disk model' with card cage and all, with a very interesting card in place. The Friday lunches that ended up at the Beer Bust by the pool at Building 2 that often spilled over into El Toro's—affectionately known as Building 4 before the acquisition of Building 4. The celebration when Don Smith was able to document and duplicate the dreaded 'split brain' problem, which led to refinements of the message system (global update protocol). What an environment and what a crew, building on wise concepts like letting responsible individuals do their jobs as and when needed, and play and have fun and a good time at the same time."

My first experiences with "unstructured communications" left me thunderstruck. The idea of an "open door policy" by which you could set up a meeting with anyone in the management hierarchy that you wanted, or just drop in on any manager without an appointment was amazing to me. The Friday Beer Busts not only helped us decompress after a hectic week, but offered a venue where you could converse, debate, catch up with or challenge any one you wanted, even the president of the company. All of this took a long time to both get used to and take advantage of. In contrast, Bell Canada was a highly structured firm, where meetings were held to plan meetings with senior executives and the idea of saying what you felt about anything was unheard of. It was as if I had moved to not just another country, but to another planet. My own experience that brought it all home happened a couple of years later after I'd left TEI to become the manager for Major Accounts Marketing.

I was launching an effort in marketing to focus on major accounts when Jerry Peterson, Vice President of Marketing and International, called and told me that Jimmy wanted to build a new marketing presentation to be called 'Tandem in the Marketplace.' The idea (then brilliantly new) was to focus on customer success stories by market segment. So with pencil and notebook in hand I trooped over to Jimmy's office in Building 2 (just outside the Customer Conference Center as I recall). We spent an hour or so while he took me through his storyboard ideas. At the conclusion of the meeting, I got up to leave and Jimmy asked me where I was going. I paused and said I was going back to my office. Having come from a large bureaucratic telecommunications provider I expected that I'd go away for some period of time, come up with a draft and return at some later date for his review and approval.

To my surprise, Jimmy pushed some papers aside on the conference table in his office and advised me that I wasn't going anywhere and that this corner of his desk would be my office for the next while. To say the least I was in shock as there I sat for the following two weeks. During each subsequent business meeting, he'd start off with a review of where we were in the marketing presentation (each part of the storyboard, now posted on the walls of his office) and ask for opinions from meeting participants. Then once the respective opinions were provided, I'd make changes on the copy on the walls and he'd move on to the substance of the meeting. It was a wild few weeks. Eventually Jimmy ran out of steam and I was able to return to my office, a bit of normalcy and my proper job. Though it was sometime later before the 35mm slide presentation and script was finally released to the field, the collaborative process by which it was originally designed has stuck with me ever since. So much so that I still own, tucked in a drawer with other Tandem artifacts, the original 35mm slide deck and the box is even signed by Jerry Peterson.

Even the structured communications were impressive publications to me. *Non-Stop News* was designed to help people deeply know other groups and what was going on, including detailed profiles of sales districts, regions and countries. The *NonStop News* team didn't just interview managers, but interviewed and named individual employees up and down the organization, outlining their roles and opinions. Detailed profiles of specific groups outlining their goals, new ideas and track record for innovation were presented each month, along with the birth announcements, promotions and other changes. New customers and what systems they had bought and the intended use was a common theme. Any heroics accomplished by Tandem staff in response to natural causes or storms or issues were a cause for celebration and recognition. Product announcements were a big thing, not just announcing the product but also introducing one to the team and how they did what they'd done. Meanwhile, the depth and quality of the articles in *Center* magazine were superior to anything I had ever seen before. In every issue was always something of interest and thought provoking. I adored the magazine and found it hard to believe that it was a company publication.

Watching Jimmy Treybig in action on stage really took me by surprise and I quickly became a loyalist. As previously mentioned, with his Texan drawl, he always came across with this down-home sensibility. One of my fondest memories of him was when we conducted our first Manufacturing TEI in Belgium. We traditionally always tried to bring Jimmy in to talk to the group on the last day, to wind them up and send them off with a big bang. For some reason, for this program, we had to have him speak over dinner at a small restaurant that the local country manager Patrick Vallaeys had reserved for the night. It was pouring rain when Jimmy showed up a few hours late. We had been expecting him to appear at the pre-dinner reception to socialize and rub a few elbows with the generally reserved Europeans. But he'd gotten tied up with a customer meeting and so appeared part way through dinner.

Umbrella-less, Jimmy looked like a drowned rat as he came in from the downpour, hair plastered to his forehead and glasses askew. Initially I didn't notice it but around his neck was this bolo-like string tie with a small creature-like figurine on the bottom of it. Halfway through his speech, this "creature" started crawling up his belly, making this odd kind of squealing noise. He didn't notice at first, but when it reached the knot of his tie, he did. He grabbed it and pulled it back down to its original location. It remained quiet for a few moments, but then started making its way back up his belly a second time. As this routine repeated itself a number of times, those of us in the back of the room started smirking into our napkins. But the participants, having never seen such a sight, didn't know what to do. Jimmy had found the tie at a local novelty shop and until that moment had no idea of the wandering tendencies of the "creature". He finally broke the tension by making some remark about the dangers of letting a Texas old-boy loose in Belgium, as you never knew what he'd pick up.

But as I soon learned, as had many before me, this was all a huge cover for one very smart, very talented and very charismatic individual. All one had to do was get him in front of an audience and he'd just glow. According to folklore of Tandem's early years, to promote his philosophical and management messages, Jimmy would arrange for large tents to be put up in the parking lots. Employees would gather, listen to him and get all wound up with energy and enthusiasm. Eventually the crowds got too big and neighbors complained, so the "tent revivals" had to stop. The last one was the "Thanks a Billion Party," which I'll talk about later.

Jimmy was intense, wore his heart on his sleeve, cared deeply about the welfare of his employees and we all loved him for it. But heaven help you if you found yourself in his crosshairs of his infamous laser focus or if you were the target of something he felt needed to get done. Ron Lapedis (#1904) shared an experience from 1985:

"My favorite story of all time (that I have never told up until now) is when Jimmy T. almost got me fired. Many will remember that I volunteered at the Exploratorium. At a Beer Bust I told Jimmy that I would trade my sabbatical for a NonStop 1 to be installed there to support the accounting department using PBL software. Jimmy thought it was such a great idea that he encouraged me to make a list of what I needed and Tandem would let me use my sabbatical to manage the project. Jimmy pointed me to a room full of surplus gear in Loc. 1 above manufacturing and told me to see if what I needed was available there. The middle part of the story is a bit fuzzy, but for some reason Dave Rynne told me to keep out of the room and stop bothering Jimmy with my idea. At every Beer Bust, Jimmy asked me how I was doing getting the gear together and I hemmed and hawed about it. At one Beer Bust Jimmy pressed me pretty hard about why I lost interest and I told him that Dave had asked me to back off the idea. Jimmy walked me upstairs to Rynne's office, threw open the door, and interrupted the meeting in progress. With me in front of him, Jimmy told Dave that I said he was getting in my way—and then told him to cut it out (in much more colorful

language). By the time I got back to my office, Jerry Reaugh (Vice President of IT) was waiting to ask for my resignation by Monday afternoon. After a very long weekend, I submitted my resignation to my manager who promptly tore it up and told me that everything was resolved and I would get my system and my sabbatical."

My own experience of being under Jimmy's laser vision took place when preparing for a Key Customer Symposium in Monterey at the Inn at Spanish Bay. The agenda had been finalized weeks before the event and I was working with each executive presenter in designing and producing their presentation with the help of Gary Bolen, Marketing's Creative Director. In those days before PowerPoint, presentations were done either on overhead transparencies (or VU Graphs as some were called) or in 35mm slide format. For the Key Customer Symposium, 35mm slides were considered the only way to product high quality visuals. Special equipment from the Illustrations Group was used to take typed copy and create the films into which any needed photos and graphics were inserted. The film was then sent to an outside firm that converted it to 35mm slides. It was a long, drawn-out process and required extensive planning to have everything together in advance of such a big event, especially when there were multiple speakers on different topics. I thought things were going fine—until Jimmy decided he wanted to see everyone's presentation. What soon became apparent was that when you ran each presentation end to end there was no overall strategy or theme. This of course sent Jimmy on a rampage. All of the executives participating in the event were quickly assembled for an ad hoc strategy session. Collaboratively, the needed themes were developed and all of the presentations revamped to reflect those themes. Gary and I, with the support of the Illustrations Group, worked all day and night to have every presentation ready for the meeting—it was unbelievable.

In 1984, professional managers started to move into roles of significant influence, and governance models started to become important (though that term never entered the Tandem lexicon). "Exec Staff" (also known as the Policy Committee) was established with a role to discuss important issues, make decisions and set priorities for the company. The highest management priorities at the time were to improve profit margins, control capital spending and better manage inventories in manufacturing. In addition, management worked on more effectively managing the travel and entertainment budget and establishing long-term product plans and marketing strategies for the various customer industry segments. For most, this process of establishing more process and procedures was welcome. As Jerry Held, Director of Strategic Planning, said in *NonStop News* in spring 1984:

"We are a bigger company and have to be more formalized about processes we go through and planning for the company's growth over the next several years. We need

to begin to introduce operational budgeting and compare actual spending against budget on a month-by-month basis."

The year 1984 also saw the development of the Third Five-Year Plan, designed to share Tandem's business strategy through 1989. Unsurprisingly, the fast growth of the company meant that once again, new employees were having a tough time getting a sense of Tandem's management philosophy and business strategy. Critical was reinforcing the company goals and priorities, which hadn't really changed since Tandem's beginning. These included being an industry leader in the following areas:

- Customer satisfaction
- Sustained profitability
- A work environment to attract and retain outstanding people
- Well managed high growth with
- A commitment to quality in all that we do

Like most strategic plans, it began with a focus on understanding the changes that were taking place in Tandem's markets and technology and provided insight as to how Tandem was going to respond to those changes. Compared to 1980, when management fundamentally believed that Tandem's only limit was its ability to manage growth, in 1984 management realized that the company needed to become more outward looking. This meant becoming aware of external challenges such as the strengthening competitive environment and changes in technology that were taking the industry by storm. As with the Second Five-Year Plan, this one was modular so that each Vice President could present a portion of it. One new change reflected management's recognition of the need to do yearly updates to the plan to reflect incremental changes of import. By spring of 1985, 85 percent of employees had seen it.

The culture remained strong as articulated by so many employees:

- *"We were expected to just get stuff done at Tandem, be direct and open with each other, treat people/their ideas with respect and not take 'no' as an answer and to have fun! Also a really unique thing I learned is that ANYONE can have a great idea—no matter what level or background they come from—and should have their ideas treated with respect. Jimmy always listened—even if he hated your idea! And anyone could bubble up great ideas that might challenge the status quo. I don't know if we all realized at the time just how unique that culture was... people really rise to the occasion when given the opportunity. Jimmy knew that this was a way to get the best from people, so it was part of our Tandem culture from the beginning."* [Melanie R.]

- "My first month on the job, I had to work almost every Saturday to pick, pack and ship binders and technical manuals to our field offices. At Valley Green Drive, the manuals and binders were stored in a few of the self-storage garages behind the Tandem building. I would use a hand-truck to move four or five cartons of binders/manuals a time from the storage areas into the shipping area of the Tandem building—quite tedious work. I usually spent hours moving cartons into the shipping area. One Saturday, Rocky, a very senior software engineer, stopped by and asked how I was doing. I told him what I was doing. He told me to put down the hand-truck. He then went to the parking lot and started up his old Chevy truck, picked me up and together we drove to the storage area. We loaded cartons of manuals/binders into his truck and then drove back to the shipping area. He then helped me unload them from his truck. Of course, we weren't done. He had a small cooler in his truck filled with Olympia beer. We slammed down a few cold ones, then Rocky went back to his programming. I will never forget that act of kindness. I was especially struck by the fact that a VERY senior software engineer would take time from his busy schedule to help someone like me with basic manual labor. Throughout the '70s and well into the '80s, Rocky was a regular on the dock at quarter's end, helping us pack systems as the clock neared midnight." [Joe Novak #117]

- "Whilst setting up for a trade show in Chicago, I asked for a little help from local customer engineers. Their typical Tandem response was two people within half an hour who stayed until the system worked (about 1 a.m. in the morning)—doing what it takes!" [Steve Rhodes]

- "The scream of 'coming through!!!' as a system was pushed at full speed down the aisleway of the Fremont Manufacturing SIT (System Integration and Test Facility) at 12:00:03 a.m., only to be suddenly stopped by an auditor and a closed door. Doing ad hoc engineering changes to circuit boards on a borrowed rework bench at 10:45 p.m. on the last night of the quarter with a system waiting for it in systems integration." [Kurt Ayers #720]

- "Jimmy is coming to Raleigh, North Carolina, to acquire an SNA (systems network architecture) software company. I call him and ask if he can spend the night and go to dinner with the team. The 'team' is one sales rep (me), two analysts, three Customer Engineers (CEs) and the admin. He agrees with enthusiasm. At dinner he looks at one of the CEs (Odell King) and asks: 'What do we make that's crap?' Odell almost chokes on his food. Jimmy explains that in Cupertino they want to tell him how great everything is, he wants to know what needs fixin' and pulls out pen and paper. Later, after a few questions about future direction, Jimmy asks, 'How far to the office and is there any beer?' Answer: 20 minutes and yes. Jimmy spends until almost midnight, at the whiteboard, diagramming future product directions. (MIPS chip, CLX, S2). Talk about leadership and respect for individuals. We're seven people in a remote office doing about $3 million a year. On the way back to *the hotel, I thank him and he says: 'It's the best part of the job.' An unforgettable experience for all of us." [Mike Greenfield #4168]*

- *"One of our teammates trying to have children. His wife would call when 'it was time.' We'd page him over the intercom and he would leave for a break. When he returned he looked like he had run a marathon. And yes, they did eventually have a beautiful baby girl and we all felt like we had assisted in the process." [Mary Cashen #3013]*

- *"My baby shower with the conference room that my colleagues turned into a labor delivery room (complete with form feed paper down the center of a table equipped with stirrups) and the phone close at hand. They wanted me to be able to work through the whole process—no medical leave necessary." [Mary Cashen #3013]*

- *"People like Jimmy, Bob and many others fostered such strong leadership and an open-door policy that encouraged everyone to do one's best. People were rewarded for a good job done, regardless of rank or job title. TOPS and stock option incentives are good examples among others that prove that point. Smart people and teamwork. Every company has smart people, but the number of really smart people at Tandem was extraordinary. In fact, you had to be smart to be 'average,' and there was definitely positive peer pressure motivating one to excel. Unlike in other companies, these smart people were also friendly, approachable and fun to work with. These teams of smart people were the reason why we were able to achieve fantastic results in development, benchmark and support. Yes, even our salesmen were smarter." [Phil Ly #1067]*

- *"I remember the times when managers, especially Jimmy, hadn't learned political correctness and spoke their minds unrestrainedly. But also the times when, in the camaraderie of shared goals, people got mad at each other but quickly cooled down and didn't hold grudges. In the late '80s, I was managing a department of developers responsible for our TRANSFER message system and associated user software at Fremont & Mary. Even though it broke unique new ground in linking all Tandem together, worldwide, in ways almost unheard of in those days, TRANSFER's proprietary nature had made us decide to retire it in favor of the new ISO OSI standard, X.400, being developed in our Bad Homburg facility. (It was a bad decision, and TRANSFER survived this particular attempt to kill it, but that's another story). It was my job to disperse the group and the associated QA and Pubs groups, totaling about 30. This was a time before the erosion of the feeling of mutual familial affection between Tandem and its employees and long before the rampant layoffs (known by a variety of creative acronyms!) So it was imperative that we find jobs for as many of the employees as possible. And, in order not to lose morale, the jobs had better be ones in which the employees happy—not just shoehorning a square peg into a round hole (to mix metaphors!) Well, my fellow managers and I managed to reposition all 30 people into jobs they were happy with. I continue to think of that episode as a highlight of my career, and representative of what was good about Tandem." [Ajit Dongre #10139]*

The mid-'80s was also a time when innovation in its varied forms was highly valued. Mike B. recalled the time that he and a group of customer engineers (Mike Gustus, Mike Wilson and Frank Bringino, to name a few) devised a state-of-the-art portable computer unit:

"It consisted of a Zentec terminal, a portable phone (which was the size of a large shoebox and weighed about 20 lbs. or so) and an acoustical coupler from a fax machine. We strapped an antenna to this and somehow managed to get the entire ensemble into a backpack affair, which could then be worn. Total weight was probably close to 50 lbs. or so. It was a precursor to the modern day laptop computer."

Another illustration of Tandem's on-the-fly innovative abilities involved a bid for 20+ distributed systems for SNOW Brand Milk Products Company in Japan. As Nigel Baker (#2700), the CLX Support Program Manager at the time, explained:

"SNOW had one interesting requirement where they required the capability for their unattended distributed systems to be remotely powered off after specific daily operations had been completed in order to save power. Hmm!! How to solve this requirement? Now here again is where Tandem teamwork clicked into immediate action. Working with the field on the customer requirement with many late nights and of course some traditional Tandem sustenance (beer and pizza), the development team came up with a solution - and it was a good one - Modify the CLX distributed systems operator panel OS to include a piece of timer code that could be remotely accessed during normal operations and timer parameters set to enable timed system power down and then power up again after a predefined power off time. Start up processes ensured that the system was restored to normal application and network operational state. This solved the SNOW requirement and allowed central operations staff to remotely set each node timers based on node power off/on requirements. It worked like a charm. They could even modify the timer parameters automatically from the central location to suit special timer requirements. For instance - say if there was a national holiday and the node power off/on regular timings needed to be changed to accommodate the holiday shutdown, the central system timer program could access each node and set the new timing settings automatically during the last day of normal operation, then revert to normal settings after the holiday power up. With this solution we won the SNOW bid."

Executive staff at a company meeting 1984 Jeanne Wohlers Treasurer, Larry McGraw - U.S. Sales, Larry Laurich Hardware, Steve Schmidt - Operations, Larry Evans - Manufacturing Tim Chen - Legal Counsel, Jerry Held - Data Base, Bob Marshall - COO

Adra Ross, Industry Marketing (l) and Larry McGraw U.S. Sales (r) - NS News September 1985

TEI founder Susan Roher (l) Program Manager Susie Farber (r) Below: Anne Perlman, 2nd TEI Director (l) and Takahiro Katoh, sales rep (r) from Japan discuss future prospect visits to Cupertino at a TEI Program - NS News April 1983

Banking TEI at Brangston Hall in the United Kingdom. L: Ellen Anderson Herbst, 3rd from L: Me - Clemson Collection

Me (middle) with customers at TEI Manufacturing in Brussels - Clemson Collection

Fritz Joern (l) and I at Manufacturing TEI in Belgium - Clemson Collection

Wildly successful computer Fat Ad campaign Spring 1985

Patty Bull Turner, Librarian (l) - NS News July 1983 and Wanda Cavanaugh, Marketing Communications (r) - NS News October 1982

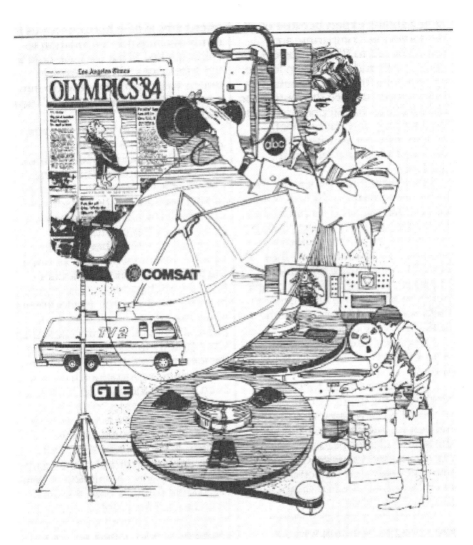

Year in Summary - NS News 1984

Jimmy (l) and Tom Perkins (r) at the 10th Anniversary Celebration - 1984 Annual Report

Closing the Gap to a Billion

Cheering squad at the London Marathon - NS News May/June1986 (photo by Communications Strategy Ltd)

THE THIRD FIVE-YEAR PLAN brought with it a stronger focus on customer support and also on quality that played out over the next few years, though it was a few years before Japanese quality themes became prevalent. For Tandem quality was built into the essence of the machine as the systems virtually never went down except in extraordinary circumstances. As William Eberwein (#5366) recalled:

"I remember the day some dimwitted electricians were working on the power in Building 1 and killed part of the three-phase power system, so our system's disks started turning slower and slower until the system said 'no more!' The power was going to be out the rest of the afternoon, so I called my wife (who was an IBM systems programmer at a nearby company) and asked if she wanted to go home early. When she asked me why, I told her my system was down and I couldn't do anything. She said, 'Why don't you do what you NORMALLY do when the system goes down?' (spoken like a true IBMer). I thought for a moment and replied, 'I don't know WHAT to do when the system is down—it hasn't been down in almost two years!'"

Another example of this obsessive emphasis on quality came through in a story shared by Bob Marshall (#32) at a 2012 Association of Corporate Growth Silicon Valley meeting:

"In the 1978/79 timeframe we would test all of the 50MB disc drives (which came from Control Data Corporation (CDC)) before they were shipped [with the Tandem Systems.] About half would fail, in which case we would put them in the corner to wait for servicing. Pretty soon we had 50 or so disc drives in the corner. Coincidentally, the new president of CDC was in the valley and came by to thank us for our business. While he and I were talking in my office, Jim walked in wearing a construction hard hat and carrying a sledge hammer. After I made introductions, Jim commented that since it was Friday, that day at Beer Bust he was going let all of the service people take a swing at one of CDC's disc drives. Once they'd beaten the hell out of it, Jim intimated that he was going to wrap it in plastic and put it in the lobby with a sign dedicating it to the worst supplier in the world. He suggested to the CDC president that if he wanted to he could come along and take a swing at one as well. After extensive discussion of the problems, Jim was talked out of smashing the disc drive. The president of CDC then went back and launched a quality program that turned things around."

By 1984, Japan's "Quality Circle" ideas were getting traction in western business so a task force was formed to figure out how to leverage some of these new concepts, with Bob Marshall, Chief Operating Officer as chairman. One ritual, which seems both quaint and funny now, was the reciting of Tandem's quality commitment before the start of each task force meeting, *"We in this room do not impact quality. The entire company impacts quality. All employees must be involved in this process."* The impact of the commitment was immediate. For the first time in company history, a new product introduction was delayed because the required level of field support and customer education expertise was not in place. This despite the fact that it affected short-term revenues for Tandem.

Leading the quality charge on the customer support side was Randy Baker, another former IBMer, who strongly believed (and was quoted frequently in the NS News) that *"quality technical support as a way of life was as important as the product itself and began with a focus on three elements:*

* *Customer and Tandem support people with strong technical skills through strong education program*
* *Dissemination of accurate and timely information*
* *Continuous streams of feedback to and from technical support people in the field"*

He introduced a number of customer support programs that, like so many other Tandem efforts, were lifted from more traditional players like IBM, but then molded and enhanced to suit a nimbler Tandem environment. Some of these as outlined in *NonStop News* in February 1985 included:

- **QUEST:** An easily accessible online information retrieval service that archived technical information with a Q&A service for selected product areas, handled by technical specialists in corporate headquarters.

- **Systems Support and an Early Warning Reporting System:** New processes that were used to track product installability, defects and quality.

- **Sensitive Account Program:** A weekly meeting from each functional area to develop action plans to resolve sensitive account situations identified by Division Vice Presidents.

- **Problem Reporting to Executives:** A monthly summary of unresolved software problems presented to COO Bob Marshall to identify problem areas and inform appropriate development or support groups so they could take corrective action quickly.

- **Systems Assurance Program:** A support requirements planning document on potential problem areas completed before products are shipped to customers.

- **Productivity Council:** Selected customer engineers and systems analysts from the field that helped identify product and support improvements that enhanced quality of the support organization and increased field productivity.

- **Customer Support-Specific Customer Survey:** New questions added to the standard customer survey gathered feedback about the quality of the support function (availability, technical expertise, professionalism and software education).

Reading all of this in 2012 makes me laugh as the importance of effective customer support programs with appropriate issue escalation processes now seem so self-evident, not just for fixing problems and making happier customers, but also in providing feedback to product developers. But at the time many of these ideas were leading-edge concepts in the industry. Tandem's focus on customer support also generated an entire mythology about the hard work and antics of customer support engineers who were called in to save the day in countless situations. Their ability to roll up their sleeves, assess what needed to be done, get the work done or the problem solved—regardless of the time it took—were hallmarks of Tandem's commitment to customer satisfaction. As Phil Ly (#1067) shared:

"The Customer Support mantra was 'Fix the Customer's Problem First' instead of focusing on bureaucratic rules or finger-pointing. I remember many occasions working with other support folks on a problem all through the night until it was solved. When customers' business depended on our systems, we viewed it as our top priority to fix their problem as soon as possible. This is a motto that I carry with me to this day as I try to serve customers under the same guiding principle. While many companies may want to claim to have these similar traits, very few can actually say that they can 'walk the walk' the way Tandem did."

Some of the more vivid examples:

- *"We moved to the Oasis building in Culver City. I had a Tandem Internals class starting Monday and the system was not hooked up. At the same time, there was a crisis at Long Beach Memorial (an important local customer) so the rest of staff was tied up with a mysterious TMF failure. So, left to my own devices, I installed the system, ran the terminal wires through the ceiling and brought the system to life Saturday and Sunday and was ready to start my class on time Monday."* [Justin Simonds #4521]

- *"The screams from Cupertino after the time I chartered a DC-3 to get from Melbourne to Sydney for a customer meeting. (I was chartering due to an Australian airline strike and could not find any other transportation to Sydney). I ended up covering the cost of the charter by selling the other 18 seats on the plane to other folks who needed to get from Melbourne to Sydney. One memorable line from my boss was: 'Damn it John, we're a computer company, not an airline!'"* [John Haverland #4512]"

- *Spending 72 hours straight trying to get the original FedEx Zap Mail benchmark/demo running (an innovative idea for faxing via a national satellite communications network instead of flying documents between major cities that never got to market) before Fred Smith, the President of FedEx, arrived. At one point I fell asleep on a running line printer and got woken by Dave Mackie."* [John Haverland #4512]

- *"Becoming the Flying Dutchman—I'd been working on a benchmark in Australia and flew up to Hong Kong for a division meeting. In typical Tandem fashion, I got very little sleep in Hong Kong and was totally exhausted when I crawled onto the flight back to Sydney on Sunday. When I woke, I was well rested but it seemed that the sun was on the wrong side of the aircraft. Yup, I had slept through the turnaround in Sydney and was now en route back to Hong Kong. The look on the steward's face when I asked him how long until arrival in Sydney was priceless. Calling the office on Monday to tell them that I had encountered a slight delay returning from Hong Kong resulted in a lot of ribbing." [John Haverland #4512]*

- *"World-class support was never so evident as the time that a timing problem in Guardian caused the computers to stop at stock exchanges. As the world turned, the problem reported in Tokyo was found, code rewritten, patched, sent, installed, and operations were restored by the time New York opened." [David Mathes #10510]*

- *"It was Friday and I was in London for a meeting of the CODASYL COBOL Committee (I was chairman) and was not leaving until Saturday, so I decided to attend the Beer Bust at the London office. I was having a fine time enjoying it all when someone came up to me and said I had a phone call. The call was from my boss and she said that a customer in Des Moines was having problems with COBOL and I had to go there on Saturday. How she knew I would be at the Beer Bust has always been a mystery to me. Anyhow, I managed to arrange a flight from SFO to Des Moines as there was no way I could change my London to SFO flight. (I suppose they could have issued me a parachute or something). Anyway, I flew to San Francisco, my wife met me there with a suitcase with clean clothes and then I flew on to Des Moines and headed to the customer site. Talk about jet lag. It turned out the problem with not with COBOL but something else in the system. I hung around a couple of days to make sure all was OK, and flew back home." [Don Nelson #4534]*

- *"My first project was installing Wells Fargo's Branch On-Line Banking (BOLB) system. Of course it didn't help that we were using Zentec terminals for this. If anyone remembers them, the chips were not soldered into their seats, and they were loose enough to move ever so slightly, causing intermittent errors. I remember Glen Newman instructing me on the first course of action on how to repair a Zentec. It was a single unit, having the keyboard physically attached to the unit. Glen instructed me to tilt the unit up slightly and let it drop back to the desk. This action had an effect that would essentially reseat the chips on the logic board and the damn thing would work fine." [Mike B.]*

- *"Phoning corporate support in the afternoon and getting a fix the next day. One I remember is the customer's application being written to use TMF file locks which just did not work and getting a code patch that fixed the problem in less than 24 hours—amazing by today's standards." [Keith Payne #1739]*

- *"A hardware dude who drew a customer complaint when he used a Swiss army knife to fix a disk drive—just a few months before they became company issue." [Ray Glasstone #5106]*

In the mid-1980s, Tandem was being accused of being a "one trick pony"—in other words, it had one product to address one technological problem. To fix this perception (supported by the introduction of the CLX for low-end distributed systems), Tandem introduced the idea that from small to large, Tandem had the right size of system to meet a customer's online transaction processing (OLTP) needs. Marketed as the "Pyramid of Needs," Tandem's product family could fulfill any customer's requirements. In addition, it was the first time that Tandem participated in head-to-head competitive positioning in its marketing materials by showing precisely how its product offerings compared to those of other vendors such as IBM. The width of the Pyramid corresponded with the number of systems, and the position to the level of cost and performance required per unit. The top corresponded to the small number of very large mainframes at a customer's location and the bottom, the very large number of small systems found at the desktop, bank teller window or on the manufacturing shop floor. Between were one or more layers of departmental or regional systems. The story line was that Tandem could now cover a wide spectrum of customer needs with significantly fewer products because the architecture allowed growth by just adding more processing modules. The company also messaged that all products were compatible with one another and could operate effectively in networks with IBM systems. Of course, today the idea that systems from different manufacturers could work together seems rather mundane, but in 1985 this was quite a different way to position computers in the marketplace.

The CLX also demonstrated the high impact of Tandem's new approach to quality as illustrated in the story below from Nigel Baker (#2700):

"I was the Support Program Manager on the original CLX system program and subsequent product releases of that excellently engineered low-end system. We were in a 'Proof of Concept' bid with IBM at United Parcel Service (UPS) for a new automatic letter sorting application and database. UPS had setup two test beds in separate data center rooms that were identical except for the systems attached to this huge letter sorting machine in each room (it was a French design). IBM was bidding an AS400, and we were testing with a standard two processor CLX 600 cabinet. IBM was popular with UPS so I was really anxious to learn how IBM were doing next door, but there was a cloak of secrecy. So we just kept focused with our test programs with the UPS' IT organization overseeing the test runs and results. Then suddenly in the middle of a test run there was a loud thump noise and then complete blackness and silence. Emergency battery lighting came on and we were told to evacuate the building. It turned out that the county had lost electrical power, and for some strange reason, the UPS plant did not have back-up power. So, we had to wait outside the building for several hours until electrical power was restored.

Once it was restored we all dashed back into our test rooms to see what had happened to the test machines. To our surprise the CLX, bless that superb machine's little heart, had powered up automatically as part of the power fail recovery design (the CLX battery supplied power was applied to memory during the main supply down time period – preserving system and data state) and had restored the system to a power fail recovery checkpoint restart and was waiting for input from the letter-sorting machine. Once the French team had restarted their machine, the CLX carried on without any operator intervention. The INSCRIBE database was completely intact and all data was secure - including in-flight transactions at the time of power fail. The UPS team just could not believe it and it took some explaining of our power fail recovery design and review of data for them to believe it. Next door in the IBM room, all hell had broken loose. It took FIVE DAYS for them to restore and reconstruct corrupt and lost data and to be able to carry on with the test. Guess who won that deal."

Though Tandem's great products offered marvelous features and benefits, the continued shift to market and industry-oriented marketing and product development (rather than a technology-oriented focus) was relentless. To increase revenues and profits, the company refined its marketing strategies to focus on high-growth industry sectors in which Tandem could be a leader. The idea was to pinpoint industries or niches within industries where Tandem had a superior product compared to the competition and could capture large revenues by offering full business solutions. For Tandem, the focus was on financial services, manufacturing, telecommunications and retail point of sale. As shared by Jan Seamons (#442), who had moved from Corporate Marketing to the USA Sales Division:

"To help jumpstart company knowledge on these industries we created and launched various industry forums and vertical training programs. Often these were more popular than the corporate product education programs. Industry 101 was an introduction to the specific industry (infrastructure, terminologies, segmentation, etc.), 201 was modeled to include how Tandem sold into the industry (strategy, product fit, industry positioning, etc.), and the 301 module included information on all of the related industry partner solutions."

One ICON colleague shared her experiences introducing Tandem to the telecommunications world:

"At the time I joined, there were three of us in the company who knew how to use 'Touchtone,' i.e. knew anything about the telecom industry. Dick Dworak was the specialist in the USA, Robert Lane was in Europe and I had the rest of the world. Up to that point, Tandem had been successful in telecom without any focused marketing. The company was just about to join the International Institute of Telecommunications, a global non-profit organization that provides services for development of

*the telecommunication industry, and form its own development arm, Tandem Tel-
ecom Systems Inc. (TTSI)—so it was time to get serious. Over the next few years,
many people from the industry joined the company and made tremendous contributions. In those days we had to beg country managers to put dedicated sales and pre-
sales resources on the telecom accounts, beg third-parties to port their applications to
Tandem and beg existing application developers to resell their applications to other
companies (to sell in other countries). Then we had to REALLY beg the switch manufacturers to OEM our stuff. We trained, we wrote presentations, we made plans, we
begged some more and then we conquered.*

"*My first trip to Asia was with the infamous Roger Hewitt and our first stop was
Taipei. I had never tasted sake before, but I became quite familiar with the drink
when Raff Liu, his lieutenants, Roger and I went out for dinner my first night. We
toasted everyone we knew, wherever they were, in the free world! I was such a trooper,
I was invited to party on with the team. All I remember (besides being the only
woman in the Love Boat Club that night who wasn't working) is I was the only one
who had presence of mind to put a matchbook from the hotel in my purse before we
went out. Somehow I managed to get us all back to the hotel that night.*

"*After Taipei was Hong Kong and then the next stop was Seoul, Korea. Roger
forgot to tell me that I needed to reconfirm my flight reservations, so I missed our
scheduled flight. Roger assured me that our distributor would pick me up when I
arrived on a later flight. Luckily I made friends with a German sporting goods buyer
on the plane, who kindly took me to the hotel because no one was at the airport
flashing me any welcome signs. When I got to my room, I found matchboxes with 'Mr.
.......' embossed on them. On a later trip to Japan, where I was doing a tutorial on
virtual private networks, I walked out the door to have lunch with the only other
woman in the meeting, in front of the men. When I asked her, in what I thought was a
whisper, if men didn't usually precede women in Japan, a guy behind us piped up and
said, 'She knows it is only for today!' And so it was for women in Asia in 1987.*

"*During my first two years in ICON we won some deals and closed some new
accounts—a testament to the dedication of the field operation and support from
Headquarters. A little company in Perth chose our platform for their Metropolitan
Area Network management system and both Alcatel and Siemens became the distributors of the bundled solution. It was a backdoor route into the account but it worked.
We went to the Telecom '87 trade show in Geneva and roped everyone within a three-
mile radius into our little booth. Bruce Dougherty had joined the team by then running Telecom Marketing in Corporate and what a fearless leader he was! Later when
Bob Lane resigned as Telecom Marketing Manager in Europe, I was asked to join the
team in Holland. My husband moved sight unseen to Amsterdam with me and we
never looked back. Who could ever forget Martin Fennel and his wild and crazy tel-*

ecom team in the United Kingdom, or Rob Hoogstratten muscling every last dollar out of us at the end of the quarter, or Joan Garrett, on loan from the United States, running the Telefonica Account Team in Spain or going to all of those meetings with Siemens where Frau Gerner and I were the only women or the Telecom TEI in Vienna that broke attendance records and we were taken to the Schoenbrunn Palace for dinner in horse-drawn carriages.

"I'll never forget my first trip in Europe to Italy, leaving my passport and luggage in the office when we called on our customer and not being able to get back into the office afterwards. Can you imagine (a woman) trying to check into a hotel without a passport and luggage? (Not to mention Paulo Donzella, the Country Manager, trying to explain all of this in Italian to the desk clerk). We ended up at the police station on a Friday night, where I was finally granted permission to stay in the hotel. I never had more fun or felt more professional satisfaction in my life. I became, to quote Jimmy, 'that Telco lady.' I wasn't the first perhaps, nor the last, but I was an original."

After a couple of years with successful TEI programs held in London, Belgium, Texas and Reston, Virginia, I decided that it was time to move onto something new. Though the 1982 business downturn had been difficult, the major economic downturn in 1986-87 affected the company in a big way as growth once again started to slow. Though the company had gone from $200 million to $600 million in four years, it was challenged in figuring out how to keep profits growing at the same time. The business opportunity was there—the number of transactions that companies would need to process was expected to rise rapidly over the next several years, driven by deregulation and competition, availability of solutions and integration of systems, networks and personal computers, as well as adding voice and fax systems to networks. Yet Tandem dropped the ball in a number of key areas, as was voiced in *NonStop News* in December 1985:

- Not as effective as we could be in winning large accounts
- Not adjusting fast enough to a world that is changing to selling solutions not product features
- Unwilling to do joint projects with customers
- Not generating enough growth at the low end for the new distributed network strategy
- Challenged in understanding well enough that customers' business and support applications were getting more complex, driving up the cost of support
- Way too xenophobic

One of the causes was determined to be that corporate was too disconnected from the field sales organization. The solution was to encourage some field district sales managers to move into corporate marketing and product management positions. Though it didn't feel sexist at the time, this move to bring in 'field expertise' resulted in the sidelining of a number of female middle management leaders since just about all of the new imports were male sales managers and directors. The fact that many of these women had sales experience prior to joining Tandem, didn't seem to matter much. The resulting reorganization also moved some key individuals from product management into marketing, including John Kane, who had been responsible for Systems Product Management and became the head of Marketing Communications. Bob Jolls, who had run Database Product Management, took over the Industry Marketing Team. This changed the dynamics of 'corporate' quite substantially - at least on the marketing side. At the senior levels, a whole crew of experienced people joined the management team from large competitors such as IBM and DEC. "Promoting from within" was the first Tandem Philosophy management practice that bit the dust. There was at the time a feeling that only outsiders had the right expertise and promotional opportunities seemed to disappear. The days of lateral moves to learn on the job, say from marketing to manufacturing, were long gone.

An important contributor to the turnaround was Gary Bolen, a creative genius and a key driver behind the company's move to more proactive "Industrial Design." The idea was to establish an unmistakable Tandem image that was embedded in all of its products—as *Center* magazine put it in 1987, a "*consistent visual image that met market, environmental and human requirements and complements the superior technical capabilities of Tandem products not just in the USA but internationally as well.*" This led to a new company logo with standards around the use of color, type style and all sorts of other marketing elements. The announcement of the new logo caused an internal uproar. Though opinions were of course always welcome, in most areas of the company final decision-making was reserved for those who had the expertise. Unfortunately, though this practice worked in engineering or in software development, when it came to marketing and the selection of a logo or company color scheme, it was a whole different story. Throughout the ensuing firestorm, Gary had this amazing ability to be totally unfazed under fire. I don't think that in the nine years that I worked with him, I ever saw him lose his temper as he guided these marketing neophytes through the basics of brand management. He told me later that having survived the Vietnam War, there wasn't much in his current life that could upset his cool demeanor.

Within marketing two new positions were created—one to manage and rebuild the Major Accounts Programs, and a second to develop and execute a strategy for selling to small to medium accounts. Though I thought I had the skills to take on the Major Accounts Programs job, having been with a large customer, Bell Canada, for a number of years, the belief was that field experience was needed to ensure that corporate became more responsive to field issues. So, though a little disgruntled, I accepted the more junior small to medium account program management position and went to work. After a few months, when they couldn't find a field person to take the major accounts job, I became the de facto manager of the Major Accounts Programs, which included Major Accounts Planning, the Key Customer Symposium and the Executive Sponsor Program.

I loved Major Account Marketing. I don't know if it was the acting training that I had had in my youth or what, but it turned out that I had a real knack for facilitating account planning sessions. The process of getting teams together to develop common sales goals, strategies and action plans gave me a tremendous sense of accomplishment, especially when a global account team was involved. Though of course it may be just ego talking, but I believed that my successes during those two years contributed to both the revenue achievement in 1987-88 and the shift in Tandem's image among some customers to being not just a vendor, but a real partner. John Kane, now running Marketing Communications, was a Brit with the most incredible sense of humor and was a riot to work with and for. Other team members included Jim Bourgeois in Sales Training and Phyllis Witherspoon at the Customer Conference Center. I look back at photos of us all in those days and I just laugh. So young! Phyllis and I dressed the same in blue or dark suits with white shirts and bow ties. We women were "dressed for success."

For those not aware, in the 1980s, fitting in was deemed to be a huge part of the way to gain, as noted in Wikipedia.org, *"acceptance in a male dominated workplace and break what became known as the glass ceiling."* The book, *Dressed for Success for Women* by John T. Molloy, was required reading for all women interested in getting ahead in those days. Published in 1977 as a follow on to his book *Dress for Success*, it provided insight into the effect that what a woman wore had on her potential success in business. It rocked to the top of the bestseller lists and popularized the notion of power dressing, i.e., *"the idea that the style, color and nature of clothing and hair could make wearers seem authoritative and competent, especially in professional settings such as business, law and government."* Out went flowered prints, dresses, pink, yellow or baby blue. In came brown, gray or navy pant or skirted suits (hemlines no more than two inches above the knee), with white or beige blouses, flat shoes or pumps. The only admission to color were the funny bow ties that we all wore—the idea being, I guess, to match the male business uniform or look as much as possible like a guy from IBM. Now of course such guidelines are considered silly and the jury is out as to whether or not any of it made any difference.

The other two key parts of my job, the Key Customer Symposium and the Executive Sponsor customer support program, were also critical customer engagement programs. By this time, the Key Customer Symposium was an established program and my role typically involved defining the agenda for the two to three days, then working with the executive presenters to ensure an integrated flow to the proceedings. Since the objective was to share the company's direction, key product and marketing plans as well as provide an opportunity for unstructured workshops, socializing, and leisure activities, it all had to hang together to be effective.

Most of the time, the Key Customer Symposium was a positive morale-boosting affair, though one year, after the first few sessions, a couple of the customers took Jimmy aside and advised him that they hated the product direction the company was pursuing. All hell broke loose and overnight, during mad backroom brainstorming sessions, the entire product strategy was revamped to meet customer needs. Talk about being online and real time. It was an amazing experience.

By 1987, things had started to improve. As *BusinessWeek's* Jonathan B. Levine wrote in February of that year:

"In the past two years, Jim Treybig has trimmed the firm. He's replaced its line of products with a broader array, revamped its xenophobic marketing strategy by working with outside vendors, honed manufacturing efficiencies and tightened financial controls. Tandem's efforts have also catapulted it to a new respectability in the market."

In addition to revamping the marketing organization, the company also changed its views on the role of third-party organizations in the sales process. Instead of focusing on how much Tandem could sell to third-party software houses and other alliance partners such as systems integrators, the company did an attitude adjustment and started to think of them as extensions of the sales and software development organizations. Management started to think about how Tandem could help third parties support new account generation. More focus was placed on finding value-added resellers for the low end of the product family. In less than a year, the Alliance Program tripled the number of software houses with Tandem applications to 225 companies. As reported in *BusinessWeek* in February 1987, this new strategy of establishing a separate group of specialists and support centers around the world whose purpose was *"to do nothing but pamper software houses"* was a success.

The company also removed a management layer in the sales organization, added more "sales feet on the street" and created a new Global Sales Organization that I soon became part of. It was headed by Jack Chapman, who moved over from Europe. In response to new globalization trends, the idea was to create a small cross-functional organization that could provide consolidated input from a global perspective into the management of the company. The team would become a focal point for input about international marketing, sales activities and issue resolution concerning sales strategy, product planning, legal matters and the sales organizational structure. For the first time, Tandem had an integrated approach to pricing, discounting guidelines for multinational customers and consistent engineering support. The days of country managers running their operations like little fiefdoms were over. That's not to say that the transition was easy, as it wasn't. I remember one new hire who rubbed country managers the wrong way was "banned" from visiting Tandem Europe offices. Even Dave Peatrowsky, who had a successful track record running sales in Asia Pacific, had a tough time gaining acceptance in Europe when he was transferred there to help initiate turnarounds in Italy and Spain.

Another big announcement in the fall of 1986 was the Sunnyvale Benchmark Center grand opening at the South Mary Avenue facility in Sunnyvale. Jack Mauger became the manager of a facility that conducted large performance benchmarks, which were becoming more important for selling into major accounts. The facility contained two large conference rooms with the latest in rear-projection screen technology that could be used for delivering 35mm slides, video presentations, could show terminal output, high-resolution color graphics or be site nodes for teleconferences. There was also a large viewing room so customers and prospects could watch NonStop systems at work. According to *NonStop News* in January 1987, the Benchmark Center's hardware included a NonStop VLX, several TXPs and enough other equipment so as to be able to conduct three or four benchmarks at the same time. As Justin Simonds (#4521) recalled:

"I was assigned to the Security Pacific benchmark. It was composed of 40 Cyclone computer systems and we were the first to hit 1,000 transactions per section. It was six months of 20-24 hour days, seven days a week—work, slink back to hotel, sleep a few hours, repeat. My first job was labeling 1,600 tapes. Had to swap out all the drives over a weekend. Air conditioning guy did a quick and unannounced PM (preventative maintenance) routine and the computer room went to 117 degrees in about 12 minutes. One day we found a way to get into Jack Mauger's 'wine cellar' and consumed it all. We were still able to win the benchmark."

The company was changing, and so was Jimmy. He stopped smoking, took up jogging and adopted a whole new management style, though he continued to worry about Tandem employees' welfare as much as ever. Though still always happy to give "stem-winding" speeches, there was less managing through inspiration and a greater realization of the difference between motivation and management. As Jimmy himself said, *"I thought everyone would do the right thing if they appreciated the company's goals and their place in the organization. It took [me] awhile to learn that people would abuse that…"* As *Fortune* magazine's Brian O'Reilly wrote in May 1987:

"Jimmy began grappling with details and holding his executives more accountable. He became less of a cheerleader and more of a manager. Management by inspiration was over, management by perspiration was in. Suddenly every part of the company was exposed to incredible scrutiny. It used to be you could stand up at a meeting once a year and state your goals and nobody ever came along and asked if you met them. Now there are weekly staff meetings and quarterly staff reviews."

Another innovation was the introduction of a twice-a-year employee survey whereby employees were asked their opinions about their jobs, their perceptions of their own and senior management, quality of Tandem products, benefits and their work life at Tandem. This barometer of employee feelings provided more insight into the attitudes of the workforce and helped to ensure that people weren't being lost to competitors.

However, neither Jimmy nor Tandem gave up on having fun though over the years; some of the stories and pranks seemed to get wilder and wilder. The Tandem-sponsored celebration during the Los Angeles Marathon was a classic. As recounted by Henry Norman (#2827):

"At the Los Angeles Marathon in 1987, sponsored by Tandem, a bunch of Tandem employees were volunteering in various positions at the race. Jimmy was one of the racers with a new record time of 1 hour and 190 minutes. [Author's Note: One of the company's long-standing jokes was Jimmy's running time. Under 2 hours was his goal, so no matter what his time, it always got converted to 1 hour and xxx minutes, to the amusement of all employees.] *We had been having a good time, and in the elevator on our way up to the hospitality suite reserved for Tandem people, I reminded Jimmy about the great stunt he'd pulled off at a Frankfurt party five years earlier— that of smoking a cigarette with his belly-button. 'Can you still do that?' I asked. 'No, I quit smoking,' he said, 'but I can write with my feet!' Everybody demanded a demonstration, and outside the closed hospitality suite door, Jimmy took off his right shoe, a piece of paper was placed on the floor, where Jimmy promptly wrote 'I Love Y'all!' His shirttail was sticking out the back, in the well-known Jimmy style, shoe tucked under one arm, not really radiating the picture of your typical high-tech company CEO. Suddenly the suite door opened, and a hotel functionary of some sort stuck their head out saying, 'You can't come in here yet.' 'Why not?'" Jimmy asked. 'You have to wait for permission from Tandem management.' 'No problem,' Jimmy said, 'I'm the CEO of Tandem, permission is hereby granted!' The hotel guy looked at us, at Jimmy, with his shoe under one arm, with a doubtful and condescending look on his face. 'I don't think so,' he said. 'I have proof!' Jimmy said. 'Here's my Tandem ID card. See, employee number one, that's me!' Slowly the hotel guy realized that Jimmy was the real thing, and began a hilarious display of groveling, bowing deeply, excusing himself. 'I didn't know! I didn't know!' It was so funny! The party went on well after that, of course."*

The culture of pulling pranks was also still alive and well. Some of the funniest included:

- *"Being set up by a certain management person to pick out an anniversary gift for his wife only to discover I was set up by Jimmy and Bob and the entire QA team to bring back a Victoria's Secret catalog. I embarrassed the daylights out of myself. I think I blushed the first three months I worked at Tandem...OK, maybe longer."* [Cheryl Kay Mullins #2134]

- *"Going to lunch with my team and Jimmy at Cicero's and having him discover that he had a $900+ bill on the tab from previous people charging lunch to him."* [Cheryl Kay Mullins - #2134]

- *"When we filled Kurt's office to the brim in helium balloons and sold off his Corvette on third-class mail (to his surprise)."* [Cheryl Kay Mullins #2134]

- *"A certain manufacturing software person was getting married and the Friday before, his group presented him with a ball and chain. Unfortunately, the bowling ball was handcuffed to him and he was stuck with it until the end of the day. I remember him getting ready for vacation, trying to carry a couple of those green and white lined printouts, while balancing the bowling ball. Or the time a software manager came back from sabbatical to find his office set up as a campsite. Tan bark laid over some heavy plastic, a pup tent, sleeping bag and a Tandem terminal. I don't think I ever heard where they hid his desk and office furniture."* [Linda Blanke Walton #3274]

- *"A Beer Bust in Reston, Virginia at which Kay Khandpur was describing growing up in Nigeria and the various edible delectables he indulged in. Sue Daniels was really grossed out by his assertion that goat's eyeballs were the best. So the next Monday morning, Kay comes in early to prepare 'breakfast' in Sue's cubicle. Two Ping-Pong balls with black dots drawn on with magic marker and then covered with Spaghetti-Os and a side of Visine made a unique picture. When Sue got to work I'm sure you could have heard the scream in the next county. Or the time that Mike Arnwine discovered that going on vacation was risky. He went on sabbatical and by the time he came back, his office door had been removed and its opening completely dry-walled in, repainted, and decorated with a potted plant. No more office. Who needs a manager anyway?"* [Mary Ellena Ward #4362]

By fall 1987, the outlook for Tandem had changed dramatically. Business was booming again. Though a few years late, the company had finally reached its goal of generating a billion dollars in revenue. It was a watershed moment of joy and a time to celebrate, so the company organized what was called the "Thanks a Billion Party" in the parking lots behind the Vallco Parkway Buildings in Cupertino. As mentioned previously, these kinds of parties had been relatively common in the early years, but with neighborhood complaints their frequency had grown few and far between. That year an exception was made and in October, after the end of the fiscal year, an incredible party took place. The entertainment included Kenny Loggins, The Charlie Daniels Band, Chuck Berry and a local band called the Cool Jerks. Unfortunately Chuck Berry only performed for 20 minutes, which was a letdown to many. This spawned an incredible set of rumors, which by 2002 had him refusing to go on without cash in hand. According to the story, in order to get him the cash, dozens of Tandem folks had been corralled to spread out across Cupertino to hit every ATM in the neighborhood for the maximum $200 individuals could withdraw until they had enough money to pay him his cash. Of course none of that was true, but is sure made a great story. The truth wasn't quite so exciting. According to those close to the action, Berry was contracted to perform for an hour from 10:30 p.m. to 11:30 p.m. Because of a delay, his start time had to be moved back by 30 minutes to 11 p.m. No one thought to confirm that this meant that the stop time would also be extended by 30 minutes. By Berry's reckoning, the end time was the same—the organizers had just moved the start time. Not exactly a cooperative performer.

Barton Sarto, the lead Thanks a Billion Party entertainment organizer and closest to all of the action (with help from William Eberwein), knew all the details and reported the following:

"His contract asked that we provide everything including amps and a backup band that knew his tunes, At one point the backup band had asked if Berry had music, or could provide them with a song list or something to rehearse. Berry looked at them and said, 'Just play Chuck Berry music!' The plan was that Chuck would show up with his guitar and just plug in at show time and play for 45 minutes to an hour. After the show he would collect the balance ($20,000 in the form of a cashier's check). Come show time, he shows up by himself in his Cadillac. We had two stages designed to keep music playing throughout. Charlie Daniels was on Stage 1, finishing his set. Chuck tells me that he wants the check before he goes on stage. He wasn't friendly and I don't blame him. He looked like he was tired of being 'Chuck.' He didn't want to meet anyone, not even the other bands. He didn't want to sign autographs. No pictures. No 'meet and greets.' He made that very clear by using four-letter words. He wanted to do his thing and go. Everything was running smooth. He was there and ready to play so I said sure and gave him the check.

"As soon as Charlie Daniels finished, Chuck jumped out on Stage 2. It was a trip. The backup band never even saw him until he hit the stage. Kenny Loggins was now setting up on the Stage 1. Twenty minutes into the show, Chuck starts doing the low 'Chuck walk' thing with his guitar and he keeps going and going until he disappears

behind the amp. I waited for a second, but I think I already knew what was going on. I hustled backstage to find him loading his guitar into the Cadillac. He'd done this before and was ready to pop me if I stood in his way. I'll never forget his face screaming at me so loud above the music the spit was coming out of his mouth. The guy was 60-something years old back then but he dwarfed me. There was no way he was going back on stage, so I had security let him out before something bad happened. I felt so lame but what do you do? I think Kenny Loggins came on a little early to make up for the gap. Looking back on it now though we're lucky Chuck even showed up."

The party went on into the night, with beer and food flowing. Eventually the neighbors had enough and called the local police who showed up part way through the final act, the Cool Jerks. Their ultimatum was pretty simple—*"Shut it down or go to jail!"* For a split second, the organizers considered the jail option, but thought better of it. Alas the plug had to be pulled in the middle of the Cool Jerks set to the disgruntlement of all, most of whom *"had a good hour or two still left in them"*. There were even rumors that breakfast had been organized, which had to be canceled. Every employee received a 1,000-share bonus option and a special commemorative gift—a clear Plexiglas rectangle with an embedded gold swoosh labeled $1,035,495,000 with a signed congratulatory message from Jimmy—so it was a wonderful close to a great year. Some of reminiscences include:

- *"'Watering the Ivy' behind the bank of portable toilets side by side with good old Jimmy T. He was a HOOT, talking about intolerable queue-times and buffer over-flow."* [Pete Kronberg #6276]

- *"I do remember the Thanks a Billion Party—well, most of it—it gets blurry toward the end. But wasn't it the Cool Jerks that wrapped it up? In preparation for the party, I was asked to set up a database of current Tandem employees so that the security staff could check each person off online as they entered. The thing that really struck me was that there were still 51 of the original 100 employees with the company."* [Bob Davidson #7061]

But the real show of Tandem's strength came a few weeks later, in October, when there was a major stock market correction on Wall Street. Tandem's technology, focus on quality and superior customer support enabled the Securities Industry Automation Corporation (SIAC), which managed all of the securities trading applications, to save the day for the New York Stock Exchange. Over a few days record trading volumes were recorded and as reported in the *San Jose Mercury News* by staff writer Josh Gonze:

"The computer and communications system used to support the NYSE withstood the strain of record trading volumes set in the frenzied stock market last week. A record volume of stocks, 604.8 million shares, traded hands on Monday (worth $7.6 billion). This is more than triple the volume on a typical day and another 608.1 million shares were traded on Tuesday. More than 600,000 separate transactions were made on both days. A two-hour transaction processing time lag, widely reported in the news last week, existed only on ticker tape machines, deliberately slowed to allow reading by the human eye, according to SIAC VP James Squires.... For Wall Street, the system as a whole worked very, very well."

Quality in its many forms Top - Leo Martinez analyzes the quality of a printed circuit board - NS News Februrary 1988
Bottom: Cabinets awaiting shipment to SITs - NS News May 1982 Right:1991 Quality Award

VLX Tandem Hits New Highs

VLX Launch Party - NS News May/June 1986

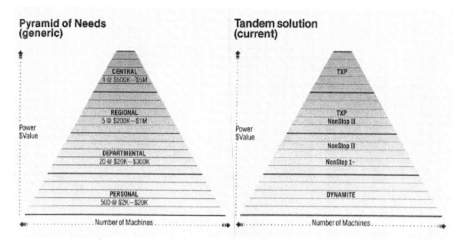

Pyramid of Needs Marketing Campaign. Tandem was no longer a 'One Trick Pony' - NS News February 1985

Award Winning Brochures - NS News May/June 1986

Jack Mauger Benchmark Center Leader - NS News January 1987

Harald Sammer Germany High Performance Center - NS News January 1987

Top: Sunyvale Benchmark Center - NS News Jan. 1987 Bottom: Me leading an ICON management planning session with Chip Greenlee standing - Clemson Collection

Top sales people join the Presidents Club - Clemson Collection

Jimmy Trebig (l) and Ed Sterbenc (r) at President's Club Reception - Clemson Collection

Top: Cartoon - NS News January 1987 Bottom: Swiss Army Knife to celebrate No. 1 in Customer Satisfaction

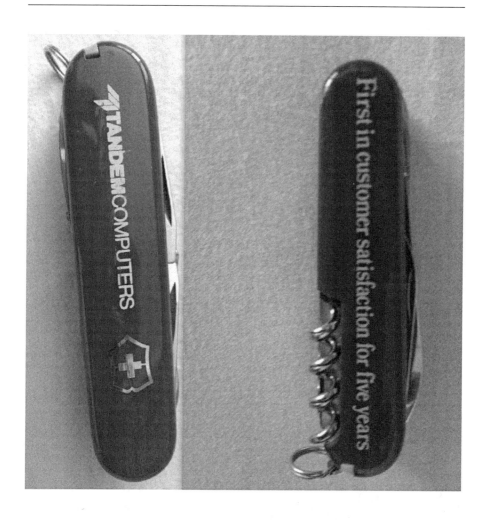

Top: Yvonne Mathieu (l) and Kirk Cunningham (r) launch the first customer survey - NS News May 1985 Bottom... John Kane Takes over Marketing Communications 1986 - Clemson Collection

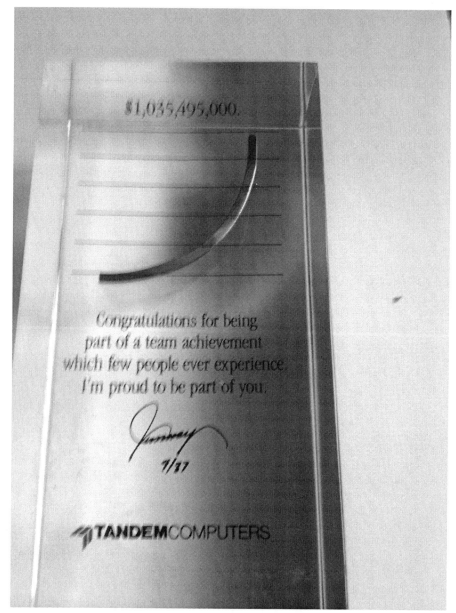

Billion Dollar Achievement commemorative gift given to all employees

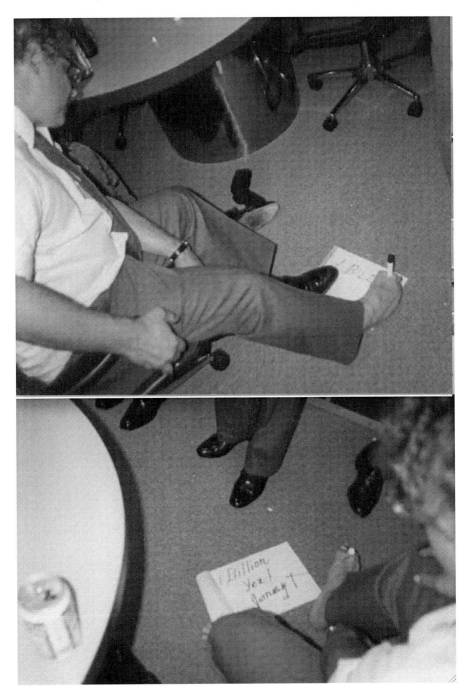

Jimmy writing with his feet 1987 - Cradin Collection

Jimmy celebrating a big win in the NYC sales office 1987 - Cradin Collection Next Page: U.K. Marathon finish line and a Tandem 2-handled mug

Tandem Grows Up

New Cyclone System Messaging

ALAS, ONCE AGAIN THE good times didn't last very long. New storm clouds were triggered by a worst-case nightmare scenario—a massive NonStop failure at the Toronto Stock Exchange. As reported in the Toronto *Globe and Mail* newspaper in August 1989:

> *"The Toronto Stock Exchange (TSE) was shut down for almost three hours yesterday due to the worst breakdown in 26 years of computer assisted trading. Pearce Bunting, TSE President, estimates that the exchange lost between $30,000 and $40,000 when client orders had to be rerouted to other markets. Video display terminals refused to respond properly at the 9:30 a.m. opening bell and almost all trading was halted 11 minutes later and remained closed until 12:31 p.m."*

The *Globe and Mail* described the failure as follows:

> *"The company's three-year-old Tandem VLX machine crashed after failures in subsystems of its disc drive and failures in backup systems. To say that what happened to the Tandem computer was not supposed to happen is an understatement of significant proportions. 'Up until yesterday the reliability record of TSE systems was excellent,' says TSE spokesperson Mary Revell. 'Our reliability figures were over 99 percent. Last year with 253 trading days, the system was down only 20 minutes.' The exchange is replacing the entire subsystem and may have it done by the weekend. Peter Richards, Tandem Canada President, said the disc drives suffered three separate failures that 'were once in a lifetime events.' The first two failures occurred in the early morning hours and were rectified before the TSE opened, but a third failure in the backup drive happened just before trading began leading to some of the data being*

unavailable. Yesterday's failure was not a computer crash. The whole system minus the data on the one drive was up and running and available to the exchange during the entire morning. Tandem technicians are continuing to work with the TSE to figure out why the disc drives suffered three failures."

This failure totally shook up Tandem and made everyone aware that large installations were a completely different kettle of fish and needed much more attention than they had been getting. In particular, multinational companies that were trying to install applications in multiple countries were growing very unhappy. Globalization was the hot new trend and starting to get some traction. Driven by customer need, Tandem embarked on a globalization effort of its own. Up until that point the company had generally operated more like a collection of independent subsidiaries than an integrated global company. Sales compensation strategies and the selling process discouraged communication and cooperation between subsidiaries and distributors out of a fear of having to split revenue credit and possibly lose control over the account relationship. The entire sales process for global deals was all getting very messy with commission split fights (arguments between account managers in different countries as to who should get revenue credit for specific sales) the order of the day, wasting tons of people's time and energy.

Joint account planning at headquarters was no longer enough. Customers now wanted single purchase contracts, with standard pricing and markup worldwide, regardless of whether or not a Tandem subsidiary or distributor was involved. They wanted "one voice"—a single point of contact who could speak on behalf of Tandem support and sales regardless of where in the world the customer were headquartered. They wanted efficient account administration so that, for example, Tandem could tell them quickly how much they had purchased worldwide and where. They wanted Tandem overall to be far more flexible and responsive than it had been. In addition, in 1992 the European Union was going to come into being, which was going to create one unified European economic entity.

In the summer of 1989, Jack Chapman asked me if I'd join his Global Sales Operations team, both to continue to run account planning activities, but this time for multinational customers, and also to try to figure out how to resolve these globalization issues. To globalize Tandem's sales approach for major accounts, 15 large customers with installations across all three sales divisions were identified and a pilot program tested with the field sales organization. The program was designed to demonstrate how managing, selling to and supporting these customers from a global perspective instead of on a country-by-country basis could gain competitive advantage. As I wrote in 1989 in the November-December issue of *NonStop Magazine,* a new employee communications periodical that had started in 1987:

"Tandem's multinational customers expect to do business in a certain way. They want master contractual agreements that define the global relationships, consistent worldwide support, joint planning activities with flexibility and responsiveness to their changing needs. This requires resolving several key internal issues including international pricing, compensation programs, resource allocation processes, account management and better streamlining of procedures. It is hoped that this global attention will lead to more revenue for Tandem, improve cross-organizational links, foster understanding of differences in cultural and business practices and help determine how account teams located in various parts of the world can work better together."

Beneath a gruff exterior, Jack had a heart of gold. As mentioned previously, he'd joined the firm to establish the United Kingdom office and over the years had been given more and more responsibility so that by the mid-1980s he was leading the entire European sales organization. As befits all fine sales people, Jack hated bureaucracy and didn't want to set up another management layer (he had three Vice Presidents of Sales reporting to him) nor did he want a big organization. His solution was to structure his small staff around issue resolution. Sally Shorthill handled sales administration issues, Phil Cardman handled legal ones, Pete Van Kuran worked on product management and product marketing issues, Eric Chow became the guru of all technical support issues and I joined the group with the responsibility to sort out the multinational account and compensation splits mess. Later on Vic Para, former Regional Director for the Southwest Region in the U.S. (who'd gone to Europe for a few years to help with sales management issues there), would join us to handle sensitive global sales management issues. What a motley crew we were. We all had strong personalities, didn't quite fit the traditional corporate mold and had burned a few bridges along the way to our current assignments.

In hindsight, both personally and professionally, I have to say my years with Jack were the highlight of my entire Tandem career. For three years I was footloose and fancy free and had the opportunity to travel all around the world—New York, Chicago, Dallas, London, Paris, Madrid, Zurich, Holland, Hong Kong, Thailand, Singapore, Mexico, Venezuela, to name just a few. The only key places I missed that I would have liked to have visited were Japan, New Zealand and Australia. I facilitated planning sessions. I coached and cajoled country managers into accepting global pricing and standard support arrangements. I standardized commission splits for certain types of multinational accounts (with scars in my back from the multiple arrows flung at me to prove it). I visited customers to test new ideas on how to globalize Tandem's business. I developed and sold management on adopting a whole range of new global policies and procedures including an innovative approach for purchase agreements for global customers and partners.

I had a hard time with jet lag so couldn't just fly to Europe for a week nor, as a result of a divorce, did I have any family that I had to get home to in California on weekends. So all my trips were usually for two to three weeks at a time, with lots of free time to visit some exotic locale. Zurich was a favorite, as were London and Paris. It seems now like it was a big dream. One remarkable trip to Europe was to attend the European Sales Rally, held in fall 1989 in Braunlage, a town in the former West Germany on the border with the former East Germany. A few weeks previously the Berlin Wall had fallen and the town was full of East Germans who were venturing for the first time into the west with their little smoke-belching diesel cars, called Ladas. Going to see the no-man's land that was the border, with its great expanses of treeless land and barbed wire, was really unnerving. Though empty now, one could easily imagine the guard towers staffed with rifles ready to shoot anyone who ventured across. The astounded look on the faces of the East Germans was remarkable as they crossed the bridge into town and saw for the first time grocery stores full of fruits and vegetables and all manner of goodies. The idea of self-service was totally foreign to them as I found out the next spring after venturing through Checkpoint Charlie at the Berlin Wall. Stores on the main street in East Berlin contained only samples of goods available to see thorough glass cases. The actual goods were ordered from a clerk and usually took weeks to obtain.

The next spring, I ran my first Global Account Management training class in Holland for the top 15 newly appointed Global Account Managers. Memorable to this day was the closing celebration. I'd asked each Global Account Manager to bring with them inexpensive mementoes, to be given to other participants that represented the culture of their home country. The responses were amazing. The boys from Chicago brought White Sox baseball caps and the folks from Canada brought hockey pucks. Those from Switzerland brought these huge cowbells and the guys from Italy brought pasta. The English contributed Beatrice Potter tea and the Japanese chopsticks. But the crème-de-la-crème and winner of the culture prize were the French. It turned out that the account manager had a relative who owned a vineyard and had made up a special label upon which the names of everyone who had attended the class had been inscribed. The whole experience brought tears to my eyes.

When it was over, a few of us with a free weekend jumped on a train to Berlin. There was a special celebration taking place to celebrate the bringing down of the Berlin Wall and we wanted to join in on the fun. The train was packed as thousands of young people converged on Berlin. This meant sitting in the train car hallway the entire overnight trip. Finding an affordable place to stay was a nightmare, but what fun we had. We rented hammers and helped smash down the wall. I still have a sample of the grafitti covered concrete as well as a pair of jeans I bought with a map of Germany on the thigh and a zipper that connects the two parts of Germany back together again—a marvelous memento.

Another wild trip during those years was to the Asia Pacific Region Sales Rally in Phuket, Thailand. It was the first time that all of the Asia-Pacific region direct and distributor country sales teams had gotten together, a group that were planting seeds for tremendous new growth for Tandem. Susan Hailey, Jo Carol Conover and myself (the few women still remaining in marketing) had been invited to participate in the proceedings. Susan and Jo Carol were part of the Industry Marketing Group (Susan in HQ and Jo Carol in ICON). Jo Carol and I decided to meet in Hong Kong to spend the weekend before the meeting shopping for jewelry. I remember vividly that she'd gotten the name of a reputable jeweler located off of the beaten path and therefore hopefully less expensive, from Roger Hewitt (the Latin Distributors Sales Manager). We ventured out to his shop, which turned out to be in an apartment building north of the main part of Kowloon, complete with barred windows and doors. It seemed almost clandestine, but when the door was opened we were let in after showing our personal introduction card from Roger. Inside, the staff brought out cases of jewelry that was priced way out of my league. At one point I tried a gold bracelet with a jaguar whose spots were embedded rubies. It cost a mere $25,000. Eventually I settled on an $800 lapis lazuli necklace with accompanying earrings, which I still have to this day.

Our first indication that the Phuket trip was going to be extraordinary was the scene when we arrived at the hotel, a couple of hours south of Bangkok by bus. Out front was an elephant, upon whose back was Glenn Grimme. Jack Baker, the Director of ICON Customer Support, was trying to arm twist arrivals into joining Glenn up on the back of this elephant. Apparently it was a surprise birthday present for Grahame Bennett, the Australian Country Manager. His Australian colleagues had set up the elephant visit and ride as a birthday gag. Our adventures were just beginning.

The first night after dinner, a small group including Susan, Jo Carol and I gathered in the hotel lobby bar for drinks. Awhile later several sales reps showed up and asked us if we wanted to go out on the town with them. Wanting to prove ourselves as "one of the boys," Jo Carol, Susan and I jumped at the opportunity, having no idea what was in store for us. We all piled into various taxis and pulled up in front of what looked like a nondescript nightclub. Little did we know that we were in the heart of Bangkok's sex trade district. As we walked into the club, we were too shocked to do anything but stare. On stage was an act that defies description in public company. Let's just say that a cigarette was being smoked from a place on the human body that I would never have thought possible. Susan, Jo Carol and I took one sly look at each other, whilst all of the guys had their eyes on us trying to gauge our reaction to the spectacle. The three of us played it cool and on our way to find a table, I nudged Susan and signaled for her to take a long look around us. In addition to the main act, there were all of these women wandering around the room with numbers pinned to their very skimpy dresses, mixing with the crowd. It took awhile for us to realize that men would signal interest in a specific number and then disappear with that woman to rooms adjacent to the main club. We were the only Caucasian women in the place—all the rest were either hostesses serving drinks or sex workers. Of course the sales guys had expected us to bolt, but we stuck it out and in the process apparently earned a bit of respect.

The next evening, after a long day of presentations, we were presented with another male vs. female test when introduced to the Team Drinking Relay contest. The pressure to join the contest was extreme, such that we couldn't refuse without losing face. This turned out to be one where brains rather than a strong constitution won the day. The rules were simple. Each team member had a tall glass in front of them, while at the beginning of the line was a pitcher of beer. One at a time, each team member had to pour beer into the glass, chug the glass of beer, place the empty glass upside down on top of one's head, which would leave one's hair soaked in beer if it wasn't empty, and then pass the pitcher down to the next person on the team. The team that moved the pitcher of beer the fastest down the table won the contest. We knew that as a woman's team, that we'd never be able to drink the quantities that were expected in anything close to times of the men. However, we were fearsome competitors and didn't want to lose. So we spent time with the Rules Chief making sure that we understood all the rules and then retreated to a quiet part of the bar to strategize as to how we could win without breaking any rules. We eventually came up with the perfect plan. We knew that our competitors in about the fifth or so heat would likely be the awesome Australian team, which had already been drinking for hours. At the appointed time we took our places with the pitcher of beer set in front of the first drinking team member. The room became deathly quiet. The looks on all of their faces made it clear that no one thought we had a chance. Regional Vice President Dave Peatrowsky, the appointed referee, rang the starter bell and the competition commenced. Unbeknownst to them all, we'd each borrowed a shot glass from the bar. After the starting whistle blew, we pulled these shot glasses out of our pockets set them down on the table, filled them up instead of the standard issue beer glasses, and started chugging one at a time. Of course we won our heat hands down.

The room erupted in howls of dismay with the Rules Chief nearly apoplectic. He and the judges huddled in a corner to decide what to do about this flagrant rule-bending. After extensive discussion the Rules Committee had to agree that we hadn't broken any of the official rules and had won our heat legitimately. However, there would now be new rules in place for the second round. The Australians went crazy as this meant that they had lost and likely now wouldn't make it into the final round. The women's team met again in the bar to plot our next move. Given that the Rules Committee had thwarted us, we decided that we couldn't win, but wouldn't go down without a fight. We ran back to our rooms and each grabbed our bathing suit tops. After the starting whistle, instead of chugging beer we all tore off our blouses to revealing our bathing suit tops and did everything we could to try to distract the opposite team. Again the room erupted in howls with everyone shouting foul play, while the three of us stood there hugging our sides in laughter. This time all agreed that those moves were definitely against the rules and we were swiftly eliminated. But our credibility and reputations as equal players in Asia was set, which made our business lives from then on so much easier.

Another highlight of working for Jack was the months that I spent on assignment as "special envoy" to Italy. The idea was to try to help the Italian subsidiary turn around their business model, reduce dependency on the local distributor, which operated mostly in the south out of Naples, and get them back in the corporate fold. Paolo Donzella was the newly appointed Italian Country Manager, hired to jumpstart the direct subsidiary. Dave Peatrowsky, with Jack's approval, had decided that the group needed someone to help translate Tandem's corporate policies into local practices as quickly as possible. Tall, lithe and handsome as only the Italians can be, Paolo was a mixture of charm and sales acumen, with an aristocratic yet down-to-earth air about him. He turned out to be one of the finest human beings I'd ever had the chance to work with before and since. His family roots were in what has been called the Italian Riviera, in the small city of Sanremo, just west of Genoa and east of Cannes, France, on the Mediterranean coast.

Prior to my duties as "special envoy," I'd had very bad memories of Italy that Paolo set out to fix. While a traveling summer vagabond just after graduating from university, I'd gotten seriously ill with blood poisoning that I'd acquired in Vienna. We'd gotten stuck on a train from Vienna and by the time we reached Venice, I was deathly ill. With the help of a kindly gondola pilot who took pity on us, I was rushed to a local charity hospital where I hovered between life and death for several days. Luckily there was a very smart doctor who spoke a little English, and with good care and great antibiotics I lived to see another day.

So with some apprehension did I venture to Milan, where the Tandem Italian headquarters was located. Well, Paolo was a marvelous host, but trying to figure out how the Italian business culture worked and use it to my advantage was a challenging exercise. Women in business were for the most part unheard of in Italy at that time. Women as secretaries and getters-of-coffee, yes, but equal business partners, forget it—especially a tall, blond and young North American one.

My first visit was during the month of August, a time when Milan basically shuts down, as most citizens abandon the city for the coastal towns or head north to the cooler mountain villages. The place was just about empty, quiet as a tomb. It gave me a good chance to spend time with the staff and understand their perspectives on the world. It also enabled me to experience being entertained by my Italian hosts. I have many fond memories of extraordinary food, great wine and beautiful vistas, especially in Naples. It was customary to drink wine at lunch and at dinner, which after a few days was a challenge for me. I used to joke that I'd have to return to the United States to "dry out." There was one restaurant called Casa Fontana in Milan that only served risotto. It was fabulous. They gave me an English-language booklet containing many of their recipes that I still have and covet today.

Over the course of several quarters, I visited Italy every few months for a few days of sales coaching, training and problem solving in an effort to improve sales, with an occasional visit to customers. It sounds so odd as I write this, but real success occurred when Paolo's team felt comfortable enough to allow me to present on Tandem's culture and leadership practices at a local seminar they were hosting for leaders in the manufacturing industry in Turin. I had no idea at the time what an honor that was nor the extent to which my strengthened credibility may have improved Paulo's stature in other parts of the Italian business world. But the net result was that various sales opportunities that were in the pipeline seemed to be progressing. But eventually after several more visits, more talk and lots of dinner meetings, we still had no signed orders. One afternoon I lost my cool and put my foot down. With a booming voice and hand motions to match the Italians, I advised Paolo in no uncertain terms that I could not return to the United States the next week and face Jack without having closed a big deal. Something must have sunk in that I was serious as a few days later we closed a major piece of business with the SIA, the Italian financial payments systems processing entity, a huge success for the Italian subsidiary. Now the truth was that I'm not sure that my hand waving really had that much impact. The real assist came from the Japanese subsidiary who had hosted a visit from SIA. As Dave Peatrowsky, a Sales Director on special assignment to Europe, who had previously been the Asia Pacific Regional Sales Director, said:

"Watching the Japanese, especially Taka san and Izumi san, sell the Italians was a thing of beauty. Paolo even became a fan of sushi from then on."

As Tandem continued to grow and looked forward to attaining $2 billion in revenue, the company had to continue to quash market concerns about its ability to preserve and protect the best of its culture but still generate high quality, innovative products under professional management practices. It had been a number of years since the Understanding Tandem Philosophy classes had been introduced and the general consensus was that the program needed some refreshing. Using the core Tandem Philosophy as a basis, Focus Programs were born, spearheaded by Debbie Byron, the Manager along with Ed Martin and Candace DeCou. Eventually named the Philosophy Department, the group, reporting directly to Jimmy, built a series of four core Focus training programs called Focus on Fundamentals, Focus on Customer Satisfaction, Focus on Leadership and Focus on Values. With all employees expected to attend Focus training, the programs were designed to ensure that employees were on the same page with regard to fundamental company direction, values, leadership and customer service principles. From these four programs it was expected that Tandem employees would explore other training programs and seminars provided by the company.

The first one, called **Focus on Fundamentals**, was designed for new hires. It was an intensive one-day program to provide employees who had joined Tandem in the previous 90 days with high-level overviews about Tandem's corporate goals, products, strategies and values. The program was also a place to experience the Tandem Philosophy first-hand in an interactive format. It featured participation by senior level managers for each module with lots of time set aside for questions and discussion, both during the sessions and over meals. Jimmy was often a key contributor and usually presented the Tandem goals and values part of the program. The class included an end-of-day reception and dinner, where employees were encouraged to bring a family member or guest and mingle with company executives. A special part of that program was an after-dinner talk on career management by Jimmy.

The second program was called **Focus on Values**. It was designed to provide employees with a common code of behavior and through those values build trust and relationships. The modules tried to answer the questions such as:

• Why a company needed values
• What Tandem's basic beliefs and values were
• Live examples of values in action
• Details of key programs (Shared Success) that supported those values

The adoption of these values included both rights and responsibilities and began with a set of basic beliefs about people. Though the language was somewhat different, the principles were the same ones that had been communicated since Tandem's beginning and revolved around a series of basic beliefs, namely that:

• People were the company.
• People wanted to be successful and share that success
• People wanted opportunities to grow and learn

- People would take responsibility and accomplish goals when they are having fun and are challenged
- People would make good decisions when they have good information and trust

Along with these core beliefs were a set of actions that were needed to make them really work such as:

- Respect for people and their diversity
- The importance of the individual, fairness, honesty and trust
- Open and effective communications
- Responsible action and ownership
- Hard work, flexibility, innovation and creativity
- Quality in all that was done
- Shared success

Values also drove key management practices, which again hadn't changed much since the early days such as:

- The importance of "erring on the human side," which gave employees the freedom to take prudent risks
- The importance of teamwork
- A commitment to only hire outstanding people and promote from within
- A focus on keeping people whole, while encouraging self-management
- An open door and an open management structure

Tandem also tried to build organizational structures that accommodated varying management styles and kinds of work. It also tried to balance structure for business and management efficiency with flexibility that would encourage creativity and innovation. Though the employee/manager continued to be the primary relationship and source for direction and communication (such as work and career planning and performance feedback), peer management was also important. The program tried to instill an awareness that Tandem succeeded because of a "common fate" culture—in other words, we were all in this together. As had been a hallmark of the company since its beginnings, structured and unstructured communications continued to be key drivers. The sharing of myths and war stories that illustrated the company success was a key component of every program. Core communication programs that were now well institutionalized included:

- Electronic mail
- Pipeline to senior management
- TTN teleconferences (quarterly results) and special events
- TTN First Friday Marketing
- Beer Busts
- Town meetings and manager update meetings
- Publications such as the monthly *NonStop News* & bi-monthly *Center* magazine

In addition were a series of Shared Success Programs that included:

- Stock options and stock benefit programs
- Sabbaticals (six weeks of paid time off every four years)
- Special health benefit programs
- Employee recognition programs including not just cash or prize awards but special events like TOPS, President's Club, ICON's Reach for the Peak, First Cabin Club

Again with a 2010 mindset, this all seems so self-evident. But in those days, most companies didn't particularly caring to any degree about any of these types of management principles and people motivation programs.

The decade ended with a bang and an opportunity on October 17, 1989, to demonstrate Tandem values to the utmost degree. The morning started with the introduction of the Cyclone, the newest computer system in the Tandem family, and ended in the afternoon with the Loma Preita earthquake. As shared by Ed Sterbenc (#11136) Jerry Peterson and Ghery Pettit (#5816):

"The big customer show in Cupertino for Cyclone was held in Loc. 55 in the space behind the brand new ten meter RF semi-anechoic chamber in the new EMC lab. We had a pair of Cyclone cabinets on the turntable in the chamber for customers to look at. The half of Building 55 that was not yet fitted out was turned into a theater of sorts for that day's introduction of the Cyclone family of computers. The announcement was held at 10 a.m. in the morning to accommodate a simultaneous satellite TV hookup to a venue in London for the European customers and press. John Kane was Master of Ceremonies in London and the stage there had a hydraulic trap door allowing the Cyclone to rise dramatically through smoke and laser light effects. The London and Cupertino audiences were treated to both 'product reveals' via the satellite link. John and I had a carefully choreographed conversation via the satellite link to prove to everyone this was live and not videotape! In Cupertino a stage was constructed onto which rolled a Cyclone through a haze of smoke as the climactic ending to the incredible short piece called 'Cyclone Coming' which was accompanied by a tre-

mendous soundtrack played through a monster sound system including a garbage can-sized super-woofer under the seats. The theme of the 'Cyclone Coming' video was 'Big, Fast, Powerful.' It featured a team of black-shirted rowers powering a shell (Power of Parallelism) on the Crystal Springs reservoir, a black Ferrari Testarossa and an SR71 Blackbird. Black was the featured color and the opening scene had thunderbolts coming from a stormy sky (Cyclone coming...), thus the thunderbolt over the Building 55 driveway.

"Facing the stage were temporary bleachers where a couple hundred press and honored guests were watching in breathless awe as we announced the new Cyclone system, our IBM mainframe-killer with the internal tag line 'Be One of Three' remaining competitors in the mainframe computer industry along with IBM and DEC. This all happened right after lunchtime with the entire product launch event moving across the street to Jimmy's building for a fantastic reception. The last guests probably exited Building. 55 at about 3:30 p.m. which was fortunate because if they were still in those bleachers at about 5 p.m. ... I'd rather not even speculate. There was a photographer working in the chamber taking pictures for advertising materials. His camera on a ladder when the quake hit and a $1500 lens was scattered all over the floor. A floor made of 3/8-inch steel plate. The lens lost. Those who participated in the events of the day received crystal medallions on a black and gold ribbon, as I recall, a few weeks later with an inscription memorializing the day that read: 'Tandem Computers. I survived a Cyclone and an Earthquake on the same day. October 17, 1989.'"

For those of us who lived in the Bay Area, the Loma Prieta earthquake certainly changed us all. The earthquake, 6.9 on the Richter Scale, struck at 5:04 p.m., during warm-ups for the third game of the baseball World Series between the Bay Area's two teams, the San Francisco Giants and the Oakland A's. The epicenter was about a mile from my house in Capitola in the nearby Santa Cruz Mountains, Nicene Marks Park to be specific. Though technically not the "Big One," it was big enough to scare most people badly.

Of course earthquake preparedness is a basic part of life in California, but none of us ever thought that we'd experience a major quake. Yet here it was. I was in the office that afternoon when the building began to shake and the shaking didn't stop. Looking out the office window, I saw the parking lot turn into what looked like a large undulating black wave. But fifteen seconds later it was over, and everything was quiet, scarily quiet. In Cupertino we had no idea of the terrible damage that had been wrought just up the road in Oakland where a major bridge had collapsed and in downtown Santa Cruz, where many buildings had collapsed. The main route to my home (Highway 17 over the Santa Cruz Mountains) was closed due to landslides, so I spent the night in Los Gatos at the home of Dave and Fran Peatrowsky. One eerie memory that still haunts me to this day was waking up the next morning to the sounds of a lawnmower. Even though there was no power anywhere and no businesses were open, somehow Dave's gardeners felt so responsible to their clients that they still showed up for work. A day later, the back roads opened up and I was able to get home to find a home badly shaken but not seriously damaged.

Steve "Woody" Woodson [#1570], who was in Watsonville when the quake struck, provided a different perspective:

"Fred Sheppy and I were looking into a board problem when it hit. We crawled under a table. He was holding two legs and I was holding the other two. That didn't matter the table was dancing all over the place. It was all we could do to hang on to the damn thing. Then the lights went off and it starting raining. The ceiling girders had sheared the sprinkler head off the pipes. By the time it stopped shaking enough for us to try to get out there was half an inch of water on the floor. We headed out the back door. On the way out we thought it would be a good idea to shut off the sprinkler system. It wasn't going to do much good now anyway. You have all probably seen it that big red thing in the back of every building with a big wheel on it. Anyway, first you shut off the water going into the system, then you drain the system. We did everything right.

"Now, we're all standing in the parking lot. Since it was near 'quittin' time,' we weren't quite sure if everybody got out. So we decided we had to go back in to check... aftershocks and all. That was one of the scariest things I ever did. Since we didn't have keys to open locked doors, we starting using fire extinguishers to smack the doorknobs off and bust the doors down to make sure no one was left in the building. No one was in the building. While we were searching I noticed that all of the system battery packs were still on. I had the bright idea to start shutting them down. I grabbed a 2x4 (so I wouldn't get shocked, remember the water?) and starting shutting down batteries. Then a big aftershock hit and I got the hell out of there. I got home and the home and family were safe.

"I got up the next morning and tried to go back over Highway 152 to Watsonville but the road was closed. I worked my way down Highway 101 and through the back roads (Highway 129 had been closed for construction for some time). I drove through Watsonville and was devastated by the destruction. Tandem Watsonville was designated an emergency relief center for Watsonville, which made it even more important for me to get there. After I got there, we went inside to video record the damage for the insurance company. We also gathered all of the bottled water we had to give to the people of Watsonville. And they did come.

"At this point, we set up a war room in the cafeteria to decide on our next moves. Bruce Taylor had made it down there somehow and had booked a room in

town somewhere for the duration. Next, I get a call from my dear friend Ron Labby. He had flown down to Watsonville airport and wanted a ride from the airport just down the street. I went and got him and Scott McMillan who had come along. When we got back, Bruce gave us orders (anyone who knows Bruce knows what I mean) to go get batteries, smokes and candles for his hotel room. We drove over to the grocery store and saw long lines coming out the door. We figured that there was no way we were going to get what we came for. Then Ron had a brilliant idea. 'Let's fly to Los Banos. The airport is right across the street from several stores.' We drove over to the airport and took off, literally. It was amazing to see the damage from the air. The list is too big to present here. We got to Los Banos, walked across the street and into the store. It was like nothing had happened there. The contrast was unbelievable. We got our stuff and flew back looking and still seeing more damage.

"We got back and starting the long process of putting things together. \WATSON had tipped forward at a 45-degree angle. It was about 12 cabinets. Somehow we were able to tip it back and it booted right up. Tandem Computers... the most amazing machine and people in the world... ever."

For Bob R.:

"When the earthquake hit in 1989 I was upstairs in the back hallway in Loc. 2. I was knocked back and forth in that hallway so hard that I decided to get the heck out of the building. I jumped the two flights of stairs in the back and ran out onto the basketball court next to the pool. Looking at the pool I was mesmerized. The water was shooting up about 20 feet in the air (or so it seemed) and there were two employees in the pool shooting up with it. When things settled down I yelled out to the guys to see if they were OK as they crawled out of the pool. Thank goodness they weren't hurt. I never did find out who they were. I know one thing for sure, that had to be the water ride of a lifetime."

From the perspective of Austin, Bill H. reported:

"Just before 7 p.m. Central Time, I was on the phone with some colleagues in the Forge Building (Loc. 55) recapping the events of the day. About 6:55 p.m. we bid adieu and I grabbed by belongings and headed to the car. I hopped into my car and turned on the radio to listen to the World Series game. The announcers were suddenly gasping and groping for words as the quake was just hitting the stadium. At first they didn't know what was occurring but shortly gained their composure and assumed it was an earthquake.

"My reaction was to pick up the cell phone (one of those big ones with batteries that weighed almost as much as a CLX) and call our Second Shift Supervisor, Dolores, in

the TNSC. 'Dolo,' I said, 'have you heard what's going on in California?' 'No.' 'Well the announcers on the baseball game said there is a pretty bad earthquake going on right now, let's implement our disaster plans. Start calling all of the Tandem Customer Engineers in the Bay Area; make sure they are all right and find out their availability.' My staff in the support center were terrific. Not only did Dolores and her staff know what to do, she put one of her people on the task of recording what occurred and especially taking comments from customers. They contacted every CE and Field Service Manager they could before the phone lines got clogged by the general public checking on their friends and relatives in the area, made arrangements to have them call the support center periodically as we would try to coordinate as much as the phone lines would allow.

"Close to 5:30 a.m. Pacific time the next morning, Bob Marshall called me to go over the announcement to Tandem customers that he was to make in the Bay Area over the radio stations. We concurred on a statement that encouraged Tandem customers to call the support center and we'd do our best to serve them. Around 6:30 or 7 a.m., Randy Baker called from Forge. He, Pete Schott and others were setting up a 'war room.' About a half-hour later, John Elkins and Scott Thompson called from Building 98 (if I recall) and they were going to set up a war room over there. I suggested that they might be safer in the one-story Forge building, besides there was already a coordination center being set up. The available staff from Customer Support Operations and Customer Service gathered in the Forge facility. One of the Field Managers from the Eastern Region was in town for a class and logged into the 'dispatch' system. His efforts were superb and made communications from customers through the support center to those field service people who were available rapid and accurate. To say everyone pitched in is an understatement. Everyone came together for the benefit of Tandem's customers. A day or so later, the needed spare parts, identified through all the calls between us and customers, were loaded on two vans, one for the East Bay and one for the peninsula. The comments from customers, as recorded by Bill in the dispatch operations, were unbelievable testaments to the reason customers did business with Tandem."

David Hodge [#12801], who worked out of the United Kingdom office, also reminisced:

"Tandem being the international community that it was caused all of us to have friends 'over there,' so I think the mail trunks were probably hot that day with us mailing our friends to see how they had fared. Mercifully, I did not hear of anybody I immediately knew that was affected. One of my friends was very ho-hum about it, having been born and bred in California and grown up with earthquakes like I have the rain and fog. Clearly the news was painting a different picture for us and we knew what had really happened. I think one of the most captivating messages I ever read *was from a Brit, who along with another had been doing some testing in the High Performance Lab. Most Brits don't experience earthquakes so for this gentleman to describe a unique event was riveting. I don't wish to sound disrespectful to those who lost life or property at that time. I remember the description of him standing in a room and everything around him shaking until he was knocked off his feet. He promptly got back up again at which point one of the locals practically rugby-tackled him and hauled him underneath a desk to comparative safety."*

Or as Ian Evans [#12776] shared:

"Not spilling my coffee as I ducked under a table in the Loc. 3 computer room and watched the waves of floor tiles and rolling system cabinets. The Illinois native next to me went back to Illinois shortly thereafter."

Despite the incredibly difficult time, Tandem's customer support organization came through with flying colors. As Steve Benasso explained:

"Everyone could easily recall examples of how the human element at Tandem was displayed. For me, I will never forget helping staff the Earthquake Hotline following the Loma Prieta earthquake. It was the Tandem Human Resources department that came up with the idea but the entire Tandem employee family contributed to its success. The epicenter of the quake was in Santa Cruz just north of Watsonville, the location of Tandem's printed circuit board plant. As a result we obviously had a very high percentage of employees that were impacted. As I recall, the largest need was for drinking water, since the local water supply had been compromised. Many, many employees showed up in Cupertino with car, truck and van loads of bottled water that were then ferried over to the Watsonville and Santa Cruz areas. Shelter was probably the next biggest need for many of our employees and their neighbors. With a significant number of homes seriously damaged, people were not allowed back into them until overworked inspectors could assure them they were safe to re-occupy. Tandem employees donated their own or purchased sleeping bags and camping tents so that people could camp in their backyards and front lawns until given the all clear. Lots of employees simply donated money and asked that it be spent on whatever was the greatest current need. It was an amazing experience and one I felt honored to be part of. I don't know of any other company that put forth such a sincere effort to assist others and link those that needed help with those who could offer it."

Buster Maness was a brand new space planner and in his first week at Tandem when Loma Prieta struck. This caused the closing of the Triangle Building and forced consolidations in Loc. 4 and several other buildings across the Cupertino campus. We had to use the cafeterias in Loc. 4 and Loc. 200 and many of the conference rooms around the campus to accommodate the closing of the Triangle Building and the Loc. 4 overflow. As Buster shared:

"Jerry Peterson, Dave Rynne, Tony Smith, Bruce Dougherty, Barry Ariko, Bill Heil, Bryan Ball and Bill McNally were not really happy with what their groups needed to do to accommodate the employees who had to move into their office space but in the end they and their employees decided to pitch in, follow the Tandem Values, and got the job done. As of course you can imagine, implementing this compression strategy was not exactly a great way for a new planner to make friends."

Though not related, in late December 1989 an earthquake struck in Newcastle, Australia, about 200 kilometers north of Sydney. The epicenter was very close to the site of Tandem customer Australia Wire Industries (AWI), situated among industrial slag heaps next to Newcastle Harbor. As Ken Vaughan reported:

"They had a small multi-story building set aside from all the main works. AWI was a model Tandem NonStop user, they embraced all the features and were proud of their setup. Everything was running normally in their site until the quake hit. Just after, I received a call from their systems manager who curiously said, 'Hi Ken, I am calling from a telephone post in the middle of a slag heap; we have had an earthquake, our building is cracked and the civil engineers will not let us go back in there to run the systems.' 'Go back?' I queried and he said, 'Yes, I have been in there and the Tandem was on its side but still running, the other systems all were down. The engineer made everyone leave immediately.' 'The question comes to mind, why are you on the slag heap?' He continued, 'We had set up the NonStop part in detail to every specification, however, we forgot to put in a remote operating terminal in case we could not get into the building.' The only local telephone operating was an emergency unit on a pole in the slagheap. Meanwhile, as the management, civil engineers and the IT people all dithered, that magnificent Tandem NonStop whirred away... who needs an operator, who needs a level platform, who needs a building? That Tandem really was Non-Stop. This story made a lot of media space and the fun part was everyone speculating on how AWI managed to use the communications line on the pole to run the system? We speculated on using the words—'new platform.' Everything was fixed and back to normal once the building was cleared a day or two later. Later AWI added a proper remote control facility as well."

But the ultimate earthquake story came from Joe Massucco [#3772], who phoned Tandem Support in Austin after another quake rattled the Bay Area. As Joe related:

"After reporting my problem the Austin guy told me about a call he'd taken just a few minutes before from someone else in the Bay Area. As best as I can remember, this was his conversation:

CUSTOMER: I'd like to report that my CLX system is down and I need to know how to get it up again.

AUSTIN: OK, do you have power?

CUSTOMER: Yeah, we have UPS (uninterrupted power supply), so when the quake hit we didn't lose power.

AUSTIN: Have you tried to reboot the system?

CUSTOMER: Huh?

AUSTIN: You reported that your system was down.

CUSTOMER: Yeah.

AUSTIN: Do you need help rebooting the system?

CUSTOMER: No, I know how to reboot the system. The system is running just fine. That's not the problem. The problem is my system is down.

AUSTIN: I guess I'm not quite understanding your problem, then.

CUSTOMER: OK, let me explain this carefully. When the quake hit, our CLX when down on its back. Well, the disk drives moved all over the floor, but they're still okay. But the CLX fell over backwards and is now lying on the floor on its back—it's running just fine and we haven't lost a transaction. I just want to know the safest way to get it back up on its rollers without damaging the cabinet.

Maybe we should have taken Timex's slogan as our own: 'Takes a licking and keeps on ticking.'"

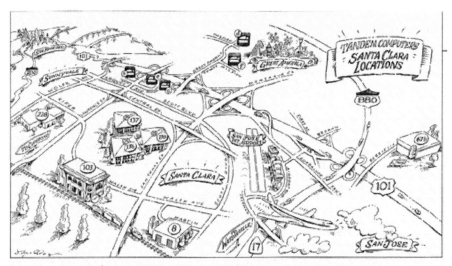

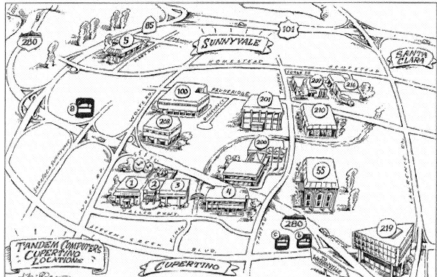

Artist's rendition of the Cupertino and Santa Clara building sites.
(Illustrations by Joe Murray, Murray Communications Group)

Tandem Headquarters Campus in Cupertino - NS News February 1988

TSE halts following computer failure

BY GAIL LEM
and HARVEY ENCHIN
The Globe and Mail

A stunning malfunction in the Toronto Stock Exchange's computer shut down Canada's premier equity trading floor for almost three hours yesterday, and sent stockbrokers scrambling to process their orders in Montreal and New York.

It was the worst breakdown in 26 years of computer-assisted

Trading resumes at the Toronto Stock Exchange after three-hour computer breakdown.

Fail-safe Tandem system fails

Toronto Stock Exchange fails 1989 - Globe and Mail September 1989

'MAKING OUR MOVE' North American Sales Rally - Seamons Collection

Cyclone Systems in all their glory

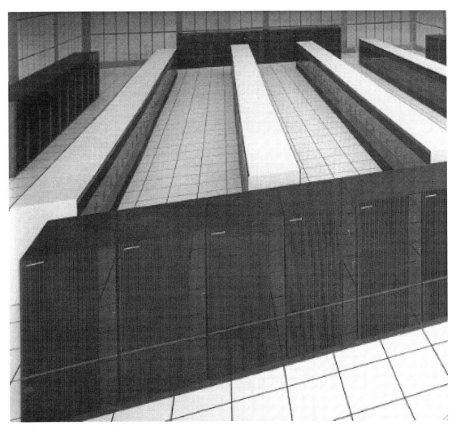

Cyclone Systems in all their glory II

Tandem Introduces the Cyclone 1989

Jimmy getting ready to give his barnburner his 'VARMINT KILLER' speech complete with rubber snakes that he kept throwing out into the audience - Seamons Collection

Top: Welcoming elephant outside the Hotel at the Asia Pacific Sales Rally in Thailand. - Clemson Collection Bottom: Sales Reps Mingling L-R: Bob Bloom, Mitch Slutzky, the rest unknown - Seamons Collection

Asia Pacific Sales Rally 1989 L-R: unknown, John Kane, Pete Van Kuran, RIchard Hellyer - Clemson Collection

Asia Pacific Sales Rally 1989 L-R: Grahaeme Bennett

Post Asia Pacific Sales Rally - A day at the beach before heading home L-R: Jo Carol Conover, Frank Penner, Richard Hellyer, Susan Hailey, water ski boat driver, Pete Van Kuran -Clemson Collection

Tandem Logo in Ice - Clemson Collection

Previous Page: Women's Drinking Team wins their heat at the Asia Pacific Sales Rally Men's Team wins the final round -
Clemson Collection

Dave Peatrowsky Asia Pacific Regional Sales Director, Ellen Martinez - ICON Marketing, Myra Rodrequez - Singapore District Sales Office - Clemson Collection

ICON Management Roger Hewitt (Latin America Sales Manager), Kevin O'Connell (Regional Sales Manager) and Mike Moore (V. P.) - Clemson Collection

Jack Chapman, V.P. Worldwide Sales - NS News January 1987

L - Wine gift from Philippe Tour for all of the Gobal Account Managers Training participants R- Neil McGowan helping knock down the Berlin Wall - Clemson Collection

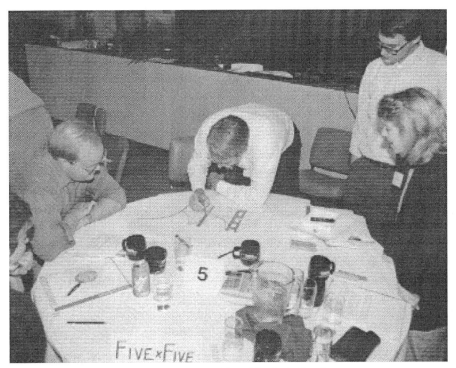

Focus on Fundamentals team poster design competition - NS News (photo by Jim Howell)

TANDEM'S VALUE
SYSTEM is composed of an interconnected set of Core

Values and the business relationships in which they are applied. Our Core Values are:

• Respect for people and their diversity • Importance of the individual

• Teamwork • Fairness • Honesty and trust • Open and effective communication

• Responsible action and ownership • Hard work • Flexibility

• Innovation and creativity • Quality in all we do

• Shared success

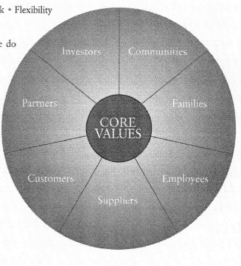

Focus Series - Focus on Values Wheel

Tandem Pulls the Plug

Tandem Reunion at Bay Meadows September 2002 - Tandem Alumni YahooGroups Posting

As THE LAST DECADE of the 20th century began, once again the computer industry was going through another period of tremendous change. Jimmy's ability to paint a picture of the future and the opportunity therein continued for the most part to be on target. As he outlined in a speech at a company annual meeting in 1988:

"PCs are going to continue to increase in power. We're going to have massive mainframes on the desk, with continual, dramatic improvements in the human interface. Behind that workstation of the future will be a huge amount of communication with shared databases that must exist to make that communications possible. This movement from terminals to PCs will trigger a desire to connect heterogeneous databases across different systems with reliability in performance. Everyone knows that the computer in the 1990s will become your HDTV set. That TV set will become your PC in the home. Try to imagine, just for a second, the database capabilities and the amount of database that is going to be out there that you will be able to access from your TV or computer in the home. There are going to be lots of PCs, but there are going to be bigger, more complicated, more rich transactions. You're going to see explosions in

queries to big central shared databases. You're going to see a change in the nature of batch in the large corporations, an acceleration in online connectivity."

While his words sounded prophetic, Jimmy missed the mark with his prediction that Tandem would be among the winners in a new and competitive landscape. He had said, *"what had always differentiated Tandem and would continue to be even more important were the core Tandem technical benefits including availability, distributed data, price/performance, security and now openness."* Unfortunately the idea of Tandem software openness proved more rhetorical than reality, as time came to show.

By the early 1990s and as the concepts behind Tandem's "Pyramid of Needs" caught hold in the marketplace, it started to become clear that if Tandem wanted to play in the big leagues with IBM, it had to be willing to take some bigger risks. One of those was an experiment in the systems integration field. Long the purview of EDS and Andersen Consulting (now Accenture), offering systems integration services was seen as a way to play with the big guys and gain credibility in the market. Set up from the beginning as a standalone profit center, the objective of Tandem Integration Engineering Services, or TIES, was to enable Tandem customers to access deep Tandem expertise along with processes, controls and tools so that they could efficiently design, develop and implement end-to-end Tandem systems. TIES was led by Neil McGowan, who'd spent over a decade in Tandem's New York sales office as a customer "bailout artist" (a consulting systems analyst who rescued large hardware accounts knee-deep in application development and struggling to get their systems up and running).

The TIES goal for the first year was to generate $2 million in professional services consulting contracts and influence $5 million in hardware revenue. To the surprise of skeptical management, the group actually closed $2.2 million in professional services contracts and influenced $9.5 million in hardware revenue. The discovery that customers were willing to pay significant amounts for access to Tandem expertise was a revelation. All customers wanted was a commitment from Tandem to help them reach their goals and assume some of the risk. This was especially important when they were building complex applications and purchasing large amounts of hardware. TIES' first customer was McKesson Corporation, a large San Francisco-based pharmaceutical company whose effort to upgrade their inventory system was completed in seven months rather than the 18 months that was projected. This effort was soon followed by contracts with Kaiser Permanente, Bank of America, Lieberman (a distributor of home entertainment products), Lockheed and UPS.

The success of these efforts made the company realize that investing in improving their partnerships with large systems integrators could significantly influence hardware sales. Teams were created in the U.S. field organization, now run by Barry Ariko, to support EDS and Andersen Consulting. In 1991, Jack Chapman decided that he'd had enough of the U.S. and wanted to return to England. A couple of grandchildren had arrived and his wife, Eve, didn't want to miss watching them grow up. He was appointed Chairman of Tandem Europe and was given the task to run a newly created Corporate Executive Advisory Board. This was a small group including global customers and a couple of outsider business leaders, separate from the Tandem Board of Directors, who acted as strategic advisors to Jimmy Treybig. The Global Sales Organization was then basically disbanded. An era had passed, and truth be told, I was getting a little tired of gallivanting around the world. An opening on a sales team that was being assembled to build a better relationship with EDS looked like a great new opportunity, which I took.

The head of the team was Jerry Gottlieb, a seasoned and very successful sales person who had been a former District Sales Manager for the Silicon Valley district. A business relationship development agreement had been struck between Tandem and EDS and the team's job was to figure out how to generate revenue across the three main EDS lines of business that had Tandem systems installed. First, of course, was their outsourcing business where General Motors, EDS's parent company, had outsourced the running of their MIS shop. These sales were managed through Tandem's Detroit Sales Branch. Secondly were EDS's systems integration activities conducted through industry-specific solution business units (SBUs) located primarily out of Dallas. The challenge here was to clarify from both a technical and market perspective where Tandem's technology fit and get that market and technology positioning strategy embedded in EDS's technology architectural roadmap. In this way it would be clear where the SBUs could choose Tandem rather than IBM as their mainframe computer vendor of choice. Thirdly was an EDS-owned stand-alone payment processing business (Payment Systems Inc.) that was one of the nation's largest credit card and point-of-sale payment processing services for the retail industry.

Alas, EDS was a very tough company to work with, though I had some funny experiences dealing with the generally uptight, blue-suited, white-shirted, wing-tipped crowd. My most memorable was a visit to EDS's Richardson, Texas facilities to do some joint sales and business planning. I'd recently decided to branch out from my "dress-for-success" staid blue, brown or grey suits and had bought one that was bright lemon yellow with embroidered native American Indian symbols on the pockets. At lunch we took a break and descended to their local cafeteria. As I made my way through the throng, I'll never forget the stir that my lemon yellow suit caused. All eyes turned my way and conversation stopped mid sentence. Luckily I was a vendor, as at the time EDS took their dress code very seriously and if I had been an employee there might have been serious repercussions.

Alas, 1990, though a record year with the company earning $122 million on revenues of $1.9 billion, turned out to be the peak of a long slow decline. Another recession was in the offing, and by 1992 Tandem's revenue was declining, costs were climbing and the company seemed to be falling apart. The company's sales strategy of head-to-head competition with IBM had turned out to be a major mistake. The computer industry shakeout that had been forecast by analyst Stephen T. McClellan (President of the Computer Industry Analysts Group in 1984) was finally happening, though it took a few more years to run its course. His prescient contribution was that:

"Any company that hopes to survive and compete over the long haul has to offer systems and network compatibility (not just within their own product line, but across other vendors such as IBM) with the ability to tie into large data communications and computer networks. Machines can't stand alone, out in the cold, unable to tie into other machines."

In addition, fault tolerance, though still important and a strong selling point, wasn't commanding the price premium it once had. According to an article by Judy Ward in the *Financial Times* in 1995, *"the market simply wanted faster machines at lower prices."* Other key Tandem features such as the ability to effectively distribute data seemed to not be able to garner enough traction in the market. Even its requester/server architecture (a precursor to what became client/server architectures), because it was a proprietary, just wasn't getting the market attention that it deserved. In Tandem's core market for fault-tolerant systems, the company was losing ground and couldn't hold its own. According to *Forbes* magazine in September 1993, half of new fault-tolerant systems sales were going to Tandem competitors such as Stratus, Sequoia and DEC. Jimmy, the charismatic Pied Piper whom we'd happily followed for years, seemed to have led us down a path that looked like it was going off a cliff. As stock options went deeper and deeper underwater, a key motivational incentive was lost. One colleague had such unwavering faith that alledgedly he had never cashed a single option in his 12 years with the firm; options that by 1992 were now likely worthless, with no perceived hope of recovery. If true he would have gone from penniless to paper millionaire and back again in a little over a decade.

Though the EDS team survived the first round of layoffs in the summer of 1991 (with about 700 employees, or 6 percent of the workforce, let go), employee morale was at an all-time low, so it was a painful work environment. Jimmy had been reluctant to make this tough layoff decision because a "no layoffs" policy had been an important part of successfully getting through the other downturns in the company's history. But eventually he realized, as shared with *The Wall Street Journal* in

1994, *"if I didn't do my job, no one would have a job."* Unfortunately, instead of ripping off the bandage quickly, his decision-making process took so long that the impact on employees (both those who stayed and those who left) was much harder than it need have been. Revenue and net income sank, hitting a loss of $41 million in fiscal 1992, the company's first ever. Another aggressive cost-cutting exercise was undertaken with more layoffs and a couple of plant closures. For those who had been at Tandem for a long time, it was almost like a sacred trust had been broken.

I fell in on myself and couldn't see a way through, ending up in a therapist's office with a series of severe panic attacks. In addition, my work relationships were turning extremely toxic and my personal life was also a mess. My grandparents on my mother's side had passed on, my youngest brother had died of AIDS, a relationship that I thought was going to last the rest of my life had ended and a dear colleague, Stephanie Steiger (a Tandem lawyer), had died of breast cancer. My second sabbatical was due, so when the opportunity availed itself I took one of the layoff packages. At the end of July 1992, my love affair with Tandem came to an end. I left the company and retreated for several months to my cabin in the wilderness north of Toronto to lick my wounds and later moved on to what turned out to be a 14-year career as an independent management consultant.

Things got worse in 1993. In July of that year the cuts went even deeper with another 1,800 employees laid off and a 5 percent cut in compensation instituted for all employees. As later reported in *Computer Weekly* in January 1996:

"It has been thought that the market for fault-tolerant systems would be better protected from the winds of open system change than more general computing environments. But it turns out that the band of customers willing to pay the extra premium for fault-tolerant systems is getting smaller both because general computing systems have become more reliable and the number of resources needed to support those systems will be fewer and fewer."

Things continued downhill even with new product introductions such as ServerNet, the industry's first system area network that enabled high-speed connections between processors and I/O devices without having to use the processor as a concentrator, and the first commercial implementation of an ANSI-41 AC to support global needs for increased network security. But as Tony Turner (#624) once again articulated so well:

"Somewhere between $1 billion and $2 billion in revenue, Treybig had exhausted his Tandem momentum. While much of the original vision was manifest, Tandem missed some big plays, really big plays. Old friends and confidants moved on. Replace-

ments were left to attend their own interests. The Beer Busts fragmented. Coherent excitement became corporate, an oxymoronic concept."

In late 1995, Jimmy was appointed Chairman of the Board and Roel Pieper was appointed CEO. Pieper had formerly worked for Software AG and AT&T and had been hired by Tandem to run UB Networks, which Tandem acquired in 1988. (Formerly Ungermann-Bass, UB Networks was the first large networking company independent of any computer manufacturer that specialized in connecting large enterprise computer systems and devices from multiple vendors). As was reported in the *San Jose Mercury News* in June 1997:

"Roel Pieper exhibited none of the sentimentality for Tandem-as-industry-icon that arguably hindered the firm's previous chief from making tough decisions. He pushed the company from proprietary computing toward industry standards that increased its marketability; then forced the incorporation of Microsoft Windows NT that pushed Tandem into a high volume/low profit margin sector."

In January 1996, Treybig finally left the firm and headed back to Texas to join a venture firm called Austin Ventures. As Jimmy (#1) said later, in June of 1997 in the *San Jose Mercury News*:

"If I had to do it all over, I really think that I should have left earlier… when you start a company and hire so many of the people… it's like a marriage. But the institution has to keep going."

Soon after, Pieper hired Enrico Pesatori, formerly Digital Equipment Corporation's Vice President and General Manager of the Computing Systems division, as President and COO. According to *The Wall Street Journal* in October of 1996, Tandem continued to *"find it hard to control costs and compete on price in new business areas."* Unbeknownst to most, the real job of Pieper and Pesatori was to ready the company for sale. In June 1996, this effort paid off and Tandem was sold to Compaq Computers (a PC company) in a $3 billion stock swap. The deal was considered a win for shareholders at the time, the view being that it was the only way the company could ensure its long-term survival. The markets reacted positively and the stock price rose more than a third in very short order.

Though I was long gone, interactions with employees who stayed behind, and some sales planning work that I did for the new Tandem in 1997, told me that life was not great under the Compaq regime, especially in the sales organization. The PC business generally involved interactions with the purchasing department whereas Tandem sales were primarily driven through the information systems department via the office of the Chief Information Officer, then a new buzzword. Though billed as a merging of equals, it soon became apparent that the Compaq folks saw it more like an acquisition. The subsequent arguments around who was going to the lead the sales process became legendary. As Gary Bonhiver, a 24-year Tandem consultant and later president of GoodWinter Database Architects, said a few years later, *"Tandem under Compaq initially was a disaster... Compaq just didn't know how to sell them."* Or as Tony Turner [#624] said:

"Compaq didn't swallow or absorb Tandem, nor did Tandem under various aliases become a parasite. Although tormented by Houston [Compaq headquarters] to the point that the sales force and a lot of other smart people left, Tandem contributed operating margins and retained an independence that most acquisitions especially DEC would have died for. It became a jewel in the tarnished Compaq crown."

Consolidation in the computer industry continued and in May of 2002, after a contentious proxy fight, HP acquired Compaq in a $19 billion deal. Tandem became HP's NonStop Enterprise Division with plans to move its NonStop servers to Intel's Itanium processors. Pauline Nish was appointed the General Manager for the now 1,500-person division (way down from the high of 9,500 in 1990). Universal belief at the time was that HP would ultimately be a better partner, especially in the area of selling and supporting Tandem systems, which generally has turned out to be true.

So with a stroke of a pen Tandem came full circle and returned to its HP roots, where it still resides today. As Tony Turner mused, *"Why would its identity persist through starvation and neglect and two very complex mergers, and emerge much as it started? Therein lies a story that is inspiring because it makes so much sense."* The division still generates several billion dollars in revenue for HP and interestingly enough, many of the key customers from the early days are still its major customers. Even today, with acres of server farms, there are some companies that can't afford to have any downtime and 99.99999% availability and reliability is still critical.

In hindsight, like a prism that separates white light into a spectrum of colors and distorts whatever is viewed through it, it's hard to really nail down what happened and why the company crashed and burned. The technology gurus say it was because architecture built on 16-bit couldn't easily shift to 32-bit processing and that the company missed the shift to desktop computing with its underlying client/server architecture. Guardian's requester/server approach was very similar, but it was proprietary in a world that was moving to open systems. Creating open fault tolerance was a difficult technical challenge. Even more difficult was creating solutions based on common standards that would enable systems from different vendors to talk to each other. Some business school pundits argued that Tandem needed economies of scale and should have partnered with a bigger firm, but with which firm might have been suitable is open to speculation. Besides at the time, Tandem had built over 20 years of sentimentality about being a independent force in the computer industry.

Few inside the company could envision a time when the centralized mainframe wouldn't play a major role. Some argued that going head-to-head against IBM had been a bad idea as it escalated marketing and administrative costs tremendously. The needed demonstration and selling capabilities via competitive benchmarks and financial support for big, complex multi-million dollar deals required deep pockets that Tandem didn't have. Service guarantees created more risk than the risk-averse finance folks were willing to take on. In addition, supporting new product development timelines took far longer than they had previously. From a practical point of view, a contributing factor may also have been that traditional large companies had trouble seeing a former mini-computer vendor taking on the mantle of a mainframe provider.

There is no question that a significant NIH (not-invented-here) mentality existed that would ebb and flow over the years, Jimmy's (#1) remarks at a TOPS event in 1992 notwithstanding:

"Every company must regularly take a new look at the future. It must re-examine its financial framework, reconsider its operating models, and reexamine its product and marketing strategies for winning. We must ask ourselves, 'How can we have advantage? Where are we the best? How can we grow?'"

For a time, client/server computing was dismissed internally as a concept that Tandem's requester/server architecture already possessed, missing completely the point of open systems. Often there was a strong resistance to spending time in a formal way assessing market forces that were constantly swirling about the company. In later years listening to industry trends unless forced to by dropping revenue or shrinking profit margins was a challenge and for all the hype about a commitment to customer satisfaction, sometimes the company became collectively stone-deaf. Many also forgot that a key to early success had been not just the elegance of the hardware and software architecture, but the fact that competitive alternatives were two or three times the price of a Tandem. Tandem at its core was a hardware company, even though much of its success was its superior software technology. Application solutions and services were not a core competency, but that was exactly the direction that the industry was going.

Inside Tandem's hallowed halls, there was also dark side at the intersection of leadership, culture and employee expectations that was not talked about much. Some have argued that things went south when the older "professional" managers arrived in the mid-1980s. Though their expertise was needed, they also brought some biases and prejudices that didn't become apparent until many years later. Lateral transfers to learn skills in a completely different function became a thing of the past as often did the concept of promotion from within. Equal opportunity for women and a proactive desire for a diverse workforce seemed to take a back seat. Sexual harassment became a way of life for some, and it took a very public lawsuit for management to begin to take the issue seriously. The unofficial political network took on a whole new set of nuances, when one also had to keep on top of friendships, interests and all sorts of other types of relationships. What began as a small problem of managers not practicing what the culture preached, or just following it for show, became much more commonplace. Many times those employees who complained were not supported by management as well as they should have been.

Upon reflection, the bigger issue may have been the degree to which the company revolved around Treybig with his big, charismatic personality. Ad hoc, on-the-fly problem solving, though great when times were good, wasn't anywhere near as workable when things got really tough, as they did when Tandem confronted the industry movement to open systems. Over the years, fewer and fewer people were able to push back effectively when they saw poor decisions being made. Meanwhile, under the surface were very real feelings of betrayal that for many of us took a long time to heal. The truth was that there were many aspects of the Tandem philosophy that just couldn't stand up to the pressure of a multi-billion dollar organization and not enough effort was placed on helping both the organization and the people in it, especially the old-timers, deal with the changes to the philosophy that were going to be needed. As William Eberwein [#5366] shared in 2009:

"The Tandem culture was great, but hindsight shows we had it backwards. A great culture does not produce profit. Profit produces a great culture. Obviously one feeds the other to some degree. But the engine is profitability. We had huge margins, and were the only game in town. As soon as we had serious competition, we had to make prudent decisions. There are any number of companies with great cultures that disappeared when their niche dried up: Silicon Graphics is a good example, Netscape, Palm are others. Today's Google is a good one to watch. As soon as things get tight, the bring-your-dog-to-work, order-what-you-want-from-the-menu, hang loose culture will change, and we'll get stories from the long-time employees on how great it used to be. Greed is one of the deadly sins, true. But making a great product to fill a market need and making as much profit as possible at a fair price is as close to unalloyed good as can be imagined. 'Make a contribution, make money and have fun,' as Jimmy used to say."

And yet under HP, "The Tandem" lives on, according to Tony Turner (#624):

"It has held some of its markets and many of its big customers. The faithful have nurtured it like Neanderthals tended a fire. Jack Mauger has a 'Mega Tandem' in the competency center that is to the transactional mind as an Atlas was to a bottle rocket. Its transactional scalability to tens of thousands per second and consistency across ter-abytes and hundreds of networked processes, about a close to zero latency as you can get. IBM, Sun and HP and 10,000 Linux guys on the open network are and have been trying to build fault-tolerant scalable servers. Treybig built one, message-based, peer-coupled and shared-nothing before a lot of these people were born in less than 20 man-years and $1 million."

The true testament to how people felt took place in September 2002. Former employees organized a company reunion at the Bay Meadows Race Course in San Mateo. Over 1,600 employees came to spend the afternoon reminiscing, meeting old friends and sharing a lot of laughs. As Mike Cassidy of the *San Jose Mercury News*, who reported on the event, picked up:

"The loyalty to Treybig and the old Tandem is deep. There was talk of Tandem's family feeling, and empowered employees and the serious fun Tandem workers had. There was a story about Treybig throwing rubber snakes into a crowd of sales people and exhorting them to 'kill a varmint'—the varmints being IBM and DEC. As Jan Seamons, one of the key organizers and long-time employee said, 'Places like Tandem only come once in a lifetime. The sort of company-as-culture that was part of Tandem or the old HP or the old Apple just isn't the sort of company being built in Silicon Valley today.'"

As Jerrianne Churchill [#2971], Tandem's long-serving manager of Trade Shows Marketing, said, *"The world has changed, corporate America doesn't value employees the way Tandem valued us."*

As noted in a graduate thesis written by Olivia Herriford (#6551):

"The core values that underpinned the culture placed equal importance on self and others, individual and organization. Self-oriented components were balanced with other-oriented beliefs. Importance of the individual was tempered by respect for people and their diversity. Hard work was balanced by the belief in shared success. The focus on innovation and creativity was given a longer view with the expectation of respon-sible action and ownership. Open and effective communication was made possible by honesty and trust. Tandem was a success and had such a positive impact on the people who worked there because it recognized (whether formally or not) the importance of balanced values. Tandem and its early leaders knew that to be effective as an organi-zation, its 'self' needed to truly engage with others."

Jimmy heads to Texas 1996 - Austin American Statesman September 1996

Tandem Memorabilia Table at the 2002 Reunion - Tandem Alumni Yahoo Groups Posting

Jan Seamons, Val Cisneros , Amy Fritz, Drew, Jimmy, jockey, Gail Ayres, Nancy Richardson, Nancy Twomey. Donna Winslow, Sandra Bachman - Winslow Collection

Reunion Tribute Sign Up - Ewing Collection

Jimmy at the 2002 Reunion - Winslow Collection

2002 Reunion Wanderings: Looking for old friends - Ewing Collection

2002 Reunion: Sharing a meal under tents Duane Binger (green), Gary Sabo (purple) - Ewing Collection

Top: Reunion Crowds Bottom: Jimmy gives another barn-burner speech- Tandem Alumni Yahoo! Groups Posting

The Wake and the End of an Era

Tandem France sponsored sailboat race in 1986 - Tournier Collection

IN MARCH 2009 A posting made its way across the internet on the Tandem_Alumni Yahoo! Groups social networking site. It advised all Tandem former employees that the Fremont Manufacturing Supply Chain facility had passed away and that on 25 February 2009 a tongue-in-cheek wake had been held with more than 150 people in attendance with Scott Davis reading a eulogy and additional comments made by Jerry Peterson and Jimmy Treybig. As Bob Wilcox (#6634) wrote:

"The facility was born in January of 1995 and has now passed to the four winds in February of 2009. Many significant accomplishments have taken place over the illustrious 15-year career of the facility. Thousands and thousands of orders have been shipped to several thousand customers made up of thousands and thousands of CPUs, containing thousands of miles of cables and generating billions of dollars of revenue with incredible margins. An extraordinary accomplishment made by extraordinary people impacting services, businesses, people, and nations all over the world. The Fremont Manufacturing Supply Chain facility has left its mark on the world. As remarked by a mourner to a certain former Vice President, 'There isn't anything anyone could throw at us that we couldn't handle.' Not to belittle the previously mentioned accomplishment, but just as significant is the impact the Fremont Manufacturing Supply Chain facility has had on the local community. They have donated 104,000 pounds of food to Second Harvest Food Bank, given 1,120 presents to the Giving Tree, supplied 2,369 backpacks loaded with school supplies, given 71.25 gallons of blood to the blood bank, and donated $16,000 to charity. They also made twice-yearly trips to local a local special needs school giving their time, talents, energy and their hearts for special needs kids providing them with fun and games. The Fremont Manufacturing Supply Chain has not only been business-minded but has been uniquely community-minded as well. Many who gathered to attend the 'wake' beamed with pride for their work with or their connection to the Fremont Manufacturing Supply Chain facility. R.I.P. Fremont Supply Chain Operations, 1995-2009."

Tandem 16 System Introduction

SUMMARY OF TANDEM 16 FEATURES

Tandem 16 Computer System (fail-safe, transaction oriented, easily adaptable)

- Two to sixteen processor modules
- Dual, high-speed interprocessor buses
- High-speed, burst-multiplexed input/output channel
- Multiprocessing, multiprogramming, transaction oriented, fail-safe operating system (T/TOS)
- Virtual file system

Processor Modules

- Microprogrammed (100 nanosecond cycle time)
- Sixteen bit data paths and memory addressing
- Up to 512k bytes memory per processor module
- Memory mapping (four separate maps: system data, system code, user data, user code)
- Up to 128k bytes addressable through each map
- 500 nanosecond semiconductor memory access time (including mapping and error correction)
- 800 nanosecond core memory access time (including mapping and parity checking)
- 122 instructions (including string manipulation and doubleword arithmetic)
- Stack architecture (memory stack and register stack)
- Procedure oriented hardware
- Memory references: direct or indirect with or without indexing to global, local, procedure parameters, top of stack, or system global data areas and to core area. Word, doubleword, byte addressing
- No machine instruction can write into code area (non-modifiable code)
- All programs are inherently re-entrant and relocatable
- I/O, bus receive, and instruction execution can occur concurrently
- Next instruction prefected while current instruction executes
- Hardware power fail/auto restart
- Hardware multiply/divide
- Maximum of five microseconds to call operating system procedures

Interprocessor Buses

- Two paths between each processor module
- 10 megabyte transfer for each bus
- Packet-multiplexed transfers between any number of processor modules
- Block transfers of 1 to 32,767 bytes
- Both buses used simultaneously

25

Features of the first T16 documentation prepared by Jerry Everett

Input/Output Channels

- Dual-port Controllers
- Data transfers occur at memory speed (4 megabytes per second with semiconductor memory)
- Up to 256 devices per processor module
- Burst-multiplexed transfers from any number of devices
- Block transfers of 1 to 4,094 bytes

T/TOS Operating System

- Multiprocessing
- Multiprogramming
- Geographical independence
- Process structure
- Memory management function makes virtual memory invisible to users
- Processes scheduled for execution according to priority (0-255)
- Sharable code areas handled automatically
- Up to 256 processes per processor module

File System

- Two paths to each i/o device; file system automatically switches paths
- All devices and programs are accessed as files
- Geographic independence
- Timeout associated with each i/o operation

For more information regarding the Tandem 16 Computer System, refer to the following manuals:

- Tandem 16 System Manual (detailed description of system from a hardware and software standpoint and information on making an application "fail-safe")
- Tandem 16 Programming Manual (describes T/TAL, using the file system, using the process control procedures, using the Tandem-supplied utility procedures, picking up the parameter message from the Command Interpreter, and using the DEBUG feature)
- Tandem 16 Text Editor Manual (describes the EDIT commands and how to communicate with the editor from another process)
- Tandem 16 System Generation Manual (describes how to configure a system and how to run the Tandem-supplied TOSYSGEN program)
- Tandem 16 Operation Manual (describes how to run the Command Interpreter program, explains the Command Interpreter command set, how to remove and mount disc volumes, how to "down" system modules for maintenance or repair, how to run programs).

26

More Features of the Original T16

Charles Johnson   - That Old Bike Magic

They tilted at windmills, that just might be giants.
Hell, they really were giants and steel-booted their pants!!!

They made redundant satellites, and Dynamites and expensive faxes.
They got Rainbowed, Crystalled, Catalysed and wrote off their taxes.

(In spite of all this, 6530's did Arabic and Hebrew against the grain,
From the right, then numbers from the left, and from the right again)

Any of these failures would have destroyed a normal corporation,
For Tandem NonStop, it was just another round of self –exploration!!!

They fought the Big Blue and the DEC and the UNIX – all flavours,
They ported to NT and really made it work, and fell into disfavour....

First they looked like a mini, a cluster and client-server machine,
A transaction system, a networked half relational database was seen,

Then a fully relational SQL RDBMS was made according to Gray/Reuter,
But for Triggers, Referential Integrity and Naming, the reconnoiter

(Thank you Franco Putzolu. And Bless You. And Keep You)

Then they looked like a database of record (not at the DMV)
A Mac Server, a Windows Server, a UNIX personality!!!

Then a worm-holed, super-cluster, by Dr. Bob Horst was sailed,
And against all belief, ServerNet scaled and scaled and scaled...

(I still don't believe that one, IBM worked on it for years.
It just can't work, but it has laid to rest all my fears)

They shipped two releases of NonStop SQL/NT, on ServerNet Clustered,
To the Paris Stock Exchange, and then pulled it and floundered.

Then with Java and open interfaces, and the ZLE they rally,
And they've made the large accounts SQL/TMF/RDF-based fully.

Finally, to the amazement of all, the Sabre account did fall.

The TPF account that no relational database, could ever replace,
Was won by little old NonStop, Right in IBM"s face.

So after spending on P-Sysplex, and DB@, a billion dollars a year,
Think they can beat NonStop? Perhaps, but listen here...

For all those wonderful Tandem people, who would never give in,
With a dream, with a vision, and the faith that good stuff can win...

We have 7 (or 15) fundamentals, with cheap hardware we still do it,
We write loosely-coupled software, with messages all through it.

This means that whatever fails, and when the traffic gets thick,
We never send our bent pointers, and step on our D**K.

So those of us remaining are determined, and wearing a new HP coat,
To fulfill that dream with Carly and Pauline, and so here's a quote:

It's always been in the cards. You know IBM will now fall.
Non one could possibly believe it will happen, Except for Y'all.

Final Musings

Almost a Hole-in-One - Tournier Collection

IT'S SUNDAY MORNING ON a somewhat dull day. It's cloudy but doesn't feel like rain. But the wind shifted over the night and is now coming from the north and with it the smell of winter. Up here 200 miles north of Toronto, even though it is mid-August, the season has shifted. Fall will soon be upon us. I'm here huddled around my coffee, stacks of press clippings and issues of *NonStop News* and *Center* magazine all around me, rereading a pamphlet called Executive View Point—"Creating, Managing and Surviving High Growth." It was a speech that Jimmy gave in February 1989 as part of a "Distinguished Leaders in Silicon Valley" speaker series sponsored by De Anza College in Cupertino, later turned into a marketing piece and distributed to employees and customers. This speech was likely one of the few that Jimmy hadn't written himself, as it doesn't have the folksy feel and phrasing that

Jimmy speeches usually did. But it's impactful just the same both for companies and for individuals and their self-actualization efforts. His basic message was that *"no matter how you look at it, your ability to survive or to win is measured by growth—by successful growth."* The four basic premises he outlined in his speech that are fundamental to achieving such growth continue to resonate with me to this day.

- **"Leadership** – *that demands, crusades for, fights for, and sacrifices for growth. To be possessed about growth starts with visualizing your goals and setting them high enough. People have to be motivated and share in the company's success, i.e., the benefits of growth. In addition, what's also important is creating an environment that accepts failure and allows for innovative people with unusual ideas to be heard. You have to be willing to listen to people.*

- **A Vision** – *that will set the framework for your potential growth rate, then execution, timing and luck determine how much growth you realize. The most difficult part of having a vision is creating it, deciding how to communicate it and educating people so that they share the new vocabulary and a new understanding of the company's direction.*

- **Proper people, teamwork and work environment concepts** – *with a philosophy that is published, shared repeatedly… through formalized systems, processes and programs and supported by management.*

- **Focus on meeting the needs of your customers, not just selling to them**– *you have to love them and measure your success as customers see you, discover what they need to make them successful.*

"As a leader, you also have to protect yourself against a number of infections caused by growth including the potential for arrogance, xenophobia (i.e. having a closed mind), and burnout and finally, figure out how to learn on the job quickly."

Some of the things that Jimmy (#1) said he'd learned that are just as true today as they were so many years ago:

- *"Hire other people better than yourself and listen to them. Avoid hiring in your own image or somebody who thinks like yourself.*
- *Use your Board of Directors and allow them to help*
- *Recognize that as a leader you go through stages and your role changes within the company*
- *Learn to be a manager using classical processes (with strong legal & financial staffs)*
- *Find some balance in your own life. Deal with your own growth and health."*

Perhaps like Icarus, Tandem flew too close to the sun. The wax on its wings melted and it fell to the earth. But Tandem's underlying values were simple, as described in the original Five-Year-Plan and repeated below:

"All people are good, but not all good people could make good decisions. People, the workers, the management and the company are all the same but at the end of the day, someone has to be accountable and lead the way. Every single person in the company must understand the essence of the business, but more importantly understand and have consensus on the strategic forces that are driving the business and the implications of them on the business. Every employee must benefit from the company's success and also share the burden of lack of success. Management must create an environment where all of the above can happen and its ability to do so over a long period of time is critical."

Until recently I was an employee at one of the next generation of Silicon Valley companies that have evolved. The company line says that people are one of its most important assets, that retaining good people is important, but the practical demonstration of these ideas is much more difficult to see. Their concept of "company as family" is nothing like what I experienced at Tandem and sounds hollow as the layoff notices attest. Unstructured communications have gone the way of the dinosaur. Beer Busts are too big a legal liability and sabbaticals too expensive. Nobody has a swimming pool for employees with their company name imprinted on the bottom - that's reserved for football, baseball and basketball stadiums. Most have no stock options, no free sodas and limited cafeteria meal choices, but there is a nice gym, a health clinic and on-site daycare, so all is not lost. Manager doors are allegedly open, but most of the time it's not clear that crossing the threshold is a great idea. Every announcement asks for feedback, but it's not clear if anyone on the other side takes heed. Annual employee satisfaction surveys take place and management teams go through the motions of reviewing the results, but few areas of concern seem to get addressed in any concrete way. Video on demand is the modern-day equivalent of TTN, while email continues to remain a mainstay. Work has become 24/7 as a result of smartphones and instant messaging technology and talking on the phone is almost a thing of the past. Travel expense funding for global or regional team meetings is rare so team building is a challenge. The idea of company loyalty seems almost archaic.

But for me, and many others, many of the collegial relationships established at Tandem are still alive and well. The Tandem_Alumni Groups on Yahoo! and LinkedIn continue to operate with over 2,500 members on each. When small groups of us get together, talk often circulates back to the early days in the 1980s and wistfulness takes over as we recall the hard work and the laughs. As Justin Simonds (#4521) said:

"It was the hardest but most rewarding job that I certainly ever had and I was always proud to say I worked for Tandem. Jimmy, if you're listening, you allowed many of us to set the high-water mark in our careers. But Tandem was the Camelot of the computer industry. For one brief, shining moment, there was Tandem."

Whatever the circumstances, it was profoundly sad to leave Tandem, but what an incredible love affair it was while it lasted. For most employees, their time at Tandem was a life-changing experience and for some, the highlight of their career. So it's best, in the end, to let the former employees speak for themselves:

- *"Tandem taught me that people could get along when they disagree. People at Tandem were passionate about their work and about quality and customer service. That often led to heated discussions (and more than a little bitching behind closed doors). But I never lost the feeling that we all shared the same goals and we could work it out. I think that has served me well over the years."* [Ian Evans #12776]

- *"Tandem, probably never to be equaled again in this lifetime, represented care for its employees, high aspirations, untiring energies and best corporate philosophies and practices that were, if not always perfect, at least diligently and thoughtfully pursued and applied. I personally interpret my allegiances to Tandem and her people in much the same way that I am bound to my U.S. Marine Corps and my buddies therein: Semper Fidelis, which translates to 'Always Faithful!' We all have much of substance in common and so many wonderful memories, but the bond we have is strong and there is a whole lot of love shared among us, one for another and one for all! We have something that is quite rare and, again, nearly, if not completely, non-existent in the corporate world, both then and now. I too am very proud and quite inspired by my years and associations at Tandem. Our systems were not the only things that were NonStop (products and culture combined for an unstoppable accomplishment, an irresistible force not to be denied)."* [Bob Cron #7061]

- *"My 17 years with TNDM were the best of my career and life. No one could touch us in so many ways. It was and still is so great to be that proud of working and contributing to THE best company ever. Jimmy would do anything for us and we would and did go to the wall, through the fire, you name it, for him and the rest of our teammates."* [Rich Giandana #772]

- *"It was a great ride for 20 years and I wouldn't have missed it for anything. Probably the greatest company every created, with some of the greatest people ever."* [Don Nelson #4534]

- *"Y'know, Tandem bled into the fabric of my life. My friends were all Tandemites, my wife (Ellen Betz) was a Tandemite. The birth of both of my kids was announced in* NonStop News, *I had four sabbaticals—fulfilling a lifelong dream of extended trekking in the High Sierra (five weeks in the backcountry...twice!). I've kept every copy of Tandem Systems Review, Focus, Atomix Comix, Center and NonStop News. I still pull Post-It notes off my Rosewood note holder, write with my Cross pen, display my 5, 10, 15 and 20 year plaques (sadly, only the first two have Jimmy's signature on them), jealously guard my CASTLE (TXP) poster, Armadillos typing on Dragons under oak trees, and assorted NonStop coffee cups—including a very rare yellow Tandem Mackie mug... before the fault-tolerant handle design! I was a kid when I started, and I've grown. Professionally and personally. Shaped by the camaraderie, the culture, the fascinating science and artful design of The Architecture... it was a strange twist of fate... and the story continues to this day, on the Itanium platform. So many challenges and opportunities. Support trips from Vancouver to Louisville, Boston to Hong Kong... and everywhere in between. My network of friends spans the globe, thanks to the Tandem family... and I am the richer for it."* [Pete Kronberg #6276]

- *"I can only say that these were the best years there ever was, working for the best company there ever was and I dare say at least 80 percent of this was due to James G. Treybig, personally, his unique style, his emphasis on the idea that people make a company (not the other way around), and his genuine interest in the people working for his company."* [Henry Norman #3827]

- *"My experience at Tandem taught me how to be a team player and have the customer interests at heart—while still bringing in revenue. We always went that extra mile for customers, and we were rewarded with being number one in customer satisfaction for many years. I was proud of that designation."* [Genie Price #8010]

- *"Tandem is my synonym for great people, hard work and fun. The first time I heard a speech by Jimmy, I realized on the spot what was the true meaning of leadership, vision and what it meant to create an environment where people can do more than they ever think they could."* [Jean Dagenais #7323]

- *"Tandem was a place where we were encouraged to take creative risks, try things we weren't sure would work, and collaborate on projects that required heavy teamwork. I worked in the Creative Services Department in Cupertino for over six years ('87–'94) where we were able to push the technical boundaries of graphical innovation. What a team! In those early days we started one of the valley's first large-scale desktop publishing departments, extended our full-service photography department to include bleeding-edge digital photography, experimented with multimedia before it was commonplace, and generally had a blast supporting the myriad corporate parties and conferences across the country and abroad."* [Annie Valva]

- *"I had worked in the Singapore government service, taught in the university, been in legal practice prior to joining Tandem as the Regional Counsel in Asia Pacific, then moved on to other U.S. IT companies but none can match up to the special bond I felt while at Tandem. It is definitely the people who make such a great corporate culture—that drives people to want to maintain ties, relive and recapture the charm, even years after they have left the company."* [Rosalind T.]

- *"Working in an environment where no one was more important that anyone else. I treasure the time I had there, and took much of what I learned to other companies I ran. I ran into a guy several years ago who used to work for me in a software company. He said he owned a software company in Washington, and that he owed much of his success to what he learned from me. Well much of that came from Jimmy, and the culture he created, and I wonder if Jimmy has any idea of how many people beyond all of us Tandem Alumni that have benefited from his visions."* [Skip Yazel]

- *"If I had to pick one theme... a theme that would carry us forth... it would be a familiar one. It would be 'change'—the need for it and our amazing capacity to adjust to it; the important things it allowed us to accomplish and the responsibilities it places on each of us. I feel incredibly lucky to have worked with such a fabulous set of people at a company that has shaped my professional life more than any other company I have worked at."* [Mala Chandra #4490]

- *"We all know that wonderfulness disintegrates in reality. There are a million stories in the naked city. Nonetheless as a zygote, 'The Tandem' had more future DNA than anything but the Macintosh and the networked workstations that came six years later. There is no doubt that Treybig was the daddy or at least one of the parents."* [Tony Turner #624.]

At most companies, executives are the people in the corner offices who are rarely seen or heard except via official company pronouncements, except to the select few who are part of the senior management team. At Tandem, Jimmy was a man of the people and we loved him blemishes and all. In the history of Silicon Valley, James G. Treybig is probably the only chief executive who has ever distilled his wisdom on everything from hiring to asset management on a single three-foot by two-foot piece of paper. In type about half the size of the letters on this page, he codified 100 management concepts into little homilies. Each little saying (like fund growth with equity, use debt for insurance, never compromise on quality in hiring) was connected with an intricate pattern of feedback loops, so that anyone who looks at the chart with a magnifying glass coiuld see how something like asset management affected employee wealth and benefits. As Jimmy (#1) said at the time:

"This chart shows how everything ties together and is important. Every employee at Tandem gets a copy. Why do we put in on one piece of paper. Because it's interesting! Asset management is damn boring, but it's important. So you want everyone to understand why it's important, what they do that impacts it, how asset management

impacts other things. It's important that every employee understands the company's direction. You truly can't manage 100 percent growth in the classical sense. There's less emphasis on management and more on information, on systems of providing information so people can work independently. You have to work to delegate as much responsibility as fast as you can. You want everyone to understand the fundamentals. You've got to concentrate on everyone understanding how to make the right decisions overall."

What can I say. It sure was something!!!

Filling in the swimming pool behind Building 2 in Cupertino Campus 2012

Tandem Timeline 1974-1997

Our Beloved Leader - Tamburri Collection

IN CELEBRATION OF TANDEM'S 10th Anniversary, an article in *Center* magazine reviewed the previous 10 years from three perspectives namely what was going on in the world, what was going on in the computer industry and what was going on at Tandem. Later in 1997, the Tandem portion was updated and provides a neat synopsis of key company historic events.

- 1974 – Tandem was one of two companies funded in this recession year by Kleiner Perkins and Pitch Johnson. Tandem created with the vision of a NonStop Computing Platform.

- 1975 – NonStop system announced in a two-page *BusinessWeek* article, which leads to an order from Citibank; Sam Wiegand starts the sales and marketing department, 39 employees at year-end.

- 1976 – Introduces first commercial fault-tolerant computer system. Year ends with 10 customers including its first F500 customer Tandy. First systems shipped to Citibank and Thyssen Steel in Germany; internal email system is born, 10 customers and 82 employees.

- 1977 – Guardian OS announced, HQ moves to Building 1 Vallco Parkway in Cupertino, Tandem becomes profitable, issues stock at $11.50 per share, with revenues of $7.7M and 170 employees.

- 1978 – First issue *NonStop News* (June), ground breaking Valco Buildings 2 & 3, First International Tandem Users Group (ITUG) meeting held, memory increased to 2MB and enhanced microcode; first 100-share bonus option for all employees. Revenues reach $24.3M with 540 employees.

- 1979 – Revenue reaches $56M with 949 employees, Neufahrn SIT and Watsonville manufacturing are opened, April 1979, Tandem is announced as #4 on the list of *Inc.* Magazine's top 100 fastest growing small companies with 137 employees $24M in sales.

- 1980 – Rated #1 in Customer Satisfaction on Grumman-Cowen/Datamation Poll (first of four successive years at #1). *Inc.* Magazine ranks Tandem as the fastest-growing public company in America, revenues exceed $100M; CCC opens and holds its first customer visit, First and Only Incredible Hunk contest won by Steve Davoli and Dennis McEvoy. The pool behind Building 2 opens. Revenue is $109M with 1632 employees.

- 1981 – Stock splits 3 for 1. First European TUG meeting. Revenues hit $208M with 3017 employees; Reston facility announced, first TOPS trip to San Diego, first issue of *Center* magazine, and Austin Facility opens.

- 1982 – Included in Electronic Business 100; first TEI held in Monterey for the Banking Industry, ICON division formed, FY revenues are $312M with 3940 employees.

- 1983 – 10,000 6530 terminal shipped, NonStop TXP and 6100 coms subsystem announced (commercial use of fiber optic extensions to build clusters of systems); First East Coast TEI for Financial Services in Reston, and in Europe (London Manufacturing and Banking); Alliance Program started, FY revenues reach $418M with 4613 employees.

- 1984 – Listed in F500, over 150 systems installed worldwide, High Performance Research Center opens in Frankfurt; Tandem systems used at the Los Angeles Summer Olympics with employee Chris Cavanaugh winning a gold in 4x100 freestyle; FY revenues reach $448.5M with 5186 employees.

- 1985 – Introduces first disk storage facilities that can be serviced while online (V8 & XL8)

- 1987 – Listed on NYSE and reaches $1B in revenue, acquires Attalla, and develops the first commercially deployed Service Control Point (SCP) outside of the AT&T network.

- 1988 – Introduces the first fault-tolerant SCP, launches the first relationship data base via NonStop SQL, Fortune names Tandem's distributed database management technology amongst the "100 products that make America Best.

- 1989 – NonStop Cyclone introduced but the company recorded its first quarterly loss.

- 1990 – Introduces NonStop Integrity S2 server, first fault-tolerant UNIX system.

- 1992 – Launches NonStop Integrity S-series, the first fully Network Equipment Building Systems (NEBS) compliant fault- tolerant UNIX system.

- 1993 – Launches Himalaya.

- 1994 – Introduces ServerNet technology, the industry's first system area network that enables high-speed connections between processors and I/O devices without having to use the processor as a concentrator.

- 1995 – Responds to the global need for increased network security by introducing the first commercial implementation of an ANSI-41 AC.

- 1996 – Brings the first commercially available system area network implementation to market deploying ServerNet architecture in the NS Integrity S4000.

- 1997 – Compaq acquires Tandem; the New York Stock Exchanges Tandem installation reaches its one billionth transaction (number of shares traded) per day.

Stock Certificate engraving when Tandem moved from NASDAQ to NYSE in 1987 - Bolen Collection

Tandem Philosophy Jimmy's Talk 1980

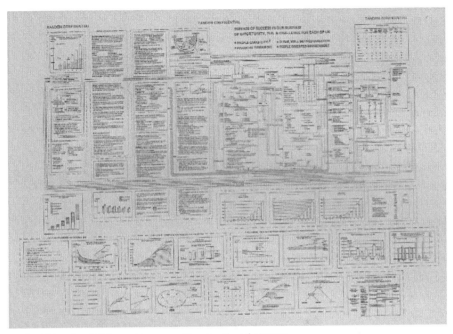

Tandem Philosophy - 1980 Success Measures and Learning About the Business

IN EARLY **1980,** JIMMY decided to document Tandem's business, leadership and people cultural tenets onto a single 2-foot by 3-foot piece of paper. Each Vice President "owned" a particular area of the map, but was required to present to small groups of Tandem employees at monthly Philosophy classes not just their own areas of responsibility but also a peer's. Below is the complete talk as presented by Jimmy in its original form.

Tandem has just completed an extraordinary period of growth taking us form $0 to over $100 million in just 4½ years of shipping. We accomplished this while maintaining attractive profits and consistency in performance. These results were remarkably consistent with Tandem's original business plan formulated in 1974 and the only plan we had during our first five years.

We are now operating under a second plan, which could put us at the $1 billion level in 1985 with over 11,000 people, an increase of ten-fold in both revenues and *people over the next five years. There are many challenges and variables in such a plan that could impact our ability to meet it or might necessitate changing it. This was, of course, also true in our first plan.*

While success during the first five years can be attributed to a combination of many things, one major reason for our success was a clear direction and philosophy that everyone understood—primarily passed through "word of mouth." In a start-up company of 30 people, passing the philosophy by "word of mouth" is easy, and with 1,500 employees it is still possible. But as the company grows from 1,500 to 11,500 it becomes a much more difficult task to share the philosophy in this manner. The second reason we met our original plan was that individuals in each function had a clear understanding and respect for the problems and challenges of other functions and an understanding of the overall company framework for growth. This enabled individuals and managers to make independent decisions that were oriented toward the total company welfare. Understanding the company's goals is crucial in a high-growth company. Only the output of those individuals working in the same direction as the company has value. And management (overhead) is expended to correct spurious work, compounding the loss of productivity. High growth requires independent, or at most lightly supervised, decision-making. This is more difficult with the number of individuals and managers we have now and will have during the next five years. Finally one of our major challenges is, and will continue to be, developing our people.

In light of the [above], we have developed an integrated "Masters in Business Administration" which encompasses the framework of our plan. This document thus becomes our five-year planning framework, our management program, and in a different format, our employee development program.

Anything good must be simple. Most five-year plans are seen by only a few, and not at all by most of the people who must make the plan a reality. Furthermore, they sit forgotten in drawers. The intent is for everyone in the company to see ours, for each of us to understand what we must do to be successful, and finally, as the title implies, how being successful translates to fun, challenge and opportunity for us all... The major factors affecting our success [include]:

- *People capability*
- *Financial resources*
- *Clear, well-defined direction*
- *People-oriented environment*

These four factors are totally [inter]dependent. As an example, a poorly financed company eventually loses its best people, which destroy its environment, which further hurts it financially.

THE IMPORTANCE OF EACH INDIVIDUAL

One problem we face as Tandem becomes larger is that individuals no longer feel important, no longer believe they impact the company performance. This is absolutely not true. As an example, if we miss our pre-tax profit margins by five systems, our pre-tax profit drops to the bottom [of the list] of more successful computer companies. If we miss by 10 systems, we move into the category of poorly managed companies. If we exceed our targets and hold expenses, our pre-tax margins could approach [the leader] IBM. Obviously, a sales person that doesn't try, a poor service job, poor system design support and/or one slipped development project or just four or five people at Tandem can move us into the poorly managed category.

INTERNAL FINANCE

The next section deals with the profit statement, cost structure, balance sheet, and especially cash flow and asset management. Every manager must learn to fill in our balance sheet given accounts receivable and inventory levels plus profitability. The Five-Year Plan has charts [that] illustrate the impacts of given levels of performance. [with] industry data which illustrates the ranges of performance. Company-wide share options [can therefore have] a range of values depending on our performance. By missing our quarterly financial performance our profitability and revenue growth rate is down. This eventually reduces R&D and benefits, which must be funded by profits. It directly impacts measures of success, which will knock our price-earnings ratio down, which in turn, lowers our stock price. This raises our cost of capital (must sell more shares to obtain cash for growth), which lowers the earnings per share, which further lowers the PE ratio. This further lowers benefit/reward (less shares for employees) which lowers motivation, which hurts performance, which goes around [and around]. Poor asset management leads to decreased profits (less interest income), a weaker balance sheet (harder to sell our product) and high cash flow (need more cash to grow). This results in less R&D and drives many of the measures of success down. This lowers the stock price and increases the cost of capital at the same time you need more cash for growth. This is a [degenerative] loop—each time it gets worse and it gets worse again. Benefits/rewards are down, which affect motivation, which combined with less R&D, means fewer new products, and on around the loop again.

A company is a complex system with a huge number of interactions, dependencies and feedback loops such as this. Most people do not understand this and almost no training programs address it.

PEOPLE AND MANAGEMENT

The key to [people and management] is people-oriented managers who like and respect all people at any level. Nothing can correct a lack of this. The major role of key managers in [a high-growth company] includes:

- *Leadership*
- *People*
- *Strategy*
- *Creativity*
- *Communication*
- *Problems by exception*

Creativity is an important one for it is not the natural state of organizations. A creative person who is stamped "deviant" in one company might be a "hero" in another. Creativity must be demanded and rewarded by key managers. Building an organization in [a high-growth environment] where there will always be a lack of outstanding people is different than in a [low growth environment]. Remember, many organizations will work with outstanding people; none will work without outstanding people. First you pick your six best people. Then define an organization built around their interests and capabilities. If you do these two things, you are delegating responsibility (and therefore developing) your six best people, which is a major contribution to our future.

HIRING

Hiring is a critical function in all companies, but especially for new companies or high growth companies. It is affected by two loops, company success, which includes quality of products, people and customers, and the second is benefits/rewards, which includes opportunity to learn and grow. Hiring is one thing that we, as a group, have developed to a fine art. It is an art which we feel includes:

- *Individual should always visit [us] several times*
- *They should be interviewed at a higher and lower level*
- *Never make an offer until they have mentally decided they want to work with us*
- *Never hire someone that doesn't have "innates" such as honesty, integrity, a work ethic, and desire for team winning, etc.*
- *Try to hire the very best we can attract and pay what they are worth.*

Remember the 10,000 people we hire in the next five years determine what Tandem will be in 1985.

MEASURES OF SUCCESS

A company is evaluated by outsiders such as investors, banks, suppliers, potential employees, potential customers and by ourselves in a multitude of ways. Each of them is important and there are tradeoffs... but they are important goals which must be kept in balance. As an example, high growth hurts profitability as one-third to one-fourth of our people are not helping product revenues at any given time. (A new development person takes a year, a new sales person eight months, a new service/software support person six months, etc.)

PRODUCTIVITY

Productivity is an overall measure of the effectiveness of a company's use of people and assets. It can be measured in many ways and from different perspectives. Classically, productivity is measured in chips stuffed per day per assembly worker. This approach doesn't consider other factors such as poor quality, which leads to unhappy customers. In development, productivity is not only how fast you develop a product, but includes timeliness, quality, proper benefit trade-off, ease of manufacturing, cost of support, etc.

Productivity comes from:

- *Enthusiastic, outstanding, hard-working people*
- *Working in a stimulating, creative environment with a clear direction and understanding*
- *Who participate in the reward and responsibilities of the company and*
- *Who understand the need and value of profit (earnings for workers) and of capital.*

Productivity in terms of revenues per person is a major challenge in Tandem's Five-Year Plan. None of us wants to have a billion-dollar crappy company. The question is how fast you can grow people and at the same time create opportunity for those people and do a good job. If we maintain this productivity we need 11,500 people at $1 billion. If productivity drops to $50,000 per person then we would need 25,000 people. Tandem can't grow people that fast and also be the best place to work. If productivity drops then we can't meet one of our primary goals (good people). If we slow down revenue growth so that our people growth does not exceed some rate this lowers all growth-oriented measures of success, which significantly lowers the stock price, which reduces motivation of option holders. This reduces productivity even more and the loop goes round and round.

QUANTITATIVE MEASURES FOR LOOPS

The interrelationships from a quantitative point of view are especially difficult. As an example, the degree of motivation of a group of people is difficult to measure, and its impact on costs, new products and lost customers is impossible to calculate. Even the stock price is difficult to measure and many people spend their lives trying to develop the quantitative relationship. If Tandem misses its quarter by 10 systems, some quantitative measures are possible:

- *Revenues would be flat quarter-to-quarter*
- *Profits would be down 50% quarter-to-quarter*
- *EPS would be down 50% quarter-to-quarter*
- *PE ratio would go from 60% to 40%*
- *Our image of consistency and ability to meet goals would be permanently lost*
- *Cost of cash would go up 50%*
- *This would reduce EPS [the following year] by an extra 8%*
- *The value of stock options for all employees here less than one year would be zero*
- *Other employees' wealth would be down 33%*
- *Future stock price would be down 10% and would impact Tandem's ability to attract new employees—over a given time span.*

STRATEGY

Strategy is the company's game plan, and it means different things to different companies. Basically it involves evaluation of:

- *One's strengths and weaknesses versus those of your competitors*
- *Trends and changes that could impact the company's position especially changing customer and technology trends*
- *Possibilities of risk, such as recession*
- *Identification of hurdles that must be overcome and many other things.*

Out of this analysis comes the definition of things that need to be done in order to succeed. The importance of strategy cannot be overstated—because no matter what your people or financial resources are, if you are going in an impossible direction, these valuable resources are wasted.

The forecast plan is to be a $1 billion company in 1985 with 11,500 people and a blank balance sheet. The PLAN FRAMEWORK is FEASIBLE because there are no strategic reasons we will not achieve these goals. But there are challenges:

- *We must improve productivity*
- *We must continue to make new product contributions for the same market*
- *We must maintain superior growth and profit performanceWe must improve asset management and*
- *We must do a better job with people.*

These challenges must flow throughout the company. For example, productivity in service is a major challenge for all computer companies.. This challenge leads to a plan involving system design technology, development and service, which hopefully allow us to do a better job than anyone. Another example of a challenge is our organization, especially in the field management and at the staff level. We have chosen an organization that optimizes the knowledge of a maximum number of people, emphasizes cooperation amongst them and enhances their ability to operate independently. This is oriented towards our challenge of having enough understanding people versus having the most efficient organization.

SUMMARY

This is a brief introduction to certain concepts and especially to interactions between concepts. This type of approach is the most important knowledge of general management. Knowing asset management, cost of capital, or cost accounting in depth is not as important as understanding the concepts, what's critical about them, and finally how they relate to everything else. A high-growth, high-margin company like Tandem must have managers with this type of knowledge, so each manager can make company-oriented decisions. At a growth rate of 100 percent, decisions come five times faster than in 20 percent growth. This then, defines what we value in managers. First and always is people orientation and then a person that takes responsibility and makes things happen for overall benefit.

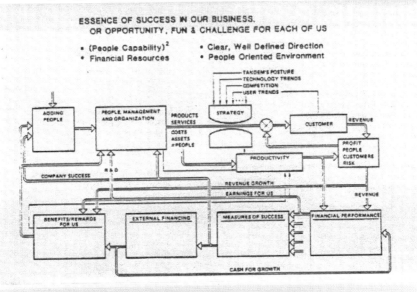

What Defines Business Success

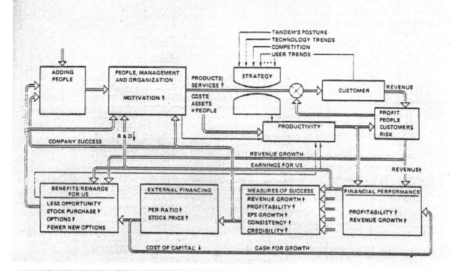

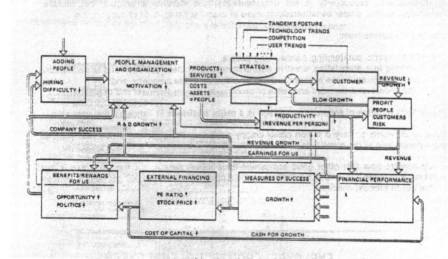

Understanding Tandem Philosophy - Top: Impact of Poor Quarterly Performance Bottom: Impact of Lower Productivity

IMPACT OF LONG RECEIVABLES

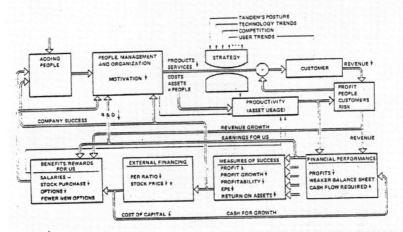

INTERNAL FINANCE

This next section deals with the profit statement, cost structure, balance sheet, and especially cash flow and asset management.

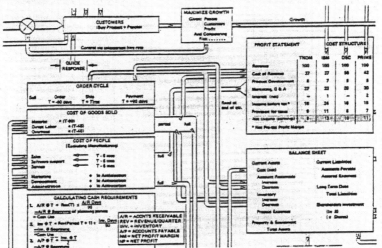

Understanding Tandem Philosophy - Top: Impact of Long Receivables Bottom: Internal Financial Measures

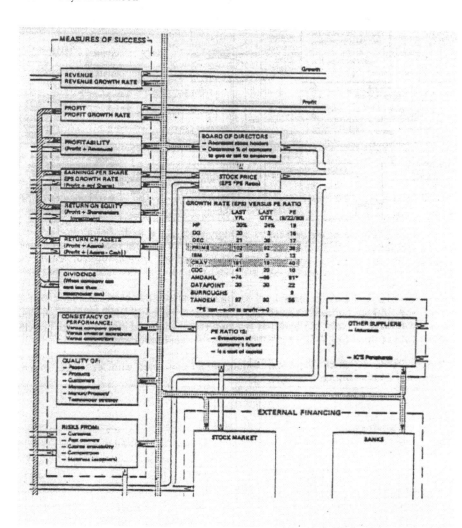

Understanding Tandem Philosophy - Measures of Success